FURY OF
THE TIGER

ERIC MEYER

ISBN 978-1-909149-68-7

Typeset by Swordworks Books
Printed and bound in the UK & US
A catalogue record of this book is available from the British Library

Cover design by Swordworks Books
www.swordworks.co.uk

FURY OF
THE TIGER

ERIC MEYER

PROLOGUE

Slapton Sands, England, April 8, 1944

"This damn country, it's either wet, dark, or cold. Most often it's all three," PFC Wenceslas grumbled aloud, "I never did like boat rides. My old man always told me..."

"Shut up, you dumb Polack," someone shouted. The Lieutenant glanced at them, but he closed his ears to their moans. He had other things on his mind.

"Shut up yourself." Wenceslas snapped back. "I signed up for the Army, not the damn Navy."

"Gimme some quiet, please, you guys," another voice sang out from the darkness.

"Why's he want quiet? Where does he think he is, the local library?"

"He's praying the Rosary, can't you see?" Wenceslas spat back at the man next to him. "Leave him be."

Like most Poles, he was Catholic, so he had sympathy for any appeal to the Good Lord for support and intercession, especially now. Although he doubted any Deity would come calling for this or any other soldier. The man was kneeling on the wet, steel deck, his hands clasped around his Rosary beads. Vomit from last night's supper mixed with seawater surged around his legs, a stinking, miasmic mess that clung to his pants and boots like wallpaper glue. It would need a miracle for anyone to escape the dank misery. And right now miracles were in short supply on Lyme Bay. They just had to endure the spiteful, storm-tossed night, afloat on the English Channel, until the exercise was over.

They were huddled in the damp misery of a British Royal Navy LCA, a Landing Craft Assault. The bow pointed seaward, further out into Lyme Bay, toward open sea. The skipper of the boat, a young Royal Navy Midshipman, stared straight ahead, careful to follow his prescribed course. He seemed oblivious to the wind and waves; the stormy seas that broke sheets of icy spray over his command to drench its suffering passengers.

For Lieutenant David Grant, US Infantry, this was his first taste of action.

Not exactly action, he corrected himself. *Just a rehearsal for the real event - the invasion of France. That will come later, probably in two or three months. When it does come, God help us all. The Germans are waiting a few miles to the south, guarding the French coast with millions of men, thousands of tanks, guns and aircraft. This is a just a pleasure trip. Kind of. At least there's no sign of the enemy.*

Ike and his staff had put together Operation Tiger to give the soldiers and ships' crews their first experience of a massed beach landing. The plan was simple, motor out to sea in the slow moving landing craft, turn around, head back for the beach, and wade ashore as soon as the flat keels hit bottom; all undercover of night to hide their activities from the Germans. A simple plan, so not likely to go wrong. He allowed himself to relax.

Lieutenant Grant threaded his way through the troops crouched on the stinking, puke-filled deck, trying in vain to avoid the worst of the chill spray washed over the vessel and drenched their uniforms. The stench of sour vomit was shocking, intense, foul and oppressive, and he felt himself hating even more the close, steel confines of the slow moving steel box that trapped them. When he reached the cramped steering position, he smiled.

Midshipman Raymond Winterton was sucking on a pipe. He had little doubt the intention was to make the young naval officer look older. More like a proper naval officer. He also sported an emerging mustache, though little more than a dark shadow on his upper lip. He looked more like a kid pretending to be a man. Which in a way he was, for it was unlikely Winterton was older than seventeen years.

Too young, much too young to be risking his life in a war zone. Although this isn't a war zone, Grant reminded himself. *It's just a practice drill. No danger, nothing to worry anyone.*

The Brit gave him a friendly nod and removed the pipe. "Nice night for it, old chap."

"Yeah, a real pleasure cruise," he grimaced, "How much longer does this go on?"

"We have a about a mile to go, maybe twenty minutes or so. I'm afraid this old tub is rather slow, and it's even worse fully loaded. We're also sailing against wind and tide, which doesn't help. However, we haven't far to go, so it won't be long before we return, and your men can paddle back out onto the sand to brew up a nice cup of tea." He smiled, "It's a lovely place, Lyme Bay. I took a vacation here once."

"I guess the sun didn't shine?" he replied, wondering what made these Brits so keen on their rain-soaked island.

"The sun?" He looked surprised, "No, as a matter of fact it didn't. How did you know?"

"Just a guess, Raymond. Just a guess."

David Grant looked out to sea, and for the tenth time that night, his thoughts turned to his brother, Josh, who was a lawyer back home in the US. They'd parted on bad terms, and he felt guilty. Men were fighting the Nazis, sacrificing everything they had, often their lives, to beat the Nazis and the Japs. While Josh was looking at a commission in the JAG, the Judge Advocate General's Corps. Military lawyers, faceless men who manned a desk while real soldiers faced the enemy across the barrel of a gun.

It was like most arguments. It started over nothing, and too much to drink. He'd made a stupid comment, and Josh hit back.

"Someone needs to do the legal work. Soldiers have to have legal representation. It's the way the military works, David. It's the law."

"It won't beat the enemy," he'd slashed back at his brother, "To beat them, we need men to do the dirty work. To shoot the guns, drop the bombs, do the killing."

"You also have to have a legal department, if it's..."

David interrupted his brother, fueled by one too many bourbons. "It's a handy excuse for men like you to avoid the front line," he'd slashed back, "Any man with guts would pick up a rifle and fight."

He still remembered his brother's angry glare. "Are you calling me a coward?"

A pause, as he chose his words. "I'm saying you're deliberately avoiding the fight. What would you call it?"

Even as he spoke, he regretted the words. Josh jumped to his feet, overturning the chair, and the table began to topple as he staggered and then knocked it over. Glass, ashtrays and spilled drinks littered the floor.

"Fuck you, David," he spat out, "If you're stupid enough to go shoot a rifle, good for you. The Army needs men with brains, too, not just muscle. They need the JAG and people like me to serve. To protect and advise the military with legal help."

Their eyes met, only inches apart. David couldn't resist the final taunt. "What's the color of the JAG flag, Josh? Bright yellow?"

He watched as his brother bunched a fist, ready to throw a punch, and then thought better of it.

"It's an honorable posting, David," Josh had mumbled. Somehow, he didn't sound entirely convinced.

"Sure it is," he'd sneered, "Stay safe, Josh. Don't go near any real shooting."

They stormed out of the bar and went their separate ways. It was the last conversation they shared, and he wished it had been different. In a couple of months they'd be attacking mainland France, and he could end up wounded, even killed. He would have wanted to make his peace with Josh before anything bad happened.

Still, it isn't too late. As soon as this little jaunt is over, I'll try to call him, assuming he's still Stateside.

A flare suddenly lit up the sky about a half-mile away. He turned to Winterton.

"What was that?"

"I, er, I don't know."

"You don't know? Why the fuck would our ships be shooting off flares. This is supposed to be a night operation held in total darkness."

The midshipman worked to keep his voice nonchalant, although it shook slightly.

Maintaining the British stiff upper lip.

"It wasn't one of our shells, old chap. Different color."

"Whose, then? One of the Canadians, or the French?"

"It was a German, I believe."

Before he could reply, a shell fired from long range splashed into the water nearby. Then all hell let loose. Shellfire, machine guns, tracers, it was as if they were entering the gates of Dante's inferno. Fifty yards away a landing craft identical to theirs exploded, struck by a salvo of shells. Men screamed, and survivors began tossing life rafts into the water and jumping over the side. As he watched, the machine guns started chattering. German machine guns, churning the sea into froth as they punished the drowning soldiers.

A huge launch suddenly appeared out of the night, the deck lit by muzzle flashes, as their guns spat hate at the Allied landing craft. The flag flying at the masthead was red, with a swastika in the center.

Germans! Fucking Kriegsmarine E-boats! How come?

They were fast attack craft, capable of almost fifty miles an hour. Eighty tons of sleek, floating battle platform, designed to strike like lightning and escape before the larger, slower moving enemy ships had time to hit back.

It's an ambush! Where are our escort ships? They'd blow these bastards out of the water, but they're not here! The stupid, useless bastards!

He looked at Midshipman Winterton. The Brit was

frozen, staring open mouthed at the conflagration.

"Start shooting, for Christ's sake," he shouted, "The Bren gun mounted on your boat isn't just there for decoration!"

"But..."

Grant ignored him. The Bren gun was mounted in a steel cupola at the side of the helmsman's position. Right now, just when it was needed, it was unmanned.

Another fuck up!

He darted across to the gun, grabbed the butt, and aimed at the fast moving German. He recalled the magazine only carried thirty or so rounds, and he hadn't a clue where they kept the spare ammo, so he fired in short controlled bursts.

The E-boat sliced through the water, racing past and turning away from them. Then it made a graceful turn, hurling up a huge bow wave as it swung back to come at them again. He waited, knowing he only had half a clip of bullets left, around fifteen .303 rounds. The only way to hurt them was to wait until they were close. His men were still huddled in the belly of the boat, numb with shock. It suddenly came to him they could all die. Unless they could do something about that E-boat.

He shouted, "All of you, shoot at that boat, murder the fucker." His voice rose to a scream. "Give it all you've got. Fire, men, fire!"

A few of them reacted, most didn't; they were too shocked by the unexpected violence. He concentrated on the German. Closer, closer, the boat was racing through the water at incredible speed. The deck guns were hammering out tracer rounds and shells, and he forced himself to ignore the streams of bullets that whistled past his head as he waited. The German machine gunner lowered his aim and emptied a score of rounds into the belly of the landing craft. Some of his men screamed, and he felt himself possessed by icy anger. This wasn't war. It was sheer murder. Still he held his fire. Nearer, nearer, and then the deck gun fired again, and a shell exploded amongst the packed men, causing scores more casualties. He had to close his ears to the screams and concentrate on only one thing. To nail the fucker who was killing his men.

The E-boat was only fifty yards away, and the landing craft was now reduced to little more than blazing wreckage, filled with dead and wounded, hot with smoke and flame. He felt a steel fragment, or maybe a bullet, slice a chunk out of his side, but he ignored the pain and concentrated on his prey. He could make out the German seamen manning the machine gun, and he aimed carefully. If he could kill them, it may cause the E-boat to veer away. Then the angles converged and he had a perfect shot. At the same moment, he saw the black, round maw of the barrel of the deck gun pointing right at him.

He squeezed the trigger, bullets hurtled out of the Bren gun, and as they arced toward the enemy, he saw the flash as the deck gun fired. He had the satisfaction of seeing the two men manning the machine gun crash to the deck as his fusillade cut them down. It was the last thing he ever did see. The German shell smashed into the front of the LCA, and his world exploded in a searing hell of heat, smoke, and shards of white-hot metal. His last thoughts were of his brother Josh, a wave of sadness as he lost consciousness. He'd never get a chance to make it up, to say sorry for his harsh words. The blackness, when it came, was a mercy.

CHAPTER ONE

The English Channel, 04.30, June 6, 1944

"Bocage."

Sergeant Josh Grant glanced at his driver, PFC Angel Montalban, who hailed from Spanish Harlem, New York City. His normally Latin face had paled to the color of putty. It was no surprise. The LCT, Landing Craft Tank, was pitching and rolling like a Coney Island rollercoaster. Angel was normally a good-looking, macho, Hispanic male, all broad shoulders and slim hips, a snappy dresser who sported a neat pencil mustache. He never appeared anywhere without his hair slicked back with a gallon of hair oil, except now. The testosterone had evaporated, and he looked sick. They all looked sick, riding in frail metal boats that tossed around the rough seas of the English Channel like discarded corks.

"What's that about bocage?"

"That's what you college boys call it, yeah? When you're puking your guts out. Bocage."

He smiled. Angel was pulling his leg. He was the crew joker, most of the time. When he wasn't wisecracking, he talked about his plans to open up one of those new fangled pizza shops in a big city. Somewhere like New York City, maybe even Los Angles. He dreamed of selling his product to celebrities, like movie stars. Grant wasn't sure if it would catch on, this new 'fast food.' The cautious lawyer inside him doubted it would appeal to enough people.

Then again, if that's his dream, I won't disillusion him.

The violent motion of the LCT carrying the platoon that included their Sherman M4 affected all of them, leaving them in unimaginable misery. They were in a temporary purgatory, their lives on hold. The vessel was a Mark 4, and it wallowed like a drunken pig when fully laden, like now. The two big Paxman diesel engines pushed the steel box through the choppy waves of the English Channel at a sluggish eight knots. Someone had suggested they could do better if they got out and pushed. Probably it had been Angel.

So far, the Krauts didn't seem to know they were coming, which was as well. Even though a New York radio station had let slip the secret of Operation Overlord, the coming invasion of Europe, in a broadcast at 03.32. The station even read out Eisenhower's Order of the Day.

'The tide has turned. The free men of the world are marching together to victory.'

Thank Christ the Germans weren't listening. So much for the 'master race.' They were probably too busy sleeping off their sausage and sauerkraut.

They were all nervous, every soldier, every sailor. He still wondered what he was doing in command of a Sherman

M4 tank. Grant was a freshly minted New York lawyer, not a soldier, yet here he was. He'd even volunteered to join the slaughter. A sudden roaring noise interrupted his thoughts and made him look up, but there was no sign of enemy aircraft. He glanced at their anti-aircraft defenses.

The gunners on the two Oerlikon 20mm cannons constantly scoured the skies, alert for the Luftwaffe. He doubted they knew their popguns would be worse than useless against a determined air raid by Messerschmitts and Focke-Wulfs. Probably. Although the biggest problem they would face this day had yet to come. The shore defenses, the huge guns mounted in hardened, concrete bunkers on the cliff tops. 88mm flak guns, or so they reckoned, their barrels pointed seaward and big enough to blow an LCT out of the water with a single well-aimed shell. That was the scuttlebutt. Every man hoped they wouldn't find out the hard way.

He leaned down to make himself heard over the howling winds, the roar of the engines, and the rapid chatter of nervous men trying to lie to themselves; trying, and failing, to pretend they weren't terrified. No one was fooled.

"Bocage isn't vomit. It's the kind of terrain we're going to encounter over there, Angel. You remember those tall hedgerows we talked about. They'll make it difficult to spot the enemy."

"Is that right? How high are those bocage things? I mean, they're just hedges, right? How big could they be?"

A pause. "Our intel says they could be up to sixteen feet high."

"Sixteen feet! Sonofabitch! So what do we do, get our stupid heads blown off if a Kraut anti-tank unit is hiding behind one of these 'bocage' things?"

"I hope not. They'll send a recon unit ahead of us to scout out the routes."

"So the poor guys get their heads blown off just so we don't, is that right?"

He smiled. The driver was winding him up, just his way of dispelling his fear.

"Tell you what, Angel. You go ahead and recon the hedgerows for us. That way, if you get your head blown off, I won't have to answer any more stupid questions."

He heard a ragged cheer behind him. The crew enjoyed Angel Montalban's joshing, but they also liked it when someone turned the tables on him. They were all sheltering from the bitter wind and freezing waves behind the solid, dark-green painted steel hull of Minnie Mouse, the nickname for their Sherman.

Corporal Solly Rothstein, their Jewish gunner, had wanted to call her something biblical, as if the Sherman was a wrathful instrument of God. Something like Zealot, after the 1st century Jewish sect that sought to incite the people of Judaea to rebel against the Roman Empire. He quickly squashed that one. Rothstein, slightly built, but always vocal about the injustices the Germans heaped on his people. Grant considered he was more than entitled to his opinion. After all, he was a Jew, and Jews had plenty of reason to hate Krauts.

Solly had wavy, dark hair, with huge, deep and soulful eyes, and the olive skin of his Hebrew ancestors. He'd told them the Nazis gave his folks in Germany a bad time, after they prevented them from leaving the country. He hadn't heard from them in years and he always worried they'd been murdered.

He was terrified, but not of fighting the Germans. On the contrary, he wanted to kill every German soldier he came across. No, his real fear was something else, capture and imprisonment in a concentration camp. If what some people were saying was true, it was tantamount to a sentence of death, which may have been the fate of his relatives. After the war, he planned to locate his family. If he found them alive, and if he could save the cash, he'd take them all to Palestine and establish a farm, what he called a kibbutz.

Rumors about the Germans rounding up Jews and killing them in the concentration camps were rife, but most thought it an exaggeration. Which was fine, if you weren't a Jew. The Germans were ordinary, civilized folk, people said. Hell, many of them had immigrated to the US, and they weren't monsters. Sure, they'd imprisoned Jews and stolen their possessions. They'd have to pay for those crimes one day, but mass murder? From a nation who'd produced some of the great names of science, literature, medicine and the arts, many of them Jews. Impossible!

Although if it were true, I'd let Solly name the tank anything he wanted. And we'd all help him go after the perpetrators. Even so, I only hope to Christ that's all it is, a rumor. The alternative doesn't bear thinking about. It can't be true. Zealot? No way.

In the end, he'd pulled rank and named her Minnie Mouse after the cartoon character. When they asked him why, he told them no matter what happened, Minnie always made it home. Besides, they needed a female around. After that, no one argued. The crew held him in some awe. He was the smooth faced, slim, tall and good-looking college-boy lawyer, who'd elected to enlist in the ranks, one of the men, almost, but not quite. They nearly forgave him his college degree, but his Germanic blonde hair and blue eyes made him the butt of more than a few jokes.

Minnie was a Sherman M4 medium tank, with three inches of armor up front, and equipped with a 75mm main gun mounted in the turret. Some said the gun was about as useful as a peashooter if they came up against German heavy armor. In the unlucky event of meeting a Tiger tank, conventional wisdom suggested a rapid retreat, although the military was careful to call it a 'withdrawal.'

They also said it would be best to reverse out of trouble, to keep their heavier frontal armor between them and the German. Grant asked the officer who'd lectured them on tactics whether the Sherman's frontal armor would be enough to stop a shell from the Tiger's 88mm main gun. He didn't get an answer.

Then again, Minnie Mouse was home. Comforting, familiar, something they could always rely on to get them home. On the LCT, they'd sheltered in the lee instinctively, putting the bodywork of the thirty-ton behemoth they called home between them and the icy sheets of water from the English Channel that constantly sprayed over them. Minnie's iron hull was also the last barrier between them and the French coastline, the long line of defenses that contained the dreaded German coastal batteries.

The gun barrels of the tanks all pointed at the French coast. They'd been ordered to aim their main guns toward the Krauts, so they could supplement the barrage from the warships when they got within range. If they got within range, before the big Krupp-made coastal defense guns blew them out of the water.

He looked to the east at the reassuring sight of the USS Arkansas a short distance away. Its twelve batteries of twelve-inch guns faced forward, ready to pound the Kraut shore defenses to scrap. To the west, the USS Texas was even closer, its formidable fourteen-inch guns bristling from the superstructure like trees in a forest. The brass said they'd turn the Jerry guns into so much scrap metal, so when they went ashore, there'd be little or no opposition. No one really believed them.

Nearer, he could see other LCTs, and the larger LSTs, Landing Ship Tanks, some of them carrying the swimming tanks, the Sherman DDs. The DD stood for duplex drive. The vehicles were equipped with a propeller to drive them through the water and a folding rubberized canvas screen to keep them dry. He shuddered at the thought of those flimsy canvas structures bolted to the steel hull, turning the tank into an amphib. Like most of the men in his platoon, he thanked the good Lord he hadn't been assigned to one of those armored deathtraps.

He checked his wristwatch. The time was 05.02. The air bombardment was about to start, and as if some God of War had read his mind, the sudden roar of aircraft engines made them all look up at the troubled sky. An air armada, warplanes, hundreds of them, thousands, they came in wave after wave. Lumbering, heavy bombers, Brit Lancasters and American B-17s, medium bombers like the Mitchell B-25 in service with the RAF, the roundels painted on their wings.

There were sleek fighter escorts darting in and out of the heavies, P-47s, Spitfires, and Hurricanes, and a couple of squadrons of ground attack planes like the Typhoons. The sky was so full of aircraft it didn't look like there was room for any more. For a brief moment, he felt a sneaking sympathy for the enemy soldiers who would soon endure the nightmare of those bombs. Then he recalled that every Kraut who survived the bombardment would soon be shooting at them, and he grinned at his stupid innocence.

Pound the fuckers into dust!

He watched the aircraft thunder toward the gloomy, dark clouds of the Normandy coastline, and then they heard the bombs begin to fall. The sky lit up with flame and smoke, and the distant 'crump' of exploding ordnance became a continuous rolling thunder.

"Hey Josh, you reckon they can survive that lot?" Dale Weathers asked him, offering him his pack of Luckies. Dale was black, a native of the wrong end of Boston. Broad and well muscled, he'd been an amateur boxer back home, a lightweight. It was a sport he took up when other kids picked on him at school because of his small stature. He kicked ass big time, after spending all his spare time at the gym, sparring and pumping iron. His duties as loader meant he had to heft heavy shells inside the cramped interior of the Sherman, so his developed muscles found a new use. If Dale had one regret, it was that he'd missed out on a college education. He wasn't all brawn; he also had the intellect to take him a long way. Sadly, he didn't have the financial resources to go anywhere, except into manual work to support his family.

Josh Grant had fought a bitter fight to get Dale on his crew. The military was not kind to blacks and saw them as lesser mortals. Of the seventeen hundred black troops heading toward the beaches with the First Army, most were posted to service companies. A few were even assigned to the 320th Anti-Aircraft Balloon Battalion. Dale was a driver when he first met him, ferrying stores to the fighting units. They would provide the essential logistical support to keep the Allied Armies fighting. They would become famous as the 'Red Ball Express'. Except Dale wanted more.

Josh ran into Dale when he was unloading shells from his truck, just prior to D-Day. His loader, Eugene Wilson, had gone down with dysentery, or so they said. The crew thought he'd caught a dose of the clap, VD. He had a reputation for spending his pay and spare time on tarts, and he wasn't too fussy about hygiene. On the day when he was searching out a replacement loader, he saw this tough-looking, muscled black man tossing wooden crates of shells around like they were cardboard cartons. He was looking at Minnie with a wistful expression. When he saw Grant, he asked what it was like, to be part of the crew of a Sherman.

"We haven't seen action yet, but my boys plan to give Jerry a hammering as soon as we get to France," he replied, patting the steel hull of Minnie Mouse.

"I'd like to fight," Dale said.

"So why don't you?"

He grimaced. "Ask the officers. They think black men are only fit for fetching and carrying, digging latrines, that kind of work."

He nodded. It was a running sore in the military, the argument about the treatment of black servicemen. Personally, he couldn't see why there was a problem. Blacks had fought in the Civil War, hadn't they? What was so different this time around? A soldier was a soldier. A man was a man. Who gave a shit about his skin color?

"My Sherman doesn't carry an officer. How about you ask for a transfer to my crew, I need a man like you. A tough man, a man who wants to fight."

He smiled. "They wouldn't go for it, not in a million years."

"We'll see about that. Wait there."

He sought out Major Morgan, who in civilian life was a college professor with views that were very liberal.

"You want what? A black man in your crew?"

"I do, Sir. I need you to arrange his transfer from a transport battalion. He's a damn good man. I could use someone like that."

"I don't know..."

He looked around, as if struggling to find a way to say no. Grant piled on the pressure.

"Unless you're a racist, like most of the brass, Major."

That earned him a sharp look, but he'd said exactly the right thing.

"I'm no racist, Sergeant. Tell him he's hired. I'll clear it with his unit. Send him to me, and I'll forward the paperwork to battalion. I suggest you keep him out of sight until it's all finalized. Colonel Lindbergh may see things differently, if you know what I mean."

"I know Colonel Lindbergh, Sir."

Lindbergh, the solid gold asshole, who was also their Battalion commander!

He looked embarrassed. "Yeah, I guess you do. Good luck, Sergeant. Maybe this could work out," he nodded to himself, "Yes, maybe it could be the start of something big. It's time the Army made some changes."

The following day Dale joined the crew. In another world, he'd have made good material for a college degree. He was intelligent and well read, but only by dint of his own efforts. He could have gone all the way, summa cum laude, you name it, and then a career as the doctor his impoverished father had wanted him to be. But it wasn't another world, the family was broke, and he'd worked as a trucker before the army called on him. Grant soon found he and Dale spoke the same language. After the war, his new loader's plan was to save enough money to put him through law college.

'I want to be a lawyer like you, Josh. Sharp suits, Cadillacs, crocodile briefcase.'

Grant told him he was still paying off his loans and hardly earning enough money to pay the rent. "It ain't all gravy, my friend. Too many lawyers and not enough clients."

Dale didn't listen. He had a dream, and no man would take it off him. So here he was, freezing his butt on a soaking wet LCT, tossing around on the English Channel. He took the cigarette Dale offered him, cupping his hands to keep the flame alive out of the wind while he thought about the answer to Dale's question.

"You want the truth, can the Krauts survive the bombardment?"

Dale grinned. "Sure. I may as well know the worst."

Grant was aware of the men standing nearby, waiting for his reply.

"Okay, here it is. I reckon plenty of Krauts are likely to survive the aerial bombardment. But." He paused for effect. "The battleships haven't started shooting yet. They're due to open up any moment now. Between the ships and the aircraft bombing and shooting up the defenses, they'll give them a shitload of grief. With any luck, all we'll have left is to mop up the survivors."

Dale didn't look convinced, but he tried a weak smile. "I hope you're right."

He smiled. "Me too."

"And if you're wrong?" Vernon asked him, in his Southern twang.

Corporal Vernon Franklin, their co-driver, waited on his reply, a redneck farm boy from Mississippi, with the prejudices and chips on his shoulder that came with the territory; including a plan to buy a small farm in the Delta, with the requisite Dodge truck and pack of slavering coonhounds. He mentioned something about raising crocodiles, or maybe it was alligators.

The rest of them craned around, their faces tense.

"What if you're wrong?" Vern asked again.

Grant winced.

I'm just a lawyer, yet they look to me as if I have all the answers. I don't. All I can do is try to keep them alive.

He tried a joke. "If I'm wrong, Vern, then you'll just have to drive a damn sight quicker."

The tension eased a little, and some of them attempted a chuckle, but it was forced. Vernon gave a satisfied nod. Now they knew it was up to him, Vernon Franklin, co-driver, to pull them out of the shit. It was enough to satisfy his stubborn pride, his warped Southern notion of bravery and honor. Which is why Grant had been careful to suggest their survival may rest on the skills of Vern. It was untrue.

What was true was they depended more on Solly Rothstein. He was a damn good gunner, the best in the 745th Battalion. If there were a chance of firing first and scoring the first hit when they met the enemy, it was bound to be Solly. He constantly brought home the highest scores in the battalion. The battalion commander, Lindbergh, even wanted him for his Sherman, and it was only with difficulty Grant kept him in Minnie Mouse.

The problem he had to wrestle with was Vernon hated Rothstein. Solly was a kike. A yid. No match for a good 'ole Southern boy. It was a constant battle to keep them apart.

As if the Germans aren't enough to contend with.

At 05.30, the batteries on board the warships opened fire, and the cold, stormy morning erupted with the thunder of more explosions, this time not from the skies but from the sea. The sky was lit up with guns firing from ships of every shape and size, warships of every type and class. Battleships, cruisers, destroyers, even motor torpedo boats fired off their deck guns. Merchant vessels, transports, LCTs, LSTs, and a host of smaller craft could only marvel and watch the immense barrage.

The noise was astonishing, as salvo after salvo thundered out from the big guns. Seconds after they fired, the massive shells struck the shore defenses, which then erupted into flame and smoke, showering the ground around them with debris. Out to sea, the landing craft plodded slowly on toward the distant beach. It was as if the men were detached from what was going on a short distance away, that they were no part of the hurricane of fire and destruction, not yet.

Grant felt like a forgotten witness in the explosive-torn hell of the morning, an unnecessary appendage amid the thunder of the shells and the crump, crump, of bombs dropped from yet more aircraft that continued to pound the Germans. Rockets surged from the wings of Hawker Typhoons, aimed at targets that were out of sight, and yet more rockets soared away, this time from the top of an LCT a couple of hundred yards away. A few of the LCTs carried rocket batteries, in a further effort to provide defense suppression.

He felt insignificant, a tiny cog, an infinitesimal part of the largest seaborne invasion in the history of man. In command of a puny Sherman M4, he was no more than an infinitesimal footnote on this historic day. Always assuming they reached the beach alive. He knew the chances of that weren't good once the big German batteries opened fire. He omitted to mention that to his crew. Let them enjoy the show while it lasted.

"They're launching the DDs."

He turned at Dale's shout and looked across at an LST with its bow doors open, and the ungainly canvas shrouded amphibious Shermans lumbered into the water.

"Oh, Christ," someone screamed, "Oh shit, the poor bastards."

A combination of the ship's wake and an abnormal wave had swamped the canvas tube of a DD, and it sunk immediately. There was no sign of survivors.

"They're too far out," Dale shouted over the noise, his expression horrified, "We're more than a mile off the beach. Those poor bastards will never make it."

They could only watch helplessly as men died. Drowned, for no good reason. Defeated not by the enemy, but by nature, by wind and wave. Another DD went down when an LCT rammed the fragile canvas and tore it to shreds, plunging the tank to the bottom of the sea. Abruptly, another LST carrying DDs raised the front ramp and altered course. The vessel picked up speed, heading straight for the beach.

At least that skipper has seen the danger and plans to take them all the way, Kraut guns or no. He should be running this show.

Grant grinned at Dale, trying to offer encouragement. The loader was standing next to him and they'd both lit more cigarettes, both men sucking feverishly at the tobacco as they watched the carnage. Grant's hand shook as he again raised his cigarette to his lips, but he ignored it.

"We'll be there soon, my friend, are you ready to make history?"

PFC Dale Weathers shook his head. "Nope, and I never will be. But I guess someone has to do it. Hey, you reckon we're gonna meet any Tigers?"

He stared back at him. "I honestly don't know, Dale. But if we do, I intend to beat the crap out of them. And don't mention Tigers to Vern, you know what he's like."

"Yeah, they scare the shit out of him."

They scare the shit out of me too. Truth is the Tigers outmatch us, but what else am I supposed to tell them? That if we tangle with one of those monsters, we're as good as dead? Better to let them spend what time they have left in blissful ignorance.

"They're just tanks, machines," he said. "Relax, we can beat them any day."

The black man gave him a skeptical glance. "Yeah, right."

Major Grenville Morgan's voice came over the ship's speaker system. He was the commander of A Company.

"Now hear this. We will hit the beach in six minutes. Colonel Lindbergh, the battalion commander, has ordered us to start engines and be ready to advance the moment the ramp is down. Give 'em hell, boys, and remember to move off that the beach as soon as your tracks touch the sand. I repeat, clear the beach ASAP. No exceptions."

Grant looked aft to the rear of the boat. Lindbergh was there, standing on the hull of his tank, doing his best to present the image of some gung-ho hero. Unlike Major Morgan, their battalion commander, Colonel Martin Lindbergh III inspired them with little confidence. He was a distant relative of Charles Lindberg, the aviation pioneer, and rarely failed to advise anyone of that snippet.

A scion of an old money, heir of a patrician family, he was a solid, Ivy League American WASP personified. Tall and lean, with carefully styled sandy colored hair, everything about him was controlled. His appearance, his uniform, his career, even sex with his wife, so they said, had an allocated time slot in his careful schedule. Lindbergh was one hundred percent ambitious. He was also stupid beyond belief.

Every man devoutly prayed the Krauts would target Lindbergh's vehicle first. It was not an unreasonable hope; his command Sherman was festooned with aerials, which enabled him to communicate both with his Company commanders and Division. Although Grant suspected there was some vague law of Universal Chance that would keep him alive, while other Shermans, less visible, would be destroyed. One thing they all knew was if Lindbergh survived long enough to get ashore, his ambition to win medals and glory was liable to get them all killed.

Grant's crew was already clambering into the hull. He took a last look around at the vast armada of ships and men surrounding him, all heading the same way, into the inferno. Then he stepped up onto the hull and climbed down through the hatch into the turret. Inside the dim interior, stinking of grease and rubber, sweat, and terror, Angel had taken his position in the driver's seat. Vernon was settling into the adjacent co-driver's position behind the breech of the machine gun. Solly and Dale were busy with the main gun, preparing to fire their first 75mm greeting at the German enemy. He pulled on his headphones and connected the plug. He was ready. They were ready, as ready as they could be. He recalled the famous lines of Tennyson's Charge of the Light Brigade.

Theirs not to reason why, theirs but to do and die.
Into the Valley of Death, rode the six hundred.'

He smiled to himself. *That about sums it up. We're the six hundred, riding into the Valley of Death. At least we know the reason why, unlike those poor Brit Light Brigade cavalrymen at the Battle of Balaclava, during the Crimean War. Kill Krauts, that's all they said. Kill enough of 'em, and you'll end the war. That's good enough reason.*

He could hear the ping of shell fragments, rifle and machine-gun bullets, as they began to come under fire. It was like a hail of scrap iron hammering at the loading ramp, and then underneath his feet, he felt a slight lurch as the LCT nudged a sandbar at the edge of the shallows. Morgan's voice came on the radio.

"Six minutes, men, stand by. Commanders, button up, there's a lot of metal flying around out there. And good luck."

He reached up, pulled the thick armored hatch closed, and settled himself into the cramped turret. The engine roared as Angel started up. In front of him through the viewing slot, he saw the ramp begin to lower. Minnie Mouse was going to war.

The mouse squeaks. And how!

He keyed the transmit button on his mike.

"Gunner, load HE. Stand by to fire."

Vernon's voice came out of the gloom, "Watch out for those fucking Tigers!"

Grant mentally grimaced. He was fed-up with listening to Vernon's constant whining about the German heavy armor. Although the Southerner did have a point, every one of them was rightly overawed by the reputation of the enemy heavy armor. If the Germans brought up their Tigers, King Tigers, and Panthers in one huge, armored force, they'd be unstoppable. They'd squash Minnie Mouse like a fly, as well as the rest of the Allied armor. Northern France would become little more than a massive killing ground, and afterward, there'd only be fields of scrap metal, mixed with the bloody flesh of the tank crews.

He looked ahead. They were nearly there. The ramp was dropping, and ahead of them the Germans waited, to kill them.

"Fire!"

* * *

Two kilometers outside Dreux, Northern France, 06.00, June 6, 1944

He watched the cyclist pedaling along the road past the farmhouse where he slept along with the rest of his crew. The bombs and shellfire had awakened them in the early hours, and they'd dressed and waited for the order to move. Since then, there'd been only silence from HQ in the nearby medieval town of Dreux. He'd called three times already, and the last time, the battalion commander, Sturmbannfuhrer Kleist, had chewed him out.

"I'm damn busy collating intelligence from the coastal batteries, Rolf. It's just possible this is the real thing. I do have a little more to occupy my time than chatting to my junior Panzer commanders."

"Yes, Sir, I understand! Sorry Sir."

Kleist softened a little. "I'm doing my best, Rolf. The truth is there's nothing we can do, not yet. We're all waiting on Berlin. Apparently, the Fuhrer is still asleep."

"I beg your pardon, Sir!" He was sure he hadn't understood.

"You heard correctly the first time; he's in bed, asleep. His staff refused to call him. They said he needs his rest. No, don't say a word, you don't know who's listening! I'll call you the second I hear. How are the boys holding up?"

"They can't wait to get into the fight, Sturmbannfuhrer."

"Is that right? So our brave young warriors are ready to lead us to victory, our young Nazi heroes. I feel encouraged by your assurance, Rolf."

SS Obersturmfuhrer Rolf Manhausen made no comment. Both men knew the truth. The 12th SS Panzer Division Hitler Jugend was a newly formed Waffen-SS heavy armored division. They were unique because the senior NCOs and officers were, like him, veterans of the Eastern Front. The crews were not veterans of the Eastern Front or any other front.

They were kids, all of them, some as young as only fourteen. So young they were supplied with candy and soda instead of the standard tobacco and alcohol ration. There was no doubt they'd fight with admirable enthusiasm. Everyone knew they could be relied on to make up for lack of experience with their fierce fanaticism and loyalty to the Fuhrer. Except there were times when experience was needed more than loyalty, if the enemy was not to slaughter them wholesale in their first encounter.

They had problems other than the inexperience of the

crews and the enemy. The ominous SD Standartenfuhrer Werner Schulz had arrived from Berlin. A high-ranking officer from the SS Security Office, the SD, he was also the uncle of his loader, Siegfried Lenz. Standartenfuhrer Schulz claimed to be nosing around Normandy to root out a possible plot against the Fuhrer. So far, all he'd done was make a thoroughgoing nuisance of himself. He had also found nothing. But when had a lack of evidence worried the SD or the Gestapo?

He continued to dog their footsteps and make absurd allegations. Two nights ago, he'd even suggested Rommel was planning to assassinate the Fuhrer. Rolf Manhausen started to laugh until Schulz informed him, with a face like thunder, that even his sense of humor constituted treason.

"A threat against the Fuhrer is no laughing matter, Manhausen."

"But, Sir, Feldmarschal Rommel? It's absurd. I hold him in the highest regard. We all do."

"Is that right?" Schulz's expression was almost benign, and he smiled gently, "I imagine you support him in all things."

He wasn't about to betray the legendary Feldmarschal, Schulz or no. "Rommel? Of course, I support him to the hilt."

"I see." He looked around at the crew, "You just heard Obersturmfuhrer Manhausen openly admit he would support a possible threat against the Fuhrer. Young Lenz, you heard the remark?"

"Yes, Uncle, of course. Sorry, Standartenfuhrer. It constitutes treason."

"Treason, yes." His voice cracked, like a whip, harsh and hard. "Manhausen, I don't trust your loyalty. Consider yourself under arrest until this investigation is concluded."

Rolf gaped at him. "Arrest?"

"Open arrest. You will continue with your duties. I will decide whether to take this matter further at a later stage. You will stay with your Panzer, even when the crew is stood down. Is that clear?"

"It is clear, Standartenfuhrer," he acknowledged, careful to keep his expression neutral.

It's absurd. Rommel? Impossible. And me, a Tiger commander on active service placed under arrest, and in the middle of a battle for our very survival. Insanity. Then again, it's unlikely we'll survive the coming days. In which case, all this is so much hot air.

Standartenfuhrer Schulz went on to instruct the other crewmen they could also be regarded as co-conspirators, if they did not take a threat against the Fuhrer's life seriously. Lenz, of course, nodded, his young face puffed with importance. His trust in Adolf Hitler was absolute. He would be happy to testify to Manhausen's treasonous statement.

After that night, they'd kept quiet about Schulz and Rommel; the fate of their Tiger commander was more than a warning to all of them. Having Schulz's relative in their vehicle, SS Sturmann Siegfried Lenz, made their lives even more than dangerous. Lenz took it all so seriously, a single misplace word could be reported to his uncle. The fool even thought they could win the war, when every man in Germany knew the best they could hope for was to grind the Allies into accepting some kind of peace.

Manhausen all but forgot about his open arrest. It was just a form of words, meaningless, unlike bombs and shells. A couple of his crewmen shouted questions at him about their orders, but he ignored them as he walked out the door and across to the barn. It was the only cover sufficiently large to hide their armor from the incessant Allied raids.

They'd lost scores of tanks in the last few days, especially during daylight. As soon as they were on the move, the British and American aircraft came over in waves like angry hornets, bombing and rocketing the Panzers. He'd seen too many comrades die in the blazing pyres of their vehicles, so now they were careful to restrict their movements until after dark, where possible.

He pulled open the small door in the side of the building, to be greeted by the familiar odors of gasoline, oil, and rubber. The stench of burned cordite would come later, after they engaged the enemy. A sound of metal on metal alarmed him, and he put a hand on the butt of his Luger but relaxed when the head of SS Sturmann Franz Schelling, his driver, appeared from under the front of the nearest track. He grinned as he wiped a streak of grease from his face with his sleeve. He only made it worse.

"Obersturmfuhrer! Has the order arrived to advance?"

He smiled. SS protocol was for officers to be called by their actual rank. In the Wehrmacht his rank would have been prefaced by Herr, Schelling would have called him Herr Obersturmfuhrer. In the SS, it was just Obersturmfuhrer.

A shame, I've always liked the old formalities. They are so, German.

"No, Franz, not yet. The Fuhrer is asleep, it seems. They do not wish to disturb him."

Schelling stared at him. "Is this some kind of a joke, Obersturmfuhrer?"

He shook his head, feeling exhausted.

Why am I so tired when we haven't even engaged the enemy yet?

"Sadly, no. We must wait for orders, until he awakes."

Franz was about to say something, but he choked off the retort, probably remembering the proximity of Lenz. Manhausen smiled, Schelling was a good man, well, still a boy, all of seventeen years old. A dedicated Nazi, although more fanatical about keeping the mechanics of the Tiger in good working order than the Nazi Party. Although he was a good driver, he had an unfortunate tendency to confuse right from left, which had caused them more than a few problems. Particularly at night when the error wasn't noticed until it was too late. Manhausen nodded at the steel track he'd been working underneath.

"What were you doing under there?"

He shrugged and wiped his greasy hand over his black SS tanker's uniform. "Ach, the torsion bar link to the front drive wheel was loose. I could hear it grinding every time we took a corner. I think I fixed it for now, but it won't last. A new part would be better."

"We don't have a new part, Franz," he said patiently, "You know I tried, but they said spare parts are in short supply."

Which is the same answer they've given me for the past year.

"I understand, Obersturmfuhrer. Is there any news on the gasoline?"

Rolf kept a straight face, even though he was inclined to laugh at the absurdity of it all. And the Fuhrer was asleep in bed. "We'll manage with what we have."

"Yes, Sir."

Until the fuel tanks are empty, when we'll have to abandon our Tiger. Of course, the Allies may drop a bomb on us in the meantime.

"I'm going to stretch my legs. Call the others, and tell

them I expect we'll be moving soon."

"At once, Sir."

He nodded and looked up at the formidable main gun. An 88mm shell could destroy anything the Allies sent against them, and at long range. Besides, their frontal armor was nearly a hundred and twenty millimeters thick, safe enough from the shells of the American Shermans and the British Cromwells. Although they were not safe from air attack, or long-range bombardment from the ships offshore, which even now were flinging thousands of tons of shells at targets inland from the coast. The entire region echoed to the constant crump of explosions.

And the Fuhrer is asleep in bed, while we wait for orders.

He walked out of the barn and strolled around the garden that surrounded the house. The fruit trees and flowers were fragrant with blossom, and the scents were a relief from the mechanical, warlike stench of the Tiger. It was all so different from Russia where there'd been no trees and no flowers. Stalin had ordered the earth scorched, so they won their battles only to claim empty, useless territory. He felt the ache in his bones when he thought about that brutal conflict.

He'd been wounded twice, once with a bullet in the leg, and once with a shell fragment in the left side. The leg wound still ached, and he found the only remedy was to stroll around to lessen the stiffness in his joints. It was worse in the mornings, especially during the tension of waiting to be called into action very soon.

His thoughts turned again to Russia where the Reds had finally driven all over them, despite their superior armor. They had Panzer Vs, Tiger Is, like the vehicle he commanded, and now the new Tiger IIs, the so-called

King Tigers. Yes, their armor was superior to the Soviets. Until a tank broke down and lay unrepaired for lack of spare parts, or was unable to fight because they had no fuel.

It happened too often, and there was little chance of defending themselves from enemy attack when they couldn't even start the engine. When they could move, the Russians faced them in ever-increasing numbers. What use was a heavy tank, one of the German technological marvels, when the opposition could field twenty of their useful T-34s for every one of your Tigers or Panthers? All too often overwhelming numbers of Soviet armor pulverized their heavy Panzers. As fast as they knocked them out, they replaced them with two, three, or four times their number.

It had seemed like an escape when he was transferred to the 12th SS in France, but now it was all happening again. Like his comrades, he had no illusions. Just as in Russia, they'd be faced with overwhelming armored hordes. The only difference was this time they'd be English and American, instead of brutal Communists. Once more, the Fuhrer would insist they fight to the last man, even when local commanders desperately needed the flexibility to maneuver on a constantly changing battlefield.

He mentally shrugged. They would go out and fight, and if it were humanly possible, they'd win. They were Germans, Waffen-SS, the toughest fighting unit that had ever joined battle. Their tanks were superior to those of the enemy, better armored, and better armed. He felt his spirits lift. They would prevail, his young and inexperienced HJ crew would overcome the obstacles, and if the fates willed it, they'd win.

Provided they had enough petrol to drive to the front and fight. Provided they could locate the spare parts they desperately needed to fix the frequent breakdowns. Provided the Fuhrer awoke and gave permission for them to move. Then they could take on the enemy armor. If they could avoid the enemy air attacks. He smiled to himself.

Too many 'ifs.' A pity I don't have a liter of fuel for every 'if' that awaits the coming battle.

* * *

Omaha Beach - June 6, 1944

They closed the beach, the hull of the LCT already beginning to scrape the bottom.

"Dear God!"

He never made out who shouted. The thunderous roar of artillery shut out all sound other than the ear-splitting salvos. The Naval barrage was continuous, aided by the sharper cracks of the tank main guns and the bombs and rockets from armadas of aircraft that flew overhead. They were using their combined might to smash down the German defenses before the troops left the dubious safety of the ships and drove onto the beach to face the horrors of the massed coastal defenses.

He looked back at the craft that followed them into the shore, and felt helpless as another Sherman DD amphib collided with an LCT, capsized, and sank. Straight to the bottom of the storm-swept English Channel. All that marked the grave of thirty tons of American steel and five American soldiers was just a few scraps of ripped canvas. An angry voice shouted over the radio.

"Target, eleven o'clock, up on the cliff top gun. It's a Kraut gun emplacement! Kill the fuckers!"

The shout came over the battalion net, and he wrenched his eyes away from the stricken Sherman to search for the enemy. He identified a reinforced concrete gun pit built into the top of the cliffs, overlooking Omaha Beach, a threat to all those who dared attempt a landing.

It was possible the gun inside the enclosed emplacement was a dreaded 88mm. In which case, the German could take his time and destroy them all. No tank armor gave protection against the 88, the same gun fitted in the turret of the Tiger tank. The noise grew even louder until it felt as if they were driving into an ironworks. It was like the constant clang of heavy steam hammers.

After they started engines, the fumes from the Sherman exhausts had filled the interior of the enclosed LCT, making them nauseous. The bullet strikes on the ramp increased until they were a continuous ringing noise set to jar their nerves beyond endurance. Some men huddled in corners, and a few were weeping. Other men looked away, embarrassed, or maybe intimidated. A few rounds pinged off the turret armor, a foretaste of the fiery hell that awaited them when they went ashore.

"Loaded and ready to fire!"

Rothstein's reminder jarred him back to the present. Amid the fear and excitement, he'd clean forgotten to give the order.

"Fire!"

The main gun fired a fraction of a second before he gave the order, an explosion of noise and smoke. Solly had decided not to wait. A chunk of cliff several yards from the emplacement broke away. Already Dale Weathers was loading a new HE shell, and they set up a rhythm; load, aim, fire, load, aim, fire. When the smoke cleared, the emplacement appeared undamaged.

Waste of time. Shit.

The 75mm main gun belched flame again, and this time they scored a direct hit on the gun pit. At the same instant, the fourteen-inch guns of the USS Texas fired a salvo that struck the same emplacement, a direct hit and a massive explosion followed. The sky was lit by an even greater blast as the ammunition exploded, showering chunks of concrete, steel, and body parts two hundred feet into the sky.

He looked down at Solly who'd paused for a moment, awed by the awesome destruction.

There were men inside that thing. Soldiers like us. Men with families back home.

A German shell smashed into an LCT yards away from them, splitting it in two. He focused on the shore to locate the source. The huge flak gun was half hidden inside a sunken emplacement, with only the barrel showing to give away its position.

"Target two o'clock, top of the cliff, looks like an 88."

"I see it."

The Sherman shuddered as Solly fired a round that went wide. Dale slammed in a new shell, and the 75mm bucked as they fired again. The shell also missed, but the Kraut fired a shot that grazed along the hull of their LCT and exploded in the water, only yards from the stern.

"Bastard is targeting us!" one of the sailors shouted, "Nail his ass!"

All around them the Sherman main guns were at maximum elevation, firing furiously at the 88, with little effect until the warships joined the party. Salvo after salvo rained down on the German gun, yet they seemed to possess a charmed life and continued hurling huge shells at the mass of lumbering ships. Another LST staggered as a shell slammed into the vessel. Fires and explosions broke out, and the craft lost way.

"We're getting creamed!" someone shouted. It sounded like Angel, "Someone kill that bastard!"

"I'm trying," Solly shouted, "Bastard has the luck of the Devil."

Grant could imagine Angel touching the crucifix he wore around his neck. Angel Montalban was steeped in the superstitious Catholicism of South America, where mention of the Devil not something to be taken lightly. A first generation immigrant, he was probably wondering if he'd survive to cash in with that takeaway pizza shop. Grant smiled, astonished that the absurd thought came to him at such a time.

"You wait," he'd retorted. "All I need is the cash and I'll be a millionaire. This thing is going to be big."

"You ain't got any cash, Angel," Vern reminded him. Probably because he had no money to realize his dreams either.

"Not yet, no. I was just saying if I did have it."

"Well you don't."

His thoughts snapped back to the battle as a new voice intruded on the radio net. Sergeant Ernie Elliott, an Australian immigrant to the US, he'd arrived just in time for the war. His tank was nicknamed Matilda, inevitably. He said the Australian song, Waltzing Matilda, reminded him of home.

"Shit, Solly, your lousy shooting couldn't hit a barn

from the inside. Should have put Matilda at the front. "

"Damn right. And if we meet a Tiger, I'm gonna shoot his dummkopf ass off."

He smiled at the Germanic tones of Karl 'Kraut' Lieber, Matilda's gunner. Grant had heard the Liebers were the Liebermanns when they left Germany, and they changed their name for a fresh start in the US.

Major Morgan, CO of A Company, 745th Independent Tank Battalion, snapped at them to stay off the net, and the crew of Matilda went quiet. Morgan was a good officer and all business where the war was concerned; there was nothing of the absent-minded professor about him. He was something of a hardass, but he looked after his men, who wouldn't want to serve with any other CO.

"Any moment now," the LCT skipper intoned over the speaker system.

Then the LCT would ground on the sand, and they'd drive into the hell of that lousy strip of beach, if they ever made it that far. More shells exploded all around them, and heavy machine gunfire forced the infantry to cower behind the protection of the steel hulls of the landing craft. There was a slight lull in the shooting, and he opened the hatch. The Germans had concentrated their fire to finish off a stricken LST. The craft was virtually dead in the water, listing badly to starboard, and it was only a matter of time before it sunk.

Solly climbed up beside him. "I can hardly breathe. I need a minute to get some air in my lungs. It's the damn fumes in there. The extractor can't cope."

They surveyed the fire and destruction surrounding them. Ships making their precarious way inshore, aircraft flying overhead in dense waves. In the middle of it all, somewhere, there were men. He wondered how many would survive this day. Solly took a final gulp of fresh air and went back inside the hull.

It stank of ammonia; someone had pissed himself. There'd been no groans of complaint, not today. They had bigger problems with which to concern themselves. Besides, many of them were actually looking forward to hitting back at the enemy after so many years of Nazi conquest, some with better reason than others.

Men like Solly, who thought his family could be dead after they disappeared inside the hell of the Third Reich. Karl Lieber, smarting from a legacy of Nazi oppression. There was his own brother who was killed at Slapton Sands in Devon, on a routine training exercise for Overlord. Their LCTs were shot up by a roving flotilla of German E-Boats, leaving almost a thousand men killed, two LCTs sunk, and two more severely damaged. Wasted deaths all of them, after the usual fuck ups when the escort vessels had failed to show, leaving the men exposed. When his parents heard about David, his father had a stroke and died soon after.

His relatives were surprised when he enlisted. Josh Grant was a lawyer, in his second year in a lucrative Wall Street practice after graduating summa cum laude from Yale and passing the bar. He was a natural for JAG, the Army's legal branch, everyone said, except him. They'd offered him a commission, and he was ready to go, despite his brother David's contempt for deskbound soldiers. Men who avoided the front line. Then they had the devastating news from Lyme Bay. He'd had enough; he wanted to fight the bastards, to hit them where it hurt, not spend the war in a musty courtroom. The day after the news reached them, he volunteered for active service. They said no, so he enlisted in the 745th Battalion, US Armor. The unit was desperate for leaders, and he had a track record in armor, after service in ROTC. His early promotion was inevitable after only a matter of weeks, and they shipped him to England ready for the coming invasion.

His crewmen were suspicious of the smooth, college-educated lawyer. Until he began to help some of those less fit than him who struggled through the worst parts of basic training. Some were only semi-literate, but he was more than happy to help with their letters from home. When he gave them free legal advice virtually on demand, they finally accepted the smooth faced, dark haired, and dark-eyed young sergeant.

Grant was slightly built, a whisker over five seven, and he gravitated toward armor, or maybe it gravitated toward him. In the cramped interior of a tank, it was useful to be leaner than the average soldier. Assigned to a Sherman, he quickly became expert at all aspects of operating the thirty-ton vehicle. He even came to like the noisy, smelly monsters, to enjoy the feeling of awesome power they projected. But the memory of Slapton Sands was always present. He didn't just want to fight. He wanted to kill Germans. And keep killing them.

He heard Major Morgan's voice on the net. "When we hit the beach, keep going forward. Do not stop for anything. Not for anything," he repeated.

They acknowledged. They'd heard the same speech a dozen times.

'Keep moving, and clear the beach. Hit the German defenses and send them to hell.'

Isn't that what we're here for?

"Almost there."

The crewman was standing by the ramp release, clutching the big iron lever. Then it all happened at once. The LCT shuddered as it grounded on the beach. The ramp went down the rest of the way. Angel slammed the levers into drive, and they were going forward, into the maelstrom of shells, machine gunfire, barbed wire, mortar rounds, rifle bullets, and anti-tank missiles.

Where are the Kraut planes?

So far, there'd been no air attacks, but it couldn't last. The Luftwaffe had something of a kickass reputation. So did the USAAF and the RAF. They'd seen squadrons of P-47s, Spitfires, Hurricanes, and Typhoons roaming the skies, as well as the medium and heavy bombers pounding the crap out of the enemy.

Maybe they got the Luftwaffe beat, or maybe not.

He glanced up as they rumbled forward, but the sky was empty of enemy aircraft. Forward vision from inside the turret was lousy, but there was no way he could open up the hatch if he wanted to survive. The gunfire was even more intense, an avalanche of lead and steel continuously slamming against the hull. He briefly wondered how the infantry would make out in the metal maelstrom.

They'll go to ground, dig foxholes in the sand, sure, but sooner or later, they'll have to emerge into that fiery inferno.

A shell slammed into the frontal armor of his tank, and it rocked on the springs. Angel screamed in pain.

We're hit already!

He shouted down to Vernon Franklin, the co-driver.

"Vern, check out Angel. See how bad he is."

"I'm okay, Sarge," Angel reassured him. He sounded shaken, but he was alive, "It was a steel fragment, tore away from inside the hull when that shell hit. Ripped a slice out of my side, but it's nothing."

"You can drive?"

"Yeah, I'm good. Did you see Matilda get it?"

The Aussie, Ernie Elliot. "Did they get out okay?"

"I didn't see. We were already past them. They may be okay. The shell hit them on the track."

"Anyone else?"

"No idea."

Their platoon was down to three tanks, and they'd only just started rolling up the beach. He looked up to the far cliffs, right and left, and the sloping ground in between they had to cross to get to grips with Jerry. The high cliffs of Pointe du Hoc loomed large, and further to the east, St Clare, closer to Arromanche and Gold Beach. They were the outer markers of Omaha.

Those cliffs on Pointe du Hoc will be a bastard, no question.

He knew several Ranger outfits were assigned the task of scaling the high cliffs. Under lashing fire from the defenders, it looked like an impossible mission.

Poor bastards.

A clang on the turret only inches from his head made him jump. Someone cursed. It hadn't penetrated, so it was from a smaller caliber gun. They knew a hit from an 88 would blow them apart. Like some of the coastal defense guns, it was also fitted to the Tiger I, the Germans' heavy tank. Intelligence told them the Krauts had started to field an even more formidable tank, the Tiger II, known as the King Tiger. He pushed it to the back of his mind; it would be enough to deal with the Tiger I.

Solly was determined to destroy at least one of the Nazi Panzers before the war ended, unless they were already dead. Someone told them their only chance was to close within a couple of hundred yards, to enable their 75mm to penetrate the thick armor. Although no one offered any guarantees. Neither did they tell them what the Tiger crew would be doing while they got up close. Maybe they'd be singing the Horst Wessel song and eating plates of sauerkraut. Whatever, the further away they stayed from the Tigers, the better.

"You're not scared of them?" Solly had grinned at Angel when they were discussing the German heavy tanks.

"Tigers?" the Latino exclaimed, "No, I'm not scared. I'm fucking terrified, and anyone who isn't needs his head testing before some Nazi blows it off with an 88mm shell."

Looking at that shell, bomb, and bullet-tormented beach, Grant knew there was no way they'd survive for long, even if they managed to cross the sand intact. There were too many obstacles along the way. Tiger tanks, the new Panzer Vs, which were supposed to be just as lethal. Tank hunters, assault guns, anti-tank missiles, and coastal guns, not to mention several million Germans under arms. They were supposed to be good soldiers, the Krauts, real good. They should be after several years fighting this war, including the bitter fighting reported from the Eastern Front in Russia.

Then again, Americans were no slouches. Some of them, like him, hadn't seen any action. Not until today, but the planners claimed they'd outnumber the Germans in Northern France by a factor of four to one. If they ever got off the beach, that is. There was also the fact their equipment was the best America could build, which meant the best in the world. So maybe they'd get off the beach after all. Maybe.

An anti-tank round impacted on the soft sand, narrowly missing the hull. For a few seconds clouds of debris hid the enemy positions. When it cleared, he stared through the vision slot and instantly shouted a warning.

"Target, twelve o'clock, dead ahead. Enemy gun position, hit him, Solly!"

He hardly got the last word out when the main gun fired. Vernon opened up with the Browning machine gun, spraying bullets at the enemy gun position, trying to kill his crew. Grant grasped the handle of the Browning .50 caliber in his turret, searching for a target.

There!

A coalscuttle helmet, peeping over the top of what had been camouflaged to resemble an innocent hillock of grass and sand. Another one bobbed up to take a look, then another. He could make out the barrel of a gun. No, shit, it was an anti-tank missile tube. A burst of gunfire from elsewhere on the beach ripped chunks of camouflage from the German position, exposing the shapes of the defenders.

Time to give them a taste of .50 caliber rounds.

He squeezed the trigger, and the weapon jolted in his hands as bullets streamed out the barrel.

He walked the burst onto the target. Each bullet was almost six inches in length and a whisker less than an inch in diameter. With a weight of two ounces, a single round packed a heavy punch. Grant fired twenty rounds in a continuous burst that stitched across the German position. He halted and then walked a second burst back into the dead center of the target. Then he stared at the result. The helmets had disappeared, the missile tube had vanished, and the German position was no longer there.

"How's that for shooting?" a loud voice came over the net. He recognized Ernie Elliot, the Australian.

"Hey, Ernie, we thought you were out of it."

"Nah, the engineers were alongside us in less than a minute. They hooked up a new track. We're good as new. Well, almost. It makes a racket, but they'll sort us out when we get off the beach. We just hit knocked out an enemy field gun."

"Shut up!" Major Morgan growled, "Stay off the net, all of you, unless you have something important to say."

It was good to know Matilda's crew was back. He'd assumed the worst. More shells burst around him, and he searched for the source. He couldn't see clearly, and he popped open the hatch to look out. The full devastation of Omaha Beach came into sharp focus. Burned out vehicles, tanks, equipment and LCTs lying wrecked and useless on the beach. There were also bodies, scores of bodies, hundreds of bodies. Many lay next to the strange crossed-steel structures, traps designed to rip the bottoms from landing craft. The poor bastards had sheltered behind the flimsy cover, despite all the urging to keep going forward.

A sudden movement caught his eye, out to the west. On the top of Pointe du Hoc, a turret was rotating. A German heavy tank, surely, the turret looked huge. He felt something churn in his guts, but it wasn't fear. It was something else. Fate, maybe.

What is it they say, 'someone walked on my grave.' Yeah, that's what it felt like. Why?

Then he focused his binoculars and chuckled. It was a turret fitted into a concrete base, for use as a shore defense gun. Not a tank. Not a Tiger, but still lethal. The gun fired, and close by a Sherman went up in smoke and flames.

His stomach lurched. She was one of theirs, nicknamed Cochise. The commander was Sergeant Daniel Kuruk, a full blood Indian. The hatch opened, and men started to stumble out, careful to keep the burning hull between them and the enemy guns. He counted them as they emerged, two, three four, and then five.

They made it out!

"Nail that fucker!" a voice screamed into his headset. Lieutenant Christopher Bligh, the platoon commander, riding his tank The Bounty, after his famous namesake. The order wasn't necessary. Solly was already lined up on the target, and his first shell impacted the reinforced concrete. It did little damage. He kept firing, but by now Bligh's gunner had joined in and attracted by the fall of shot, other tanks were moving their aiming points to strike the embedded turret. When the fire slackened, and the smoke cleared, the Kraut appeared undamaged. The gun fired again.

"What is that thing made of?" Dale Weathers shouted in dismay, "We keep hitting him and it barely scratches the paintwork. How about we try some AP, Sarge?"

Armor piercing, shells designed for tank on tank engagement. He hesitated for a moment and shouted in agreement.

"Three rounds AP, gunner, and then switch back to HE."

They were hurting the enemy with HE, even if the shells couldn't penetrate a hardened target. Kill enough Krauts manning the coastal defenses, and the rest would make a run for it. So they'd said back before they left England. Although if that were a Panzer V or Tiger I turret, they'd be lucky to damage it with AP. All they could hope was for it to be a turret from a Panzer IV. Thinner armor.

Solly fired off three rounds. Two of them glanced off the sloped glacis of the turret; the other missed, but it was still intact. Then the warships got interested, and the first salvo from the USS Texas exploded fifty yards from the German defenses. Someone cheered, and the gun stopped firing for several seconds, but then it fired another shell toward them. It missed, but the Texas had her teeth in the target, and two more salvos landed, one very close, and the other hit the bullseye. Concrete and ruptured steel flew into the air, and then a half-dozen secondary explosions rocked the cliff top as the store of shells exploded.

"Platoon, advance!"

Bligh's Sherman was already picking up speed as they headed for the gap in the defenses. Grant gave the order, and Angel gunned the big Continental four hundred horsepower radial engine. He could smell gasoline and thought it possible one of the hits they'd sustained had ruptured a fuel line, but when they passed another burning Sherman, the stink got stronger. They were okay, for now. He risked a glance behind him. Matilda's replacement was near enough for him to see the commander standing in the open turret. If he weren't careful, he'd take a Kraut bullet between the eyes. There were more than enough bullets to go around.

A pair of aircraft roared in on the beach and slammed the hatch closed.

Messerschmitt 109s! So they are around.

The fighters came in fast and low, and then zoomed out to the west in the direction of Utah Beach. They probably came from the Luftwaffe base on the Cotentin Peninsula. There was an airfield close to Cherbourg, one of the primary objectives of the Airborne outfits. They'd jumped early to secure bridges and other strategic targets. He smiled to himself; those Messerschmitts would get a surprise if they landed, and some hairy-assed paratrooper from the 101st or the 82nd was pointing a gun at their bellies.

Another 88 opened up, and plumes of sand were tossed into the air as the Germans sought their range.

Where the hell did that come from? Yeah, up there. Another bastard.

"Gunner, target two o'clock, up on the cliff top."

"I've got him."

Solly fired, and his armor piercing shell exploded against the cliff top. A few chunks of rock tore away and tumbled to the beach.

"Solly, you'll have to use HE. That's an open emplacement. Kill the gunners. You'll never get them with AP."

"Sorry."

The next shot impacted closer to the gun, but still the German kept firing. A shell hit the replacement Matilda yet again. This time the petrol exploded, then the ammunition store, and the vehicle became a flaming pyre. The hatches remained closed. Grant's Sherman was already at the edge of the beach starting up the long slope, behind Lieutenant Bligh, who screamed in anguish. "The fuckers, let's get 'em. Grant, are you okay?"

"Right behind you, Lt."

"Good. Did anyone get out of Matilda?"

"I don't think so."

"Shit."

They hurtled up the slope, and German defenders

popped up from foxholes where they'd been waiting to engage the armor at close range. Only twenty yards away he saw the distinctive Kraut helmet appear, followed by the long tube of a launcher; a panzerfaust, the cheap, single shot, anti-tank weapon, a disposable tube that fired a high explosive anti-tank warhead, cheap, but effective.

Before the shooter could pull the trigger, Grant swiveled the .50 caliber and riddled him with enough lead to kill a whale. The guy disappeared, and immediately he began searching for the next target. A shallow crack sounded from nearby, and he turned to see another anti-tank weapon aiming at them. This one was different, a Panzerbuchse, an anti-tank rifle.

Jesus, they're throwing everything at us.

He squeezed the trigger, and watched the target disintegrate. Scratch one Jerry.

Bligh was moving fast up the slope, and they tucked in behind him. Solly positioned the main gun over to the right, to the west, toward Pointe-du-Hoc. They'd skirted the 88mm emplacement, and now it was time to destroy the bastard before he killed any more of their comrades. Three Krauts pushed an anti-tank gun out of hiding and raced to get in a shot before the Shermans rolled over them.

"Enemy artillery, two hundred yards to the east," Bligh shouted over the net. "Fire!"

He didn't wait for an acknowledgment. The Lieutenant was charging down the enemy like hell on wheels. Two more panzerfausts popped out of hiding, and the machine guns of The Bounty shredded the gunners, brushing them aside like flies as they charged for the jackpot. The crew of the 88 had seen the danger, and they started to traverse, but their gun was as unwieldy as it was powerful. Bligh's Sherman started shooting HE. Angel stamped on the gas to draw Minnie Mouse alongside The Bounty, and Solly sent an HE shell straight into the gun pit.

Both tanks fired again, and again, and they added their secondary machine gunfire to the devastating storm of high explosive. The turret stopped traversing and fell silent.

Both tanks halted, and Bligh popped his head out to survey the damage. Grant opened up the hatch, and he could see the emplacement was a twisted, tangled mess of concrete, steel, blood and shredded human tissue. No shots buzzed and whistled past them, no shells impacted nearby. For a moment, it was as if the little corner of the battlefield was their entire world.

Grant climbed down to look. He stared with astonishment at the bloody carnage they'd wrought, and then a shell crashed into the earth yards away from where he was standing. He jumped onto the hull, ducked back inside and buttoned up.

"That was a fucking Tiger!" Vernon Franklin shouted, "I ain't kidding. We need to get out of here."

Bligh's voice sounded in Grant's headphones. "Enemy armor in front of us, about five hundred yards inland. They're only light tanks. I'm not familiar with them, but I guess we can handle them. I'll call in Able and Charlie Platoons, and we'll take them together."

"I tell you they're fucking Tigers!"

Vernon hated being wrong, especially where his favorite nightmare was concerned. Grant smiled, Bligh was right, they weren't Tigers. He identified more than a dozen French built Renault and Char Hotchkiss Model 35s. They were light tanks, thinly armored, with a main gun half the size and hitting power of the Sherman. The Germans had no business throwing those relics into battle against modern equipment. Then again, it could be a good sign. If they were that desperate for equipment, the resistance they faced inland could be less than expected.

"This is Able Platoon. We're right behind you."

"Charlie Platoon coming up on your left. Christ, what are those things? Garbage trucks?"

"French Chars," Bligh informed them, "They shouldn't hurt us, but they could murder the infantry, as well as the soft-skinned vehicles coming up the beach. Help yourselves, guys. There's plenty for everyone. Attack!"

The drivers floored the gas, and a total of nine Sherman M4s charged the enemy. Smoke appeared from the stubby barrels of the enemy armor, and several rounds chipped paint off their frontal armor, but none penetrated. The Germans could have fired M1 carbines at them for all the difference it made, and then the Shermans opened up. Within seconds, three of the Chars were smoking wrecks, and two more had slewed to a stop.

The Company A Shermans crested the low rise, and now it was a downhill race to destroy the enemy. The Germans had realized their error and turned tail, but it was too late. Someone gave out a Rebel Yell, probably Vern, as they closed with the enemy. With a top speed of seventeen miles per hour, against the thirty miles per hour of the Sherman, it was almost ritualized slaughter. The Renaults and Chars traversed their turrets to face backward, trying to hold off the vengeful M4s, but their gunnery was no more effective than before.

They caught up with them a few hundred yards away,

and Bligh led the Shermans in a charge as they opened fire on the enemy armor. They were firing AP, armor piercing shells, hitting the enemy at close range, and there was never any doubt as to the outcome. They finished off the last three vehicles inside a couple of minutes.

"Hey, some of the crews are escaping," Solly shouted, "Shoot the fuckers."

"Hold it, hold it, they're surrendering," Grant shouted before his men committed a war crime, "I'll go check them out."

"They're Krauts, only one way to check them out," Rothstein muttered, angry at the thought of a single German escaping his Old Testament wrath.

"I said don't shoot."

He opened the hatch, took out his Browning automatic, and climbed down to the road. There were five men confronting him, wearing the black uniforms that so many soldiers mistakenly assumed were SS. They were wrong; the Waffen-SS wore field gray and leopard pattern camos, not black. These men were Wehrmacht tankers, the German Army. The Heer. Grant tried to speak to an NCO using the German he'd learned at school.

"Hande Hoch! Sie sind gefangene der Amerikanischen Armee."

The Sergeant replied in English after he'd hastily raised his hands in the air.

"Please, may I translate your order?"

He shrugged. "Go ahead."

The NCO spoke rapid German, and they quickly raised their hands. He looked at Grant.

"Sir, I told them not to resist. They will not give you any trouble."

He stared at the prisoners. They were a sorry looking bunch. More like a barroom brawlers than soldiers.

"What kind of unit is this?"

The Kraut grimaced. "A penal unit, all serving out their sentences. They're under punishment for a range of offenses; theft, rape, desertion, you name it. They didn't want to fight on the Eastern Front."

"Russia? You were on the front line?"

He looked shifty. "Not exactly, no, Sir."

"What did you do?"

"I was a guard in a camp, but they transferred me."

Grant was aware of Solly standing next to him and could sense his mounting fury.

"Most of the prisoners would have been Jews," he snarled, "They take them to those kinds of places to kill them. They're murder factories."

The gunner grabbed the German with one hand and pushed the barrel of his pistol into the man's face.

"Where was this prison camp?"

Another hesitation. "Oswiecim, in Poland."

"Auschwitz," Solly breathed, "The end of the line. A death camp, isn't that right, Kraut?"

The Sergeant shrugged nervously. "I wouldn't know about such things."

"Did you kill prisoners?"

He shivered. "Some. They were Jews."

A burst of shellfire several hundred of yards away made Grant look to the west. Pointe du Hoc was wreathed in smoke and fire as a new assault began. He thought of those impossible cliffs and shivered. He climbed onto the hull of Minnie Mouse.

"Time to move out. Solly, we need to get back."

He didn't move. "What about the prisoners?"

"Send them toward the beach. They can..."

The shot made him swing around fast. Solly had his Colt automatic raised, and a wisp of smoke spiraled out the end of the barrel. The German sergeant had slumped to the ground, blood pouring from a huge wound to his head. He glared at the gunner.

"Goddamn it, Solly, what the hell did you do that for?"

His reply was stony. It was no apology. "For Auschwitz."

They looked up as Bligh's tank returned and halted next to them. He glanced down at the bloody body of the German and then at the remaining prisoners. When he looked at Grant, his eyes were cold.

"Tell me this isn't what it looks like, Sergeant Grant."

Before Josh could reply, yet another armada of large aircraft flew low, heading inland to chew up the defenses. The ground shook with the elemental roar from the engines of scores of four-motor bombers. When the noise died away, Grant gazed at Bligh.

"The Kraut was trying to escape, Lt."

"Who shot him? Was it you, Grant?"

"It was me."

He felt Solly's gaze boring into his back. He'd have to have a word with the stupid bastard. Revenge was one thing, but if he did it too often, they'd string him up for war crimes. Then again, the German had clearly been involved with killing Jews in this place called Auschwitz. If it were true, the Russians would soon uncover the evidence as they steamrollered through the Nazis on their way to Berlin. But once was enough. No more.

"It doesn't look like an escape attempt, not to me," Bligh said quietly, "Don't let it happen again, is that clear?"

"Yes, Sir."

"What the hell's going on here?"

They swung around and glanced at the officer standing in the turret of a Sherman that had just pulled up next to them. Grant felt like he'd been kicked in the guts. Of all the officers who had to come past right now, it had to be Lindbergh. Bligh pointed to the dead German.

"The German was shot trying to escape, Colonel."

"Is that right?"

He climbed out of the turret, jumped to the ground, and dusted off his immaculate uniform.

"Who killed him?"

"It was Sergeant Grant, Sir."

Lindbergh nodded in satisfaction. He'd been seeking an excuse to nail Grant ever since he found out he was a lawyer. People said he'd taken a hit from a pack of high-priced lawyers in a messy divorce back home, and he was looking for some form of revenge on the legal profession. When Grant joined the 745th, both an NCO and a lawyer, he was fair game. He stared at the Sergeant, working hard to control a smirk.

"Why did you murder this man, Grant?"

"Who said anything about murder, Sir?"

Lindbergh looked angry. "Just answer the question."

"I killed him. For your information, nobody murdered him. I shot him while he was trying to escape."

"Bullshit!" the dapper Colonel spat out, "It's as clear a case of murder as I've ever seen. The penalty is death. I'm placing you under open arrest, pending court martial. You will continue in command of your tank for the time being. I will call you to answer charges at a later stage. Don't try running away. It'll only make things worse." He sneered. "Maybe this would be a good time to get yourself a lawyer."

Grant gave him a hard stare. "Fuck you, Colonel."

His face was bright red with anger. "I'll add insubordination to the charge of murder. You will not use inappropriate language to your superior officer."

He stared back at him. "Fuck you, Colonel," he said again."

With a huge effort, he managed to control his anger. "You just disobeyed a direct order from a superior officer, and in the face of the enemy. You should know the penalty is death."

"Is that right? Which one comes first, death for the murder or death for disobeying the order?"

A few yards away someone sniggered. Lindbergh glared at him for a few moments, then turned on his heel and stomped back to his tank.

"We need to move on," Bligh said eventually, "There's a lot of Krauts to kill." He gave Grant a significant glance, "On the battlefield, I mean."

"It wasn't murder, Lt."

"I'll do my best to get it straightened out."

"Sure."

Bligh wasn't a bad officer, whereas Lindbergh was a nasty little shit. He was consoled by the fact they were confronting what some people said was the biggest, most formidable army in the world. Their chances of survival were not good. And when they encountered the Tigers, they were worse, probably infinitesimal.

He put Lindbergh out of his mind. After they'd sent the Germans' Russian prisoners walking back toward the beach, they got the tracks rolling again. Grant looked seaward; they'd come a distance of only a few hundred yards. Yet the ground was strewn with bodies and wrecked vehicles. How many more deaths would they suffer before they reached Berlin? Would any of them survive? More bombers were attacking to the south, and the landscape echoed to the thunder of heavy explosions.

The Germans are probably wondering the same thing.

The salvos from the warships kept coming, and it seemed as if they'd shoot off every shell in their arsenals before they called it a day. But the Germans were fighting back hard. Machine gunfire and anti-tank guns hit back incessantly, and when he looked south, he had a fleeting glimpse of a Kraut tank. For a brief moment he thought it was a Tiger, but then he recognized it as a tank destroyer. It melted into a small wood and disappeared. It was big, much bigger than their M10s, which were built on the hull of a Sherman. With any luck, the bombers would find it.

Solly joined him in the turret. "You heard that guy. Bastard Germans, killing Jews, he deserved it."

"Maybe, but don't do it again, Solly."

"I hear you, Sarge. And thanks for taking the rap. They would never have believed me."

"Maybe, maybe not."

"Is that true, Lindbergh could charge you with murder?"

He smiled. "Let's get on with the war, Solly. I couldn't give a damn about Lindbergh."

* * *

Franz raced around the side of the barn, his face sweating with exertion.

"Obersturmfuhrer, our orders have arrived from

61

Division. They want to speak to you."

Manhausen nodded thanks his driver and walked quickly to the farmhouse. The radio operator handed the mike to him.

"Dreux HQ for you, Sir."

He took the instrument. "This is Obersturmfuhrer Manhausen."

"Heil Hitler!" The radio operator the other end sounded excited, "We have orders at last to head for the beaches. The Fuhrer has instructed our Tigers to throw the Allies back into the sea."

He didn't return the Heil Hitler. "I assume we are to move after nightfall. We should have received those orders last night while it was still dark. We cannot leave until 22.00 at the earliest."

"Sir, the order requires you to move immediately and engage the enemy."

"In daylight, that's madness! The distance is one hundred and fifty kilometers at the least, and we can expect to have enemy aircraft attacking us every meter of the way. We may as well place charges and destroy the Panzers ourselves."

A pause. "I'm sorry, Obersturmfuhrer, but the order comes from the Fuhrer himself, direct from Berchtesgaden."

He fought down his anger. He'd sworn an oath to obey the Fuhrer. Yet to obey this order would wipe out most of their precious Tigers. He tried to picture the route they must take.

Can we make it alive to the Channel beaches? A few of us could get through, yes, but we'll lose many of our precious tanks.

They'd also have to detour, using up more precious fuel,

in order to try and stay behind cover. They'd be forced to use hedgerows and woods, darting from one to the other, always keeping an eye on the sky. For long stretches of the journey, he knew there were no trees. In which case, they'd be sitting ducks for the Typhoons, the Lancasters, and the B-17s.

"Sir?"

He realized the man was still waiting for his acknowledgement. There was only one possible answer.

"Is the Generalfeldmarschal aware of the order?"

"It came through Generalfeldmarschal von Rundstedt's headquarters, Sir."

"And Rommel?"

"He is on a visit to Germany, Sir. He went home for his wife's birthday."

With a huge effort, he prevented himself from laughing. They couldn't wake the Fuhrer from his rest, in order to repel an Allied invasion that could potentially force them all the way back to the German border. And Rommel was visiting his wife to celebrate her birthday.

Am I insane, or is it them? And they tell us we are the master race!

"Very well. You may tell Generalfeldmarschal von Rundstedt we have received the order, and will move at once. I trust the Luftwaffe will provide air cover along the way?"

The man took several seconds before he replied. "The Luftwaffe is short of fuel, Sir. As soon as they find some gas, they will attempt to put up some aircraft."

What is this, an army or a bunch of halfwits? That ignoramus Goering, he should get his fat ass over here and put a rocket under his pilots. Then again, if they had no gas, who was to blame? Not the men on the front line, that was for sure.

"I understand."

He put the receiver down after he'd heard the operator say, "Good luck, Sir."

We'll need more than good luck, my friend. We'll need a miracle. It's time to round up my schoolchildren and drive to the beaches.

When he reached the barn, he could hear the massive Maybach engine ticking over. Even at low revs, it was a mighty throb that shook the flimsy wooden structure. SS-Sturmann Franz Schelling grinned at him from the driver's vision slot. The gunner, Unterscharfuhrer Heinrich Boll, was on the deck, securing the lines that held spare equipment to the hull. He saluted Manhausen.

"Sir, we're all secured and ready to go."

"Good. The rest of the crew?"

"Wilhelm is warming up the radio. Siegfried is also inside the hull, checking the ammunition."

He nodded. "You've done well, Boll. We're moving out to the beaches."

"They're sure, the Allies are really coming?"

His seventeen-year-old face shone with enthusiasm. Rolf knew it was Boll's ambition to command his own Panzer. He also knew the kid would never survive long enough to achieve his dream. None of them would. From across the road, another Tiger of the 12th SS HJ nosed out of a haystack where they'd hidden through the night, and the behemoth moved toward the tarmac road. He climbed into the turret, adjusted his headphones and microphone, and called the crew.

"Stay alert for enemy aircraft. You can be sure they'll be somewhere overhead. Franz, follow that Tiger in front of us, but don't get too close."

"Jawohl, Obersturmfuhrer."

He was good, and the order was unnecessary. Like Heinrich Boll, Franz was seventeen years old. Both of them were the oldest kids in his crew, apart from himself. He was ancient; he'd gone to Russia an enthusiastic 23-year-old officer. He returned two years later, and twenty years older. His dark hair was streaked with gray, which he tried to conceal. It was enough his crew were so young, without highlighting the difference by having a gray-haired commander.

Their Tiger rolled onto the road and took up station one hundred meters behind the tank in front. Behind them, another steel monster rolled into formation and joined the line, and another and another. Rolf suddenly remembered the most important ritual of all, and leaned down to make his voice heard over the roar of the engine and the clatter of the tracks.

"Hals und Beinbruch!"

They laughed delightedly and echoed his words. A pagan German custom, it translated as 'break a neck and a leg.' The idea was to fool the Devil. But it wouldn't fool the Amis or the British. Not for a moment.

CHAPTER TWO

Berchtesgaden, Germany, The Second Day – June 7, 1944

Even those staff who'd observed his gradual decline found themselves shocked. Since the defeat of the Sixth Army at Stalingrad, he'd become more irritable, more inclined to fly into fits of rage. Even worse, his decision-making abilities were lessened. He was unsure, hesitant even. When he did make up his mind, he issued strings of commands without recourse to advice from his experienced Generals.

Perhaps he knew they were men who would have advised him the inevitable outcome of his insane refusal to consider tactical withdrawal would result in the loss of even more tens of thousands of German soldiers. As the Commander-in-Chief of the German Army, he'd become a liability. But they still watched him, fascinated by his effortless ability to dominate a room and to overwhelm his audience.

"It is nothing but a ruse," he told them, his voice harsh,

but under control, "I suspected the Allies would make a diversionary attack on my Fortress Europe, and they have fallen into my trap. The Panzer divisions are waiting outside Pas de Calais, and when the main Allied force lands, the armor will smash them to pieces."

Feldmarschal Keitel nodded, enthusiastic as ever. "Your genius is all we need to destroy all who dare to attack us, Mein Fuhrer."

Hitler nodded. After all, the praise was no more than his due. Before he could speak again, another voice intruded.

"Fuhrer, they are landing in Normandy in vast numbers. It is hard to believe they have sufficient forces to mount an additional attack further east. I have spoken to Rommel, and he believes this is the real thing. We should move our Panzers to the beaches immediately and repel them before it is too late."

The haunted, laser eyes flickered around and focused on Colonel Ernst Schraub, an aide to Colonel General Jodl, who hissed at his man to be silent. It was too late.

"Do you question my judgment, Colonel?"

The voice was icy, and the volume began to rise. They waited for the explosion.

"Of course not, Mein Fuhrer."

"I do not believe you, Schraub. You say that Rommel, and presumably yourself, do not agree with my reading of the situation."

His voice rose to a scream, "I TELL YOU IT IS A DIVERSION! YOU WILL CONTACT VON RUNSTREDT NOW, GIVE HIM MY ANALYSIS, AND TELL HIM TO CONTINUE TO HOLD THE PANZERS IN RESERVE."

Hitler's face was now bright red, and his eyes blazed

with a furnace-like heat, huge and filled with a terrible anger. "IS THAT CLEAR?"

"Yes, Mein Fuhrer."

The unfortunate aide stumbled toward the door to pass on the message to Feldmarschal von Rundstedt, Commander-in-Chief of the Armed Forces in France. Behind him, he heard Hitler speaking again. It was as if a switch had been thrown, and the Fuhrer's voice was almost normal.

"The situation in Russia needs to be stabilized. When we have beaten back these Allies, I will send the heavy Panzer divisions back to the Eastern Front where they are more needed."

"Brilliant, Mein Fuhrer. A master stroke."

It was Keitel again, of course. Hitler's yes-man, nicknamed Lakeitel, German for 'the nodding donkey.' Schraub stumbled into the radio room. After he'd passed on the order, he decided it was time to contact Rommel. The man really was a military genius, and Hitler respected him for his abilities. Perhaps he could persuade the Fuhrer to move the Panzers to the beaches. There was only one way to beat the Allied invasion, and that was with armor, heavy armor, Tiger and Panther tanks, and the new King Tigers. Assemble them in a single massive force and hurl them at the impudent invaders. They would pound them into scrap. Dunkirk would be a tea party in comparison to the fate they would meet in Normandy, if the Fuhrer could be persuaded to allow them to move.

* * *

Omaha Beach, June 7, 1944

They'd endured a tough night. The Krauts weren't about to fold, that was for sure, and several fierce counterattacks hit them hard. They lost two more M4s, one to an anti-tank gun and one to a panzerfaust. In the end, they managed to secure a position where their armored vehicles were hull down, protected by a natural depression in the ground. They even grabbed a couple of hours sleep. Yet there was much work to do, the Krauts were still fighting back hard.

There'd been little sign of heavy armor. The crappy French tanks the Germans captured in 1940 were outdated and easily dealt with. The STUG IIIs were something else. A mobile assault gun and tank killer, they had a low profile that made them hard to hit. They were a dangerous enemy, and their 75mm gun packed enough punch to take out a Sherman. The STUGs were issued to Panzergrenadier units, who'd made several attacks close to the landing beaches. So far, they'd beaten them all back. The real puzzle was the armor.

Where are the Tigers?

He grinned, the crew asked him the same question several times every hour. It was understandable; they wanted to know when to duck and run.

"Sergeant Grant!"

He climbed to his feet as Major Morgan approached in the dark, predawn chill.

"Yes, Sir."

"You did well yesterday. With those French tanks."

"They were nothing, Sir. Tin cans is all they are."

"Maybe. Listen, we're moving inland, some place called Gruchy. The 29th Infantry will spearhead the advance, and we'll support them as and when they need us. The objective is Vierville, you got that on your map?"

Grant took out his map case and squinted at the rough detail.

"Yes, Sir, Vierville. When do we jump off?"

"Soon. We'll wait for them to move and stay close. The objective is to link up with Utah Beach in the west, but that'll take time. The signs are the Krauts ain't gonna leave without a fight."

He seemed to pause for a few moments, and then he went on, "A warning, Sergeant Grant. Ike takes a dim view of shooting prisoners, you copy that?"

So Lieutenant Bligh ratted me out. Too bad, they can't prove anything.

"Yessir."

"If we start shooting their soldiers, they'll do the same to our men. Besides, we're not butchers, not like the Nazis."

"Nossir."

"Even if they are murdering Jews in the thousands, if what we're hearing is true." He fixed Grant with a fierce stare, "If you take a prisoner who you believe has been involved in that kind of activity, you know what to do."

"Yessir."

"Good." He grinned, "If you think he's guilty, shoot the bastard, but next time don't get caught."

He felt his eyebrows shoot up in surprise. The Major gave him a grim smile. "My wife's family is Jewish, so you can imagine how I feel about these Nazi swine."

Morgan stomped away, leaving him scratching his head in astonishment.

So much for that!

He went to roust his crew as the first rays of dawn crept across the beaches from the east. They bathed the outlines of the Shermans in a hard, harsh light, making them a perfect target for an air attack. He looked up.

No sign of the Luftwaffe, thank God. Then again, *USAAF and the RAF appear to have total air superiority, at least so far. If the Luftwaffe does come, they'll get a hot reception.*

Cheered by that thought, he roused the crew. Solly was awake, his face screwed up in thought. Grant followed the direction of his gaze, a stretch of coastline with a small fishing village in the distance. It was like a Monet painting, the impression reinforced by the soft lines of the pale dawn, the hard edges blurred by the swirling smoke smoothed the definition. He recalled Rothstein was a talented artist in his spare time, when he wasn't busy with his principal work as an accountant for a big city firm.

"You thinking about painting that scene? It sure looks good."

Solly turned around, and Grant was shocked by the grim lines on his face, as if he'd aged five years in just a few hours.

"Not really. It reminds me of something, Beach at Trouville, I guess, by Boudin. He painted it in the late nineteenth century. Before it was light, I could visualize it down there, the beach umbrellas, the bathhouses, and the vacationers. When it started to get light, I realized it was an illusion. The umbrellas, the bathhouses, they were wrecked and burned out vehicles. And the people were all dead."

He didn't reply for a few moments. Then he nodded his understanding. "You're thinking about your folks."

"Yep. It was that Kraut, his talk about Auschwitz.

People say they're killing Jews in the tens of thousands in that camp. I keep thinking about my relatives."

"It may be a rumor, Solly. You could be worrying over nothing."

The other man gave him a skeptical glance. "We moving out?"

"We are. Our job is to support the ground pounders, 29th Infantry. Their objective is Vierville. It's a village about half a mile inland. Our job is to run interference if they run into enemy armor."

He nodded, his face still etched with worry. "I guess it's time to ring the breakfast gong."

"Yeah, get them moving."

They both looked around the area. The beach and inland areas were still alive with machine gunfire, artillery, and the ships pounding the defenses, although they'd shifted their aim further inland. Aircraft droned overhead, in ones, twos, and sometimes whole fleets; all heading for the enemy positions, hitting the crap out of them, and returning to Britain to refuel and rearm.

"It's like a machine," Solly mused, "A well-oiled machine, a conveyor belt of death. Except when the belt breaks, and men fall into the cogs to be chewed up and spat out, just so much bone and gristle."

It sounds like a premonition of death, but whose death?

"Round 'em up, Solly. We need to find some breakfast. I have a feeling it's going to be a long day. At least it isn't raining."

As he said it, the first large drops splattered on his head, and the downpour followed. He grinned.

"My fault, I shouldn't have tempted fate."

"Nope. Any chance of breakfast?"

"Not one. I saw the quartermaster's truck go down with one of those LCTs. Our cookhouse gear was loaded, food, cookers, you name it."

"That's okay. We'll manage with what we have inside the lockers on Minnie. Maybe we can stroll into Vierville later and buy a couple of French loaves from a boulangerie."

"If we can beat the Krauts first and toss them out."

Solly winced and strolled off. He was a man with a lot on his mind. Any man who thought the enemy was murdering his folks would be pissed. Was he any different? He was determined to make them pay for his brother David, but at least he'd been a soldier. If the stories were true, they were killing civilians in droves.

Fucking Krauts. I hate them, I really do.

A half hour and a cold greasy breakfast inside his belly, he climbed onto the hull and slid into the turret hatch. He leaned down to shout to the driver.

"Angel, did you check the fuel?"

"We're over half full, Sarge. How far are we going today?"

"About a half-mile, if we're lucky."

A chuckle. "We could cook dinner for the Battalion with what we have, and still have enough gas for the day."

"I hear you. How about ammo?"

"We fired off about half what we had in the locker. Mainly HE, we've got plenty of AP if we run into armor."

"Dale, how about belts for the machine guns?"

"We're good. I've reloaded, and we have spares, provided we're not planning to fight all the way to Berlin. Not today, anyway."

No one laughed. "I guess we're good to go. Start engine and move up behind the Bounty."

The engine roared, and the stink of exhaust fumes engulfed them. Angel slammed the gears into forward drive, and they lurched forward. Major Morgan's voice came into his earphones.

"This is the Company Commander. Intel has reported there's an elite German unit in the area, the 352nd Infantry Division. Some of their men are vets from the Eastern Front, so they've asked us to go check them out. I'll take the rest of the Company. Lieutenant Bligh, I want your platoon to stay with the infantry. They say the Krauts have a unit of artillery up ahead. Good luck, men. Move out."

"That's just our damn luck," Vernon whined, "Why couldn't we be facing a unit of German Red Cross nurses? We could give 'em a good time, persuade the girls to desert and come over to our side."

"It'd take more than your ugly mug to persuade them," Dale growled. It was one of those times when Vern had got on his nerves a tad too much. He got on all their nerves.

"Fuck you," Vern swore in retaliation, "You find me any girl, and I'll sweet talk her into bed before you have time to spit."

"You spit at girls, is that the way you do it down South?"

"You come here, and I'll..."

"Cut it out!" Grant snapped, "If you want to fight anyone, save your strength for the Germans. You heard the Major, Angel. Move out."

"You got it," he replied nonchalantly.

Minnie lurched forward, and this time Bligh led them away from the beach, as Morgan's armor sped away at a tangent. A couple of hundred yards ahead of them, the infantry were marching in a long line, evenly spaced, hugging the verge on the edge of the road. If they hit serious trouble, they'd disappear into the ditch and call in the Shermans. At first it looked as if the Germans had pulled back. There was plenty of shooting and shelling, but all of it some distance away. It was as if they were in some kind of a dead zone when an MG42 opened up, with its peculiar buzz saw ripping noise, and a half-dozen soldiers went down.

"Ambush, get moving!" Bligh shouted, "Kraut machine gun, he's holed up in a cottage up ahead, kind of white, with blue shutters. I can see the muzzle flashes. Hit the bastard."

Grant thumbed his mike. "Gunner, load HE."

"Loaded and ready."

"Target is the white cottage, one o'clock, two hundred yards ahead."

"I'm on it."

"Fire!"

The gun crashed back on its mountings as the shell left the barrel, and already Dale was stooping forward to load the next.

"Keep firing. I want that position destroyed. Kill them."

Solly and Dale continued with a fast rate of fire while Angel kept the Sherman moving forward. The machine gun had stopped firing, and Grant opened the hatch to get a better view. He saw them, the distinctive square helmets, two men darting away from the cottage and using the garden wall as cover.

"Gunner, they've changed position, fifty yards behind the cottage, on the other side of the wall."

"Got it."

The motor whined as he rotated the turret to aim at

the new target. He was too slow. By the time the first shell hurtled out of the barrel, the two men had slipped away, carrying their machine gun with them. He felt a keen sense of disappointment. The idea of those young infantrymen cut down almost before they'd started rankled. It was something else to settle, like David's death.

What was it they said? 'Vengeance is a dish best taken cold.' Something like that.

"Cease fire, they're gone. Driver, keep moving. Follow those men from the 29th."

Angel gunned Minnie's engine, and a cloud of exhaust smoke puffed into the air, almost like he was sending out a smoke signal. They trundled slowly after The Bounty, staying behind the marching men. The Major came back on the net.

"Heads up. The Rangers just reported a sighting of enemy soldiers digging in. They're building ambush positions. The shit's about to hit the fan, so button up."

Grant ducked back inside the turret and slammed the hatch closed, not a second too soon. A bullet pinged off the thick steel where he'd been standing a moment before. He searched through his vision slot, looking for the shooter. A single well-concealed sniper could do terrible damage to those foot soldiers.

"Enemy armor!" Vernon shouted, "Four hundred yards. Jesus Christ, they're Tigers!"

He searched the ground ahead and found the target. There were no Tigers. The enemy had brought up assault guns, three STUG IIIs. The 75mm guns could do wicked damage to a Sherman, and they would murder the exposed infantry, but they were also vulnerable.

"Calm down, Vern. They're STUGs. Gunner, load AP,

open fire."

"On the way."

Dale and Solly were ready, and the shell left the gun almost before he'd stopped speaking. A miss, the AP round impacted a stone wall a couple of yards from the lead STUG. The German returned fire, and his shell also missed, but only by inches. Shrapnel from the explosion rattled against the armor. He suddenly realized they were in their first real armored duel. It could also be their last. The Bounty was firing furiously at the STUGs, and then Cochise joined in. Their combined shells knocked out one enemy STUG in an instant. A second assault gun exploded seconds later, but the third was more difficult, hidden behind the burning, smoking wreckage of his pals.

While they fought their duel, the 29th were in more trouble. The secondary armament, an MG34 of the surviving STUG was doing wicked damage to the infantry. He watched with horror as the hail of lead scythed down exposed infantrymen. He itched to close with the STUG and destroy it, but it was impossible. The gun was behind the two wrecked assault guns, well hidden with only the upperworks presenting a limited target. There was no sign of the Panzergrenadiers he knew wouldn't be too far away. They could be waiting with anti-tank artillery, panzerfausts, and more machine guns.

I have to do something.

Desperately, he surveyed the area and then found what he was looking for, a narrow path that would take them around the enemy's flank. It was narrow, much too narrow, but it was enough. Men were dying.

It has to be enough.

"Driver, steer right. Take the narrow path sixty yards

ahead. We're going to flank those bastards and hit them where it hurts."

"You got it," Angel sang out.

He pedaled the gas, and the heavy vehicle rocked on its springs as he zigzagged forward to make them a hard target. When he reached the turn, he swung onto the track, which was barely wide enough for a narrow farm cart.

"Hey, Sarge, we ain't gonna get through here. Look up ahead, those houses. There ain't room to take a pedal cycle through there."

"I see 'em. Keep moving."

"Okay."

He sounded dubious, for good reason. They'd only traveled a hundred yards when the path narrowed between two Normandy stone cottages. The Sherman was almost nine feet wide. The gap between the two houses was no more than six. Angel slowed again.

"You sure about this? I mean, we're gonna do some serious damage here."

"Keep moving, driver."

"There could be people inside those houses."

"Then they'll have to jump for it. Knock 'em down if you like, but take us through there."

There was no reply, but Angel gunned the engine to full power, and they picked up speed as the Sherman drove slightly downhill. When they hit the cottages, the big vehicle was doing almost doing thirty miles per hour. Thirty tons of high-grade American steel smashed into the ancient French stonework. Although Minnie checked, there never was any competition. The 470 horsepower, 21-liter Chrysler 30 cylinder engine punched a way through as if the houses were made of mere cardboard.

They cleared the cottages out of sight of the enemy, and he pushed the hatch open to survey the ground.

Chunks of masonry fell off the hatch as he opened up, and when he looked behind, the cottages were ripped open, as if by a can opener. The interior of each cottage was on display to the world, neat furniture, a coat hanging on the back of a door, and a burly woman, staring back at him. She caught his eye, raised a fist, and shook it at him. He waved back.

Sorry, lady, I didn't know you were there. Jesus, that was a close one.

A rifle shot whined off the open hatch cover, and he dropped back inside the turret.

"Vern, get on the machine gun. We have a sniper out there somewhere. Find him and kill him before he gets any more of our guys."

"Fuckin' A!"

Grant gripped the butt of his own .50 caliber and checked out the surrounding trees and bushes. The bastard had to be there somewhere. Out of nowhere a bunch of infantry grunts ran forward, a shot cracked out, one of them threw up his hands and pitched forward. But Grant had him now, a couple of trees surrounded by thick bushes. He'd seen the tiny movement of a branch when the bullet left the barrel.

"Vern, ten o'clock, two small trees, bushes at the base. He's inside."

"Yeah, I got him. This one's mine."

He pulled the trigger of the M1919 Browning machine gun, and the bushes danced as the barrage of .30 caliber bullets ripped into them. Grant aimed and fired his .50 cal, and the interior of the tank echoed burst after burst from the two machine guns. The foliage was soon torn into little pieces, along with anyone sheltering inside.

"Cease fire! Driver, halt!"

The stillness was strange, just the low throb of the engine on tick over, the tiny noises of hot metal as the barrel of his machine gun cooled, and a half mile away the thud of artillery and tanks as they slogged it out. It could only be Morgan's Company A, and it looked as if they'd walked into a heap of trouble. There was nothing he could do, and he kept his finger on the trigger while he searched for signs of the enemy, but it was quiet. A big black bird flew down, a crow or a raven, and landed on the ground to start pecking at some invisible morsel. Probably they'd churned up the ground and disturbed a few worms. He grinned.

Expensive worms.

He opened the hatch and cautiously poked his head up. No one shot at him.

"Driver advance. Let's go check it out."

They left the track and rumbled over a grassy field up toward the trees. The big bird heard them coming and had the sense to fly away. It hadn't been pecking for worms. The body of the German sniper lay half covered by broken branches and fallen leaves, his guts spilled out on the ground. His face was still intact, a kid of maybe sixteen or seventeen years old, too young to shave.

I only hope he got laid before they sent him out to kill our soldiers.

He thumbed his mike.

"We're done here. Let's go get that STUG."

They crept over the top of the small hill and below them was a fine view of the battlefield. Four hundred yards to the north the Channel was a car park for ships, thousands of them. Warships fired endless salvos to hit targets deep inland, and smaller vessels were coming and going, unloading more men and equipment for the battle. To the west, just inland from Pointe du Hoc, the Germans were counterattacking, and a fierce battle raged.

To the southwest, toward Carentan on the Cotentin Peninsula he could see, but it was too far away to make it out. Except it could only be Germans trucks, maybe, or more STUGs. It could be Panzers. That would make sense; chances are they'd run into them soon.

Panzers could also mean Tigers, Vern Franklin's bogeymen. No, that isn't entirely true. They're every man's bogeymen.

Their target, the STUG, lay ahead only four hundred yards away. The crew had disguised the top of the hull with branches, but from above, they could make out almost the whole of the target. To the east, he could see units of the 29th, hopelessly pinned down by a single assault gun. Further back, the other two Shermans were still firing. Their shells exploded on the ground around the STUG, churning it over like some monstrous plow. But none managed a hit.

"How we gonna play this?" Solly asked.

He smiled. The gunner's face was smeared with soot and grease. He looked more like a Special Forces soldier about to sneak up on the enemy than a tanker.

"We'll go in fast, hit them like a thunderbolt. The ground doesn't look too bad. Can the gyrostabilizer can handle it?"

"I tweaked it, damn thing was too slow. I can hit him now we can see the bastard."

"Okay. Angel, full speed; give 'em hell."

He had to grab the machine gun to prevent the sudden

lurch tossing him out of his seat. They were charging full pelt down the Normandy field, straight as an arrow and toward the STUG. The Germans were concentrating on hitting the infantry and failed to see the danger until it was too late.

"Fire!" he shouted at Solly, but once again the gunner's uncanny ability to time his shots to perfection was ahead of him. The main gun crashed out, and the recoil slammed the breech back. The first shell again missed the enemy, but Dale was already reloading, struggling to keep his balance as they bumped every time they hit a depression in the ground.

Solly fired again and scored a hit. The Sherman's main gun had a barrel length of ten feet and fired a shell weighing fourteen pounds, HE or AP. The AP shell could penetrate armor up to three inches thick. The STUG's frontal armor was a whisker over three inches, but they weren't shooting at the front of the vehicle. The rear armor was not so thick.

The Germans didn't stand a chance. The shell shredded men and machine, and exploded part of their ready use ammunition. The explosion was spectacular, and Angel brought the Sherman to a halt. In the distance, they could hear cheering from the foot soldiers running from cover to continue their advance to secure the landing areas.

A few hundred yards away, he caught sight of Major Morgan leading the rest of A Company in the direction of Gruchy, his tank distinctive because of the long, wavy aerials attached to the hull. There was something wrong, and Grant began to count the numbers.

Three, four, five...Only five?

"Solly, you see our Company over there. How many

M4s do you count?"

"Uh, five. Oh shit, where are the rest of them?" A silence, "Maybe they went somewhere else?"

"It's not likely. I think we've just lost half the Company. I think they're gone."

The enormity was almost too much to sink in. Solly gave him an incredulous stare.

"We're still only a few hundred yards from the beach."

They were all listening. Just over twenty-four hours after they drove ashore, and already half of their Company was destroyed.

"We'll get some Krauts and pay them back, don't worry. Those bastards are gonna regret the day they played around with Company A. Driver, take us back and slot in next to The Bounty."

"You got it."

Angel followed the road this time to join up with the column, and they fell into line. Bligh called him up on the Company net.

"That was good work, you guys. We watched you take out that STUG, well done."

"You want the best, you call for Minnie Mouse," Vern exclaimed with glee.

"Shut up, Vern," three men said at once.

It was bad luck to boast, especially when you were in a battle zone. Something about tempting the Devil, someone had said. Maybe it was because war was much too serious to brag about. They rejoined the Company, and Morgan called them.

"We'll halt this side of that low rise ahead. We'll laager there and wait for the 29th to call us forward."

Grant checked his wristwatch. To his astonishment, it

was already midday. They'd been fighting all morning, yet it seemed to have happened in the blink of an eye. The Shermans drove slowly toward their designated areas and maneuvered to form a defensive circle. Sufficiently far apart from each other to be safe from destruction should a shell or bomb hit a nearby tank, yet near enough to hit back in force if an enemy appear from any direction.

There was movement to the northeast, little more than a flicker on a distant hilltop, and Grant took out his binoculars. A single tank was moving west to east. It could only be a German, for Allied armor hadn't penetrated that far. It was in shadow and well camouflaged, which made it impossible to identify from the silhouette. But when the clouds cleared, the sun suddenly lighted it up, and a great, gray-green monstrous shape materialized. Solly climbed up next to him and focused a small spotting telescope on the distant target.

"Holy shit, it's a..."

"A Tiger."

The blunt, square shape of the immense armored hull was unmistakable. As was the long 88mm gun, a monstrous appendage that could hit and destroy a target from a distance a Sherman could only dream about.

"I'd best call Vern," Solly smiled, "He'll want to see this. You know the range of that gun is said to be two miles."

"Leave him alone. He'll meet a Tiger soon enough."

They watched the tank in silence. To their surprise, the Tiger halted. A flash of sunlight reflected from the turret, which meant the Tiger commander was watching them through binoculars. He shivered. It felt as if someone had walked on his grave.

What was it about that distant Tiger? It was the first one

they'd seen since they hit the beach. Yet it was something more, a weird vibe, a feeling he couldn't shake off.

Fear? No, it isn't fear. We're too far away for a fight. What is it?

He thought for a few moments and came up with the answer.

Fate. Somehow we're gonna meet up with that Tiger. Maybe not today, but our futures will be intertwined.

He shook his head and smiled. It was a crazy thought. The Nazi supertank was at least three miles away, too far for any kind of recognition. There was no way they'd ever know if they came across it again. Even so, he knew deep down in his guts something connected their Sherman to that tank.

We'll meet again, no question.

"How do we deal with something like that?" Solly asked him, "If we're ever going to beat the Krauts, we have to find a way to destroy those things."

He'd been thinking the same thing. "We have to get up close and hit them in the rear, so the experts say. Maybe we could penetrate the side armor. That's not so thick. The Brits did capture a Tiger intact in the desert a while back. A shell from one of their Churchills jammed the turret, but it was a one in a million chance. I guess the best way is to leave them to the bombers."

Solly grimaced. "Sure, the Air Force is like the cops. When you need one, they're never around. All we can do is hope we don't ever tangle with that big, bad bastard."

Except I know we will tangle with that big, bad bastard.

"We'll meet him," he murmured.

He hadn't meant to say it aloud, but the gunner stared intently at him.

"What was that? How do you mean, we'll meet him?"

"I dunno, Sol. Just woolgathering, I guess."

The both focused on the distant Tiger. It was still stationary. Watching like a predator, waiting to pounce.

Probably they're working out how they want to kill us when we meet.

* * *

The drive north from Dreux had been a bastard, and they'd already lost three Tigers to enemy aircraft. Manhausen wanted to curse the idiot who'd delayed the decision and cost them the night hours, and then sent them forward in daylight. No doubt they all felt the same, but none dared to voice their thoughts. They all knew the reason for the delay. The Fuhrer had been in bed, and they didn't want to disturb him.

Dummkopfen!

To add to their misery, some Feldgendarmerie cop, the German military police had directed them the wrong way, and instead of joining the rest of the unit on the outskirts of Caen, they'd come too far west. Right now, they were overlooking one of the invasion beaches close to a village named Vierville. They'd discovered the error when Rolf grew suspicious that the road was empty of German armor. He managed with some difficulty, and the grudging assistance of a surly French cop, to pinpoint their location on the map.

Why are French cops all so surly? I can understand it now, but I came here before the war, and they were no different. Miserable bastards.

Just when they started to retrace their steps, the engine had overheated, following the long drive. Because they had lost their way, they were separated from the mechanics that would normally have been available to make repairs. They were on their own.

"Franz, how long is it going to take? You know we're a sitting target for the bombers up here."

The reply was slow in coming. He sounded irritable, "I'm doing my best, Obersturmfuhrer. It's those verdammt valves. They're a load of crap. All of our Tigers are having problems with their engines, and it's no wonder. I'll bet they're made of cheap tin."

It was the same story, endlessly repeated. "I know, I know. How long?"

A loud sigh issued from the engine compartment. "Give me ten minutes."

"Understood. Crew, keep your eyes skinned for aircraft. Make sure the machine guns are manned and ready. Heinrich, load the main gun with HE. You may have a chance of a shot if we run into the enemy."

"Jawohl, Obersturmfuhrer. Sir, we're low on ammunition. We left Dreux with only half our normal complement of shells."

"You'll have even less if a Typhoon hits us with rockets," he snapped, immediately feeling guilty for making the angry remark.

"No, Sir. I'll unload and change to HE."

He acknowledged and continued checking the surroundings through his binoculars. He smiled, about four kilometers away, a Sherman. The American was shooting at something, probably one of their light tanks. If he were fighting a Tiger, he'd be dead. There was an explosion, and smoke poured into the air from some unknown victim.

Poor bastard. Pity it's too far away to shoot.

The Sherman began to move and joined with five similar vehicles. They all carried the distinctive white Allied star. The enemy armor stopped again, and a flash of light made him focus back on the Sherman he'd sighted first, destroying the unseen target. So they were watching him. He felt a shiver down his spine, as if someone had poured cold water down his back.

I'm getting superstitious in my old age.

The radio crackled to life, and he gave his call sign.

"Where are you, Manhausen? You were supposed to be here several hours ago."

He recognized the grating tones of Standartenfuhrer Meyer. The man was a legend in the SS Panzer Corps, a hard-charging tanker, and a man who didn't know the meaning of the word retreat. He had earned the respect of the Fuhrer himself, along with the Knight's Cross. When Meyer saw an enemy, any enemy, he'd charge in to fight, no matter what the odds. He'd enjoyed mixed fortunes. Sometimes it worked, but on at least one occasion, he'd run into hundreds of T-34s and KVIIs on the Eastern Front and been lucky to emerge with a quarter of his tank force; Tigers and Panthers that were irreplaceable.

"We were directed the wrong way, Sir. We had engine trouble, but we're fixing it right now. We'll be with you shortly."

His reply was met with a stony silence. He hit the transmit switch a couple of times.

Damn, the radio has stopped working.

Franz, the only man who may have fixed it was busy with the engine. He called to his radio operator, SS Rottenfuhrer Wilhelm Schneider.

"Wilhelm, the radio's out. You'll have to try using Morse Code. Signal headquarters, give them our position, and tell Standartenfuhrer Meyer we'll be outside Caen in two hours."

"Morse Code? I'm not sure..."

"Use the book, Schneider. It's all in there."

"Jawohl, Obersturmfuhrer."

He picked up his binoculars and looked back at the American tanks. The man was still watching him, the lenses of the binoculars catching the sunlight.

Could it be true that we'll meet in combat, a single tank from the German and American sides? How would we ever know, how would I recognize that one Sherman out of so many that poured ashore? Impossible! And yet...

In this war, the impossible was happening on a daily basis. A strong flash of sunlight reflected off the turret of the American tank, and he focused his binoculars on the strange markings. It was some kind of a drawing, but what?

He laughed. It was Minnie Mouse. He'd seen one of the American cartoons in a movie theater in Berlin. So that was what they'd named their tank.

Perhaps they don't realize it, but in the real world, the tiger always gets the mouse.

He held up his right hand, made a pistol, and in his best schoolboy English said, "Bang, bang, you're dead."

Franz Schelling climbed out of the engine compartment covered in grease. The seventeen year old stared at him, looking puzzled.

"Obersturmfuhrer?"

"I just killed a Sherman tank, Franz."

His face was serious. "Jawohl, Obersturmfuhrer."

Kids, they don't they have any humor these days. Anyone would think there's a war on.

"Are you finished in there?"

"Another fifteen minutes, Sir. I found another faulty valve. Nearly fixed.

Damn!

* * *

Bletchley Park, England, 02.55, June 7, 1944

"It looks like Morse Code from one of their Panzers. It came in ten minutes ago. They're using the code we cracked two months ago, and the message was sent to a Standartenfuhrer Meyer. We've triangulated with the Navy. They're a few miles east of Colleville-sur-Mer, Sir."

The British Army captain, part of Ultra, the signals encryption program, nodded as he looked over her shoulder. He read the decryption as she pulled it off the Enigma machine and looked thoughtful.

"Standartenfuhrer Meyer, doesn't he command one of their heavy tank units? Tigers, I believe."

"I think so, Sir."

"So do I. Well done, Corporal. I'll contact RAF liaison and see if they have anything in the area. My word, that was quick."

He ran off to find a phone and made the call. "Yes, three miles due east of Colleville-sur-Mer, at least one heavy tank, could be a whole battalion, Tigers, probably. Ten minutes ago, yes. You have a Typhoon squadron crossing the Channel right now? Excellent. Good hunting."

* * *

The men of the North Nova Scotia Highlanders looked at their new surroundings, awed by the immensity of the ancient stone abbey with the high stone tower. They were more awed by the grim faces of the stormtroopers who guarded them. Private Charles Doucette gave Corporal MacIntyre a worried glance.

"I don't like it, Corp."

He put his hand on the other man's shoulder in a reassuring gesture. "Relax, Charlie. They're just moving us to another cell."

He knew it was more complicated than he'd admit. Their captors were SS, wearing leopard-pattern camouflage uniform which they'd come to recognize as unique to the stormtroopers. The twin lightning flashes on the collars denoted them as SS. Many of the Germans were young, little more than boys.

No, they are boys, he corrected himself, *yet not like any boys I've ever encountered.*

Some, though by no means all, were the image of blonde-haired, blue eyed Nazis, as people commonly perceived SS stormtroopers. Others were dark haired and dark eyed. But they all had one thing in common. When they regarded the Canadians, their stares were hard and cruel. Merciless, like hunters eyeing up their prey, deciding how they would make the kill. Yet they weren't hunters, they were soldiers, just like the Canadians.

Surely they won't murder unarmed prisoners. It's unthinkable. Even for Nazis.

A man rode up on a powerful motorcycle and alighted.

He ignored the prisoners, strode over to the guards, and began speaking to them in a harsh, grating voice. They didn't understand the words. They were Canadians. They spoke English and French, not German. The man barked a final order, and it sounded like, 'Sofort!'

What the hell does that mean?

Then he turned on his heel. He climbed back on the bike, started the engine, and roared away. The guards approached them, their machine pistols unslung, and pointed toward a stone wall at the side of the abbey. They hesitated, but the SS squad leader, an SS Scharfuhrer who looked about nineteen years old, barked that single word again.

"Sofort!"

They got the message, but they walked slowly to the wall, expecting to be corralled there while they awaited transport to a prisoner of war camp. The guards watched them, their eyes wary. They shepherded them into a tight group close to the stonework, and then stepped back, keeping their weapons leveled at the Canadians. The Scharfuhrer opened his mouth to shout an order, but abruptly, another soldier raced out of the abbey building. A Wehrmacht captain, not an SS man, and he began remonstrating with the squad leader. They did not know it, but he was arguing for their lives.

"Scharfuhrer Bachmann, I beg you, do not do this. You cannot murder innocent prisoners."

The man sneered as another officer exited the abbey and marched up to them.

"You'd better tell that to Standartenfuhrer Schulz, Captain. You never know, he might even..."

Before he finished, the new arrival said, "Scharf, what's

going on here?"

He wore a gray-green uniform, almost but not quite SS. He had a badge on his cuff, bearing the title, SD. Before the Scharfuhrer could reply the Captain intervened.

"This is not an SD matter, Standartenfuhrer Schulz. There is no need for your involvement. It is none of your business."

The new arrival ignored the interruption. He talked quietly with the SS NCO for a few minutes, and the Scharfuhrer pointed at the Wehrmacht Captain. He was standing in front of the prisoners, staring down the muzzles of the guns. Standartenfuhrer Schulz clicked his fingers, and two of the SS men cocked their MP40s. The message was unmistakable. Reluctantly, the Captain stepped aside, but remained next to the Canadians.

"What's SD?" Doucette whispered.

"No idea," McIntyre murmured in reply, "Whatever it is, I don't think it's anything good. Why is that officer standing in front of us?"

"I don't know."

The SD officer looked across and gave the Army Captain a long, cold stare. "You will stand down, Captain Sturm. Everything that happens in this area is my business. I am investigating a plot to assassinate Adolf Hitler, which takes priority over every other consideration."

"But these prisoners..."

"You think a few prisoners are more important than the safety of the Fuhrer?"

"No, of course not. But the two matters are unrelated, you know that."

"I will decide what is and what is not related."

"Scharfuhrer, remove that officer."

The SS NCO shouted an order. Two troopers dragged the German Captain away and held him several meters from the prisoners. The SD officer gave the Canadians a casual glance, and then nodded at Bachmann.

"Carry on, Scharfuhrer. And make it quick. I am needed urgently in St-Lo. Gestapo has set up a temporary headquarters in the town to interrogate captured Allied officers."

He went to turn away, but stopped and turned back with a thoughtful expression. "Scharfuhrer Bachmann, I could do with some assistance. This Allied attack has made a great deal of extra work for all of us. If you are amenable, I will arrange with your CO to put you under my command for the duration of this emergency. It is clear you have a certain, er, ability, with these prisoners."

Bachmann smiled. "How long will the assignment last, Sir?"

He shrugged. "A week, perhaps more."

"I would be honored, Sir." He gestured at the prisoners, "So I may..."

"Shoot them, yes, of course. Get on with it, man."

Bachmann shouted an order, and the Canadians heard the ratcheting of the cocking levers as the SS guards charged their weapons.

It can't be happening. The world is going crazy. There's no way they'll kill them, no way. What is this, some kind of cruel trick to intimidate them?

The Army Captain shouted something at the SD officer, but the man turned his head away, refusing to listen.

A split second before the firing started, Corporal MacIntyre knew the truth. He drew himself to rigid attention, holding the position until a hail of 9mm bullets from the MP38s stitched a line across his chest. He fell as one of the rounds tore into his heart. His last thought was of regret that he'd been unable to protect his men from the cowardly murder. His body fell, and by some coincidence he hit the ground and lay in a neat line with the other men of his section. Soldiers, even at the end.

Had he lived, he may have seen the Wehrmacht Captain don a steel helmet and shoulder a rifle. He mounted a pedal cycle and rode away from the abbey, in the direction of the Allied lines.

CHAPTER THREE

10 Downing Street, London, England, The Third Day – June 8, 1944

Churchill smiled. "Ike, overall I'd say we're doing better than expected."

They were relaxing in the garden of Number 10 Downing Street. Churchill was puffing on his usual cigar and doing his best to defeat a half-full tumbler of Scotch whisky. Eisenhower sipped at a glass of fruit juice, wearing a frown. The customary smile he presented to the public was absent.

"We're taking losses, Prime Minister, you know that. There's another thing. So far, the Germans haven't brought in their heavy armor, especially the Tigers."

"Nor will they!" the Prime Minister chortled, like a happy schoolboy, "The little Corporal Hitler still believes we have an army in Kent, waiting to cross over to Pas-de-Calais. He could prove to be the best friend we have in this invasion. Remember, history has shown he has a tendency to get it wrong just lately. In military matters, anyway."

"Let's hope it stays that way. We need more men, more guns, and more armor if we're going to break out of Normandy. Yet already, some of our boys are reporting they're low on fuel and ammunition."

Churchill waved his cigar airily. "Relax, General. The Mulberry harbors are on the way, sailing across the Channel. Once those contraptions are in place, we'll be able to give them all the fuel and ammunition they need."

Ike shook his head. "I sure hope so. You know they're towing those Mulberries across the sea at five miles an hour. It's mighty slow, and they're a sitting duck if the Luftwaffe catches them on the way."

"Luftwaffe? What Luftwaffe? Our combined air forces have hammered them out of the skies during the past few days, and what's left is barely capable of getting airborne." He held up a hand to forestall a protest, "I know, I know, they can bring in reinforcements. But so can we. This is the largest invasion in the history of man, and it'll go down in history, famous for its massive scope and ingenuity."

"It'll be infamous if it goes wrong."

"It won't go wrong. There's a big difference between us and the Germans."

"What's that?"

"We're ready for it. The Nazis are not. This time, we've got them by the balls, General. And we'll keep squeezing until they scream for mercy."

The phone rang, and Churchill picked it up. "Yes, yes. Colleville-sur-Mer, did you say? Good, a pretty place, I once considered painting a watercolor there. Monet loved it, beautiful scenery. Let me know how it goes."

He put down the phone and grinned at Ike. "That

was Bletchley. Our Ultra people have German heavy armor pinpointed north of Omaha Beach. It could be a single Tiger or an entire division. They're sending in the Typhoons to deal with it. Our operation won't go wrong, Ike, you'll see."

The Supreme Commander looked uneasy. "Let's hope not."

"Of course it won't. You'll be the most popular man in America. Why, you could stand for President and they'd elect you."

Ike made no reply. Churchill, a political veteran, noticed the gleam in his eye.

I thought he had something like that in mind. He's a good man, too. I wish him well. However, we have a long, long way to go before we defeat that little Austrian house painter in Berlin. One of our problems is those Tigers. Despite what I said to Ike, heaven only knows why they haven't brought them to the front. Whatever the reason, they've made a huge mistake. When they do bring them up, God help us all.

"These heavy Panzers" Eisenhower suddenly said, "You know what'd happen if they did come at us in force?"

Churchill wondered if he was a mind reader. "We won't allow that to happen, General. Our aircraft will destroy them before they even get close."

"I hope so. But if," he persisted, "they did manage to assemble in large numbers, hundreds of Tigers, King Tigers, and Panthers, a solid wedge of steel, well..."

Churchill nodded. It was a question.

He has to know the truth. After all, he's the man we're depending on to get this right.

"If that happens, General, then we could lose."

Ike nodded. "Now we know what's at stake if the Tigers

come at us in force. The lives of almost half a million men, our troops in Northern France."

Churchill grimaced. "It's more than that, General. We could lose the war."

* * *

It was 02.00, and they'd been fighting for the past two hours. The infantry ran into trouble on the outskirts of Gruchy, still within spitting distance of the beach. It should have been a straightforward advance, but the crafty Krauts hit their flank with intense artillery and machine gunfire. In deep trouble, they sent an urgent call for armored support. Which meant rousing Company A, who were close. Within minutes, the Shermans were readying to move out. Grant's worry, like the other commanders, was that supplies were slow coming up to the men who were doing the fighting. They were running low on the essential stores they needed to keep fighting.

He recalled the previous evening. They'd been checking out the vehicle after the day's fighting.

Christ, was that only three hours ago?

"Solly, how're we looking for shells?"

"Not good. We used up most of our HE, and the AP was down to thirteen shells. Luckily, I scrounged up some replacements, so we have around thirty."

"They say we'll be up against artillery, so we'll need that HE."

A pause. "Too bad. Someone should have brought up more supplies."

"Okay, do what you can. Maybe the boat sunk bringing in the replacements."

Solly chuckled. "Or maybe they sent the wrong thing. Did you hear about the Jerries at Stalingrad, when they tried to reinforce the Sixth Army by air? Rumor is, they sent in an entire cargo of rubbers. Another aircraft came in with pepper. That's what they say, anyway."

"Soviet propaganda, probably, you can't believe everything they put out."

"The Sovs beat the shit out of the Krauts, Sarge. That wasn't propaganda. They're still beating them. You know they're already in Poland."

"I know. Look, the shortage of shells, it's down to ship losses during the landings, that's all. Dammit, Solly, you saw what it was like. We have to manage, like everyone else.

A pause. "Yeah, yeah, okay. Maybe you're right."

Grant understood the bigger problem on his gunner's mind. He was worried sick about his relatives in German-held areas.

There's been all the talk of mass killings, sure, but so far that's all it is. It could all be invented. Solly should stop worrying and concentrate on winning the war.

"Sarge." Angel climbed down through the hatch.

"What is it?"

"I just dipped the tanks. I know what I said earlier about having enough, but we're down to less than half, not much more than a quarter full. We're using gas at a crazy rate."

"I hear you. At first light, I'll ask around."

"Sure."

He went off to bed, making a note of what he had to attend to the next morning. He never got the chance. They rousted them in the early hours and ordered the weary tankers to go forward and help out the 29th Infantry

Division. Within minutes, they were moving.

Major Morgan's tank led off, his driver slewed around until the tracks pointed toward the sounds of battle.

"This is the Company Commander. Move out. Look for those white Allied stars, and remember, these Krauts know their business. As soon as the shooting starts, button up. I don't want any dead heroes. Oh, yeah, and there could be snipers and anti-tank crews.

It was the familiar warning. Some said Morgan was fussier than their fathers.

"Anything else we need to watch out for?"

He smiled; it was the voice of Daniel Kuruk, commander of the new Cochise, although he hadn't painted the name on the turret. He was lucky to get a replacement for his destroyed vehicle. The first platoon, Alpha, lost a commander when their lieutenant craned his head out of the turret to get a better view of the enemy. He got more than he bargained for when a sniper shot him between the eyes. Immediately, the rest of the platoon opened up on the concealed position and scorched it with machine gunfire, which killed the sniper. But it didn't bring the officer back. They gave the Sherman to Kuruk, but Morgan had refused permission for him to name the tank after a famous Indian warrior. Daniel still hadn't forgiven him.

"Yes, there is something else you need to watch for, Sergeant Kuruk. Me. Any more stupid questions over the radio net and you're demoted to private. You'll find yourself on latrine cleaning duties."

"Jerries' or ours," he mumbled, in a last act of defiance. He was still pissed.

There was a silence, then Morgan said, "Let's move out,

people."

They started forward, and within a few hundred yards came across the first casualties of the battle raging around Gruchy. Two hundred yards more, and they came under fire. The chatter of machine gun rounds hitting the steel hull was the first warning, and Grant ducked down and slammed the hatch closed. Visibility was limited at night, especially through the periscope, but he was able to pinpoint the enemy positions from the muzzle flashes.

"Gunner, target two o'clock. Load HE."

"Gun loaded and ready to fire."

As usual, Solly had anticipated the order.

"Fire!"

The main gun crashed back with the recoil, and the interior was filled with smoke and fumes from the shell. The extractors sucked hard to clear the smoke.

"Reload, HE. I can't see any armor. Fuck!"

He was shocked to see the sudden bright flash as an artillery piece fired. It was hidden between a scattering of cottages on the outskirts of the village. The shell smashed into a house behind them. A fraction of a second later, his brain connected.

There's a fucking anti-tank gun out there! Gunner, counter-battery fire and use the last HE. They're aiming at Minnie!"

"On the way."

The shell slammed out the barrel and exploded, but two seconds later the German fired again. This time the shell grazed their frontal armor, and the clang inside the tank made their ears ring. For a second Grant thought they'd been hit. The stink of ammonia reached his nostrils as someone let it go.

"Solly, hit the bastard, finish him!"

There was no reply, but the gun fired again, and he heard Dale scrambling to reload. In front of him a bunch of soldiers from the 29th raced through the darkness and dived into the shelter of a stone wall. He momentarily thought of his brother, the infantry officer. He could have been leading those men, if it hadn't been for that E-boat attack off Slapton Sands; a surprise attack on unarmed landing craft and small boats. They hadn't recovered his body last time he checked, and he doubted they ever would. All he could do was stick it down Jerry's throat. Solly would approve of it, a Talmudic revenge, an eye for an eye. Except he wanted more, a thousand eyes, and still more, until they'd ground the fuckers into the dust. He'd stop when the enemy surrendered unconditionally, as the Allied leaders had demanded. Not before.

The crack of the main gun firing brought him back to the present. An explosion up front told of a hit. Then there was a secondary explosion as their ammunition cooked off. He ordered Angel to go forward and gripped the butt of the .50 cal.

"Watch for anti-tank missiles. We're up against Panzergrenadiers, and they'll roast us if we give them half a chance."

Vernon's machine gun came to life, and a line of tracers stitched the night, impacting a spot five hundred yards away. He peered through the gloom but was unable to make out what he'd been shooting at. There were no answering muzzle flashes, so whatever it was had left, or was dead.

"Driver, advance! Take us all the way into the town. Watch out for Jerries. They're in there somewhere. We need to clear this out for the infantry. Vern, you see anyone, you know what to do."

"Hell, yeah."

The Sherman lurched forward as Angel hit the throttle. He glanced back and became aware of a dark shape charging at them out of the gloom, but before he could shout an order to engage, he recognized another Sherman.

The Bounty, no question.

Lieutenant Bligh had even fastened a small skull and crossbones to the radio aerial, a nod to the famous Mutiny on the Bounty. Bligh's tank overtook them and charged forward into the village. Almost immediately, the sparks of small caliber gunfire lighted his hull as another machine gun opened up, and a pair of snipers tried to penetrate the viewing slots with Mauser fire.

An AP shell whistled past Minnie Mouse and hit a Sherman that was closing from behind. He grimaced; another Company A tank destroyed as smoke and flames poured out of the stricken vehicle.

"Solly, hit that gun before he gets all of us."

"I'm on it. We're real low on HE, Sarge."

"You can shoot fucking K-rations for all I care, just nail his ass."

"Right."

Solly fired the HE round already in the breech, but the bright flare of the explosion showed he'd hit nothing more dangerous than an old Renault tractor. The anti-tank gun fired again and missed, but this time Solly and Dale were ready for him, and they hit him with two AP shells in quick succession. The second projectile struck the armored shield of the gun, penetrated and exploded the other side, killing the crew. Angel sent the tank surging forward. Seconds later, they were battling through the maelstrom of small arms fire, as they rumbled into the center of the village.

Bligh was engaged in a fierce fight with a STUG III, and AP shells flew back and forth. Grant saw an opening to their right, a narrow street, and decided to explore it for signs of the enemy.

"Angel, swing a right. See it?"

"I got it."

He wrenched on the control levers. The tank spun on its axis and entered the narrow lane. The hull clipped the stone wall of a cottage as they turned, and when Grant look back, the roof had collapsed, and the building was leaning drunkenly to one side.

C'est la vie, too bad.

There was no sign of any Germans, and for a few moments he wondered if he'd made a mistake. Should they turn around and get back into the village square? But he saw something move, a black shadow in the dark countryside ahead, and he decided to keep going.

Could be another STUG.

"Gunner, load AP."

* * *

"You stupid, damn fool!" he swore again at Franz, "I told you to turn right, and you went left!"

"Sir, it was the aircraft attack. You told me to take evasive action."

He recalled the attack, and it had been a close thing. One moment the sky was empty, and the next, they came from nowhere. RAF Typhoons, the markings clear when they swooped down low to release their rockets.

How had they found them? It didn't seem possible, a lone tank, moving along an isolated country lane with high hedgerows either side to hide them from the enemy. Yet they'd come, appearing as if by magic. It was only by luck they'd found the sunken road, with a thick tangle of trees and branches overhead to hide them from the vengeful Typhoons.

They'd endured a bad ten minutes with everything battened down while the aircraft rocketed the countryside around them. After they'd gone, they opened the hatches and found their covering of foliage had been almost totally destroyed. They were lucky the branches and earth had fallen over their Panzer, keeping them hidden from their tormentors.

"I didn't tell you to drive us into Cherbourg, Franz! We're overdue in Caen. They'll post us to the Russian Front for dereliction of duty if we don't make it."

"Yes, Obersturmfuhrer."

He sighed with frustration. They were good kids, and it was hard to be angry with them for long. That was the trouble; they were just kids. They had no business joining the crew of a Tiger I. They should have been in school, or right now tucked up in bed. Instead, they were driving through the night, tired, hungry, though still motivated by fervor for Germany and the Fuhrer. Proud to be part of an elite SS Panzer unit even if they were lost in the dark Normandy countryside.

He had the turret open to help navigate, but it was almost impossible to find a way through. Large parts of the defenses, the famed Atlantic Wall, consisted of areas of low lying farmland, flooded to make the passage of enemy troops and armor difficult, if not impossible. Feldmarschal Rommel had arranged for anti-tank guns to cover the narrow lanes between the flooded land, and so they effectively became killing grounds. It was impossible to strike out cross-country to change direction. Although they didn't know where they were right now, which made navigating even more difficult.

He saw flashes of gunfire ahead, and Franz slowed, waiting for orders. There was plenty of gunfire to the north around the landing beaches, but he was surprised the Allies had penetrated this far inland. Rommel had insisted the invaders be thrown back from the beaches. He'd stated repeatedly they must not be allowed to penetrate inland. Yet obviously they were here, in front of him.

He smiled to himself. *Where is 'here'?*

They rumbled past a faded road sign, and his hopes rose. He switched on the searchlight. At last he'd know where they were. The sign said Gruchy.

Where the hell is Gruchy?

He glanced up. The battle was getting nearer, so he switched off the light.

"Driver, advance. Crew, be alert, we may be about to meet the Amis."

"We'll drive them into the sea," Lenz asserted. Rolf could swear he clicked his heels together as he spoke.

"Let's just kill them," he replied, keeping his voice calm, "That will be quite enough. Gunner, load AP."

* * *

They were easing forward slowly between the flooded fields. Angel was careful to stay away from the lake each side of them. If they went in, it could be a problem getting out. There were two small farmhouses four hundred yards ahead of them, with a barn. He thought the moving shape he'd seen was further away, although distance was deceptive at night. It could have been a mile away, probably was. Then he saw the spotlight. It flashed on for a second, and then switched off.

"Did you see that? There could be a truck up ahead, maybe an entire column. Or enemy armor."

"Has to be a Jerry," Solly insisted.

"Could be a Tiger."

Vern again. Grant smiled. "It could also be a farmer driving his tractor, coming home drunk."

"So why did he turn off the light so fast? It's a German, no question."

Angel had slowed, waiting for orders.

He thought quickly, but what else could it be other than a German?

"I concur. Driver, advance. Solly, load AP. Standby to engage. It's probably another STUG."

"We're ready," Dale replied. Grant ducked his head inside the turret and saw the loader with his hand on a heavy AP shell, ready for the reload.

"Driver, forward. Let's go ace this fucker."

They picked up speed and raced toward the distant target. They were almost abreast of the farm when a shell whistled overhead and smashed into one of the cottages. His brain told him it was armor piercing, even as the awesome destructive power became apparent. The building seemed to wobble as the huge shell drove through the structure and exited the other side.

"Jesus, that was an 88!"

Pieces of masonry flew through the air and landed on the hull, and he ducked down and slammed the hatch closed. Through the vision slot he could see the dark shape coming up fast.

"A Tiger!" Vernon shouted, his voice half triumphant, half terrified.

"Maybe, maybe not. Forget what is was, just kill the bastard."

"Target located."

"Gun loaded and ready," Dale sang out.

"Fire!"

Solly did well. He'd aimed at the approaching tank, targeting the muzzle flash, and allowed for the target offset as the distances closed. His shell slammed into the dark shape and sparks flew up into the night sky. They illuminated the ominous outline of a Tiger I. Vernon was right this time. But the shell did no damage, and they may as well have spat at it. Solly fired again, but this time he missed. The Tiger hadn't fired a second shell. Probably he couldn't see them in the darkness.

"Gun loaded and ready."

"Solly, don't fire, not yet. He'll see the muzzle flash. We need to get around back of him to defeat the bastard."

"The fields are flooded both sides," Angel pointed out, "The only way through is this track. We can go forward or back the way we came, that's it. I guess back would be best. Get out of this place."

"We don't want to mix it with no Tiger," Vern snarled.

"That's a Jerry up there!" Solly shouted at him, "We're here to kill them, not run away from those murdering scum. Besides, if he reaches the village, he'll murder our guys. Infantry, armor, none of them would stand a chance."

A good point, Grant acknowledged. Except it was a fight they would lose. They'd gone over this before they shipped over from England. The only way to beat a Tiger was to sneak up from behind and ram him in the ass. But there was no way to get behind him. He opened the hatch again and chanced a look around. The only island in the floods was the farmyard.

"Driver, get off the track, turn into the farm, and stop behind the barn while we figure this out."

Angel swung the through ninety degrees, and Minnie plowed through the farm gate, trampling it into the mud, and they stopped close to the rear of the barn. The engine throbbed quietly as it ticked over.

Did that Tiger see us come in here? There's no way to know. If he saw us, we're toast.

Solly was cursing and swearing, at least it sounded like that. The language sounded weird, so it could have been Hebrew. Then again, he may have been praying, although he wasn't that kind of a Jew. He'd told them once he left that kind of religious stuff to the guys in the black hats and beards.

Angel came up for some fresh air and poked his head out through the hatch. They searched for a way through the floods, but the entire area was one gigantic lake. The driver looked at Grant.

"It's hopeless. There's no way we can get across this lot, a Sherman DD maybe, but not us. That Jerry will be along soon, and we're be trapped in the middle of a fucking ocean. We're like sitting ducks."

He glanced around, but he had to agree. There was no way out.

"Swing her around, Angel. Get ready to try and sneak out."

He returned to his seat, and the Sherman began the maneuver of slewing around. He kept his head out of the turret hatch to keep an eye out for the enemy; the big dark hull of the Tiger had disappeared in the dark. Grant suddenly saw movement close by and reached for the machine gun, but then he stopped. It was a civilian, a girl. She waved to him, and in an idiotic moment, he waved back. Angel had started to creep out of the farmyard, but he had an idea.

"Driver, halt. There's someone down there, a civilian. She may know a way around the floods."

Minnie jerked to a halt. He vaulted down to the muddy farmyard and slipped into the mud. When he picked himself up and wiped the filth from his uniform, she was standing only three feet in front of him. She wore a crumpled, belted raincoat and rubber boots, yet somehow she managed to make the peasant garments look appealing. He wondered briefly if she had anything on underneath; she must have been roused from her bed by the shellfire.

"You are American?" Her face was devoid of any amusement.

"Yes, Ma'am. You speak good English."

Her English was strongly accented, the way only Frenchwomen can do it.

He smiled to himself; *they can even make a shopping list sound sexy.*

She ignored the compliment.

"Are you lost?"

"We were trying to find a way through the flooded area."

She pointed out to the roadway. "You were already on the track. Why did you turn off and destroy my gate?"

"Sorry about the damage, Ma'am. We were in a hurry." He explained about the Tiger, "If we tangle with that monster, we'll lose."

"Why?"

"Their armor, it's too thick. We can't penetrate it unless we can come at it from behind."

She nodded her understanding. "Then perhaps I can help you. It's Mam'selle, by the way, not Ma'am. My name is Margot Caron."

"Er, Grant, Josh Grant. Sergeant."

She held out a tiny hand, and he shook it. She wore no make-up on her pale skin, yet her face glowed with a natural beauty that almost took his breath away. Even the scattering of freckles enhanced her beauty. She was short, a little over five feet tall, slender and straight backed, with a piercing gaze from two huge, shining dark-brown eyes. Her hair was styled with an urchin cut that suited her gamine, oval-faced looks to perfection.

Jesus Christ, if all French farm girls look like this one, I'm gonna enjoy this trip.

"Well, Sergeant Josh Grant? You want me to help you or not?"

He started, realizing his mind had been wandering. In the middle of the French countryside, with a Tiger tank less than a mile away, it wasn't such a good idea.

"You can show us the way through?"

"Yes."

"I see. Where is the path through the flood?"

She smiled at him, and he felt his knees go weak.

"It is there." She pointed across the lake that surrounded

them.

"You're sure there's a way through?"

"Of course I'm sure. I know this area well. There is a submerged track that is very shallow. It will take you to the other side of the lake, and you can circle around and come up behind your German tank."

"How would you know we're on the track?"

"I will come with you and show you the way." She smiled again, "I take it you have no objection to giving a girl a ride on your tank?"

"Er, well, I..."

Before he could object, she skipped up onto the hull, and he followed her. She held on to a stanchion behind the turret. He shrugged. She'd evidently made up her mind. He climbed into the hatch and took his place in the commander's seat. He glanced at Margot to make sure she was secure, shook his head, and ordered the driver forward.

"Take it slow, Angel. Miss Caron is up on the hull, and she'll guide across the flood."

"You got it."

He engaged the tracks, and they lumbered forward. The girl leaned close to him and gave directions in a husky voice.

"Left. Yes, that's it, straight ahead now; bear a little to the right. Not too much, come back a couple of degrees to the left."

It took them almost thirty long, grueling minutes before they cut the road. Angel swung onto the dirt track and headed back toward Gruchy, and they strained to look ahead, searching for the Tiger. Every man knew they'd get only one shot. After that, the monster tank would swing their main gun around, and an 88mm shell would destroy them. The girl still clung to the hull, and he didn't know whether to order her to get off or tell her to shelter inside the cramped interior. In the end, he decided the risk of engaging the Tiger was too great.

"Driver, halt."

As they slowed to a stop, he explained it to her.

"It's for your protection, Mam'selle. We don't want anything to happen to you. But we're mighty grateful for the help. I mean, really grateful."

She grimaced but nodded her acceptance.

"I will find my own way back. Good luck, Sergeant. Perhaps when you are back this way, you will come and see me, and let me know how it went."

"Sure I will."

She bent forward, kissed him on the cheek, and then skipped lightly to the ground.

What a woman!

"Driver advance. Heads up, guys, that Tiger can't be too far away. He has to be in front of us, somewhere."

They approached the section of track next to the farm, but there was no sign of the German tank. He glanced idly around, and gaped, German armor, coming straight at them. Not Tigers, these were three Panzer IVs. Their Sherman was outnumbered and outgunned. He wondered if the Krauts had seen them. Probably not, they were backlit in the moonlight, which meant Minnie Mouse was in dark shadow. They needed reinforcements. He grabbed his mike.

"Company Commander from Sergeant Grant. Three Panzer IVs, approaching Gruchy from the northwest."

Major Morgan replied almost instantly, "Acknowledged.

Can you engage?"

He sounded tired, a different man from the stern, serious academic who'd landed on Omaha Beach.

"Affirmative, Sir, but we need support. A platoon should be enough."

A chuckle. "We're a little short on armor, Grant. Lieutenant Bligh is with me, and I can't spare him. I can give you Sergeant Kuruk. I'll detach him to your position now. Good hunting. Three Panzer IVs, you said?"

Four Shermans, all that's left for the entire Company! Shit, almost three quarters of our strength gone. They sure hit us hard.

"It looks that way, Sir. We didn't get a good look at them."

"Understood. Do your best. Sergeant Kuruk will be with you in a few minutes."

"Roger. We're also short on ammunition and fuel, Sir."

"So are we all. Morgan out."

They needed somewhere off the road to hide until the Panzers came into range.

"Driver, swing back into the farm. We'll keep out of sight until they go past us." He switched to the Company net, "Kuruk, this is Grant, do you copy?"

"This is Kuruk, receiving you loud and clear. We're heading out of Gruchy right now. We'll be up with you soon."

"Negative. Hold at the edge of the village, and wait until the shooting starts. I'm planning to wait for them to go past and bushwhack them. When their attention is on Minnie, bring up Cochise and hit them hard."

"They wouldn't let me name this one Cochise."

"They'll change their minds if we pound those Panzers. If we don't, we'll be dead."

"Uh, okay. We'll be there."

His mind was still reeling from their losses. What did they leave England with, fifteen, sixteen Shermans? Now they were down to four. And they were facing, what? Three Panzer IVs, which were tough opponents, and there was still that Tiger out there somewhere. All they needed now was for a battalion of Panzergrenadiers to happen along. His mother would get the knock on the door, the sympathetic glances from the family support officers, and they'd leave her to shed tears for another son lost on the altar of Hitler's ambitions to turn the world into a Nazi paradise.

No way, José! Adolf ain't got us yet.

Angel drove past the wrecked gate, which gave Grant a brief feeling of guilt, and halted behind the house out of sight of the track. Fifty yards away, the barn swayed as a gust of wind hammered at it. And then it started to rain again, a humdinger of a downpour, reducing visibility to less than fifty yards, perfect ambush weather. Besides, it would wash some of the mud off his uniform jacket, which was out in the open. The engine note quietened from Angel throttling all the way back, and he strained his ears to listen for the enemy. At first nothing, and then he heard it. Heavy, powerful gas engines, and the heavy mechanical clank of steel tracks chewing up the unmetaled roadway.

"Solly..."

"I hear it."

He switched to the Company net, "Daniel, how're you doing?"

"I estimate we're eight hundred yards from your position. Can't see much. The rain is pretty bad."

"Bad for them, too. Keep coming, and when the fireworks start, come in fast and hit them hard."

"Roger that."

He watched and listened. They'd be here soon. There was one thing that bothered him.

Where did that damned Tiger get to?

* * *

Rolf Manhausen peered through a gap in the side of the wooden barn. Behind him, Franz dropped a spanner and he cursed. Even though the rain drummed hard on the roof, kicking up a racket, he knew the sound of dropped metal could alert the Amis.

"Quiet!" he hissed, "They're fifty meters away."

"Sorry."

Rolf thought back to only a half hour before when he'd almost had them in their sights. A Panzergrenadier unit alerted him with a radio message. They'd seen the Sherman cutting through the floodwater. Their intention was clear, to attack the Tiger from behind. Obviously, they had a local who knew a way through the flooded water. Rolf directed his crew to drive to the farm and wait there in ambush. A nasty surprise for the Amis, just when they thought they had the Tiger cornered. They'd left the road and driven into the farmyard to set up the ambush. That was when it all went wrong, and the engine began making the familiar rattling sounds. It was like someone had filled a steel drum with nuts and bolts and was shaking it violently.

"What is it this time, Franz?"

The driver sounded flustered. "The valves,

Obersturmfuhrer. We've lost another one, at least. Could be two. We have to stop, or we'll wreck the motor."

"I thought you'd fixed the problem."

"Sir, I said at the time, the spare parts they send us are useless. You know the Maybach engine. It's a precision piece of machinery, not some worthless Soviet junk."

It was true, the Maybach 12 cylinder, 21-liter gasoline engine was well made and powerful, but it was also prone to breakdowns.

Yet we have tens of thousands of Soviet prisoners of war working in our factories, making these spare parts. Is it any wonder they're useless? They sit in comfortable factories while German men and boys go out to do battle with the enemy. Crazy!

"How long to fix it this time?"

"At least three hours. Obersturmfuhrer. We must shut down the engine, otherwise it'll be damaged beyond repair."

With no engine, they'd be helpless even to defend themselves. No engine, meant no power to the eight-ton turret. Nothing. He glanced around and saw the barn.

"Drive over to that wooden structure. Wilhelm, Siegfried, get the doors open. We'll hide in there until Franz has the engine fixed."

The two men leapt out to obey the order, and Franz eased the big vehicle into the barn until it was completely inside. The men closed the doors, and the driver switched off the engine. In the silence, he heard the ticking of the hot machinery cooling in the cold, damp night air. He climbed down and stretched his legs.

"Franz, three hours, not a second more. Wilhelm, radio Headquarters and advise them of our situation. Heinrich, Siegfried, find a good place to keep a watch on what's happening outside. You'd better unmount both of the MG34s, in case the Amis come."

"Obersturmfuhrer, that was a Sherman we saw. The machine guns will be useless," the gunner, Unterscharfuhrer Heinrich Boll objected.

It was a fair point. "Agreed, we have an MP40 and a couple of KAR98 rifles in the locker, use those. Move it, we need to watch for the enemy. And make sure you wear your steel helmets. You never know."

"Jawohl, Obersturmfuhrer."

They removed their sidecaps, donned the helmets, and one man doubled to each end of the barn where they could observe through the cracks in the ancient timbers. He smiled. They'd magically transformed from boy tankers to German infantry. All it had needed was the addition of helmets and weapons. How easy it was to become a warrior.

But these are child soldiers, he reminded himself, *I wonder if I should advise them to surrender if the Amis come.*

Posting a guard was more to keep up morale than anything else. If a Sherman happened along and caught them with no engine, they'd have a single option, and that was surrender. At least it would mean these children would survive the war. He walked over to join Heinrich, who was watching through a gap in the center of the big wooden doors. They looked at each other as they both heard a rumble and clatter that meant only one thing. Armor.

Ours or theirs?

* * *

"AP loaded and ready."

"Roger."

The clanking noise came nearer, and in a break in the sheeting rain he saw them, three Panzer IVs, moving slowly along the track. Their frontal armor was slightly thicker than that of the Sherman, while the main gun was about the same caliber, 75mm. Theoretically, an equal contest, except there were three of them.

Grant had no intention of making it an equal contest. At long range, there was no guarantee the Sherman's 75mm gun would penetrate the frontal armor of the Panzer IV. At close range, fifty or a hundred yards, it was no contest, and that was the way he intended to play it. Besides, when he started to shoot, Daniel Kuruk's Cochise would attack from behind, and the 75mm shells would slice into the Panzers like a knife through butter.

Theoretically. So why did he feel so uneasy? It was as if they were being watched, yet he knew the farm was empty. He glanced around at the abandoned house and the big semi-derelict timber barn. There was no one around now that Margot Caron was gone, presumably walking to the nearest friendly village. He felt a pang of loss. He'd like to have known that beautiful, feisty French girl a bit better. Now he never would. He shook his head to focus.

"Driver, advance. Gunner, fire as you bear."

"Roger."

The tank lurched forward, taking them beyond the shelter of the farmhouse, and there they were. Three targets, the Panzer IVs lined up like ducks in a shooting gallery. They had no room to maneuver; the flooded fields meant they had no chance to escape. Solly fired, and the first AP shell smashed into the lead Panzer. The vehicle slammed to a stop, and roiling, black smoke and flame poured out of the turret. The Panzer behind halted, blocked by the wrecked Panzer in front and the tank in the rear. The turret began to turn toward a panicked attempt to engage.

Minnie's gun crashed out, and a second shell hit the center German tank, but the hit was on the thick, sloped frontal armor, just below the glacis. The AP shell glanced off, and tore away part of the track as it exploded. But the tank was still able to fight, even if it couldn't maneuver. They fired, and the 75mm shell skidded off Minnie's turret, only inches from Grant. The projectile whistled away into the darkness. Solly fired again, and this time his shell slammed into the armor plated side of the Panzer, penetrated, and exploded inside the vehicle.

The third Panzer was better prepared. Already the turret was rotating as the driver maneuvered to get a shot at them from behind the wreckage of his two comrades when Kuruk's shell slammed into his rear, and the German armor suddenly stopped. There was no explosion, no flames, but the enemy tank was motionless.

Probably the shockwave from the exploding shell killed them, he thought, *At least it killed them before they could kill us.*

He called Kuruk on the radio.

"Nice shooting, Dan. Old Cochise himself couldn't have done better."

"Just a hundred years too late, white boy. Next time, it'll be different."

He grinned. It was a standing joke between them.

"It looks like they're all dead, but we need to make sure. We'll go and check them out."

"Roger. I'll come up to your position in case you need me."

Grant called Vernon to grab a rifle and join him. He climbed out of the Sherman, drew his Colt .45 1911 automatic, and together they walked over to check out the wrecked armor. The first and second vehicles were totally destroyed, their hulls blackened and riddled with holes when they exploded. The third Panzer was weird and looked almost unscathed. When he opened the turret hatch, two of the crew were apparently uninjured, although fragments from the AP shell had ripped apart the rest of the Germans.

Vernon climbed up beside him, glanced inside, and nodded. "Dead, those two in the turret."

Grant holstered his Colt. "Yeah, no doubt. This lot won't be shooting at any more of our boys."

They looked up as a loud rumbling noise announced the arrival of Daniel Kuruk. The Indian climbed out of the turret and walked up to them as they dropped to the ground and nodded a greeting. He looked at the wrecked Panzers.

"Looks like we're done here. Any survivors?"

"None."

"A massacre," he grimaced.

"Like fucking Little Big Horn," Vern Franklin snarled, "Shot in the back."

Ever since he'd joined the 175th, there'd been friction between him and Daniel, the redneck and the Indian. Although it was true Vern managed to create friction with every soldier of Company A who wasn't a good ole boy like himself. Kuruk decided to let it go, and he smiled at Vern.

"You're right. Didn't we Indians win that one, too?"

Franklin gave him a nasty look and then turned away.

It was as well; if he'd tried to push it, Grant would have broken it up. He'd considered on several occasions forcing Vernon to transfer to another unit, which would probably mean he'd go to the infantry. However, so far he'd held back. They were in a war, and if there was any fighting to be done, they needed to concentrate on the Germans, not beat up on each other. It was the only way to get the job done. Kill as many Germans as possible, reach Berlin, give Adolf a bloody nose, and go home. End of story.

He glanced at Daniel. "You okay?"

"I've seen worse. He's just a cracker asshole."

"Yeah. We need to rejoin Major Morgan. There's unfinished business in Gruchy. It sounds like the 29th Infantry have something of a fight on their hands. Let's move."

He ran back to Minnie Mouse, vaulted up on the hull, and held on grimly as Angel drove out the farmyard at speed. The wrecked Panzers partially blocked the track, but Minnie nudged them aside. Angel was careful to avoid sending them into the water at either side of the track, and they drove at speed back to Gruchy. Grant had his turret open, and the sounds of battle were loud and fierce. They neared the village, and the track they followed sloped down until it became a sunken lane. They were surrounded on both sides by high, impenetrable hedges.

Bocage.

* * *

Two hours later, Manhausen cautiously stuck his head out the door and surveyed the area around the farm. It was clear. He boarded the tank, climbed into the turret, and gave the order to advance. Franz drove away at slow speed out onto the track and turned right, away from the burning Panzers, away from the conflagration at Gruchy. And away from their intended destination.

He was starting to get worried. They'd been separated too long. He had to find a way around the local battles to rejoin his unit outside Caen before they got the wrong idea. He'd known of tank commanders in Russia who got lost, and when they returned were accused of desertion. On the front lines, desertion was a crime that carried a single penalty. He shivered, but there was nothing he could do. They would link up with Division when they could, and if the Allies blocked him with armor and aircraft, that was too damn bad. He smiled.

There is an alternative. I could always surrender; at least that would allow the kids in my crew to survive.

Then he dismissed the thought; he'd made an oath to fight. He was a member of the Waffen-SS, not the League of German Girls.

It had rankled watching the Shermans destroy those Panzers, and he'd have given anything to be able to go out and engage the enemy, to wipe out the arrogant Americans. It wasn't to be. Without an engine, the Tiger was just so much junk. Siegfried Lenz, the most enthusiastic Nazi of them all, had wanted Franz to jury rig the engine, so they could at least drive out of the barn and use their main gun to destroy the Amis.

"They're our enemies!" he'd spluttered, "We must engage them, drive them back into the sea!"

Rolf smiled. Siegfried was all of fourteen years old, even more of a Hitler Jugend fanatic than the rest. Even so, he had to be careful; they all did. As long as his uncle,

Standartenfuhrer Werner Schulz of the Sicherheitsdienst was in Normandy, they had to guard against an innocent slip. Lenz was quite capable of reporting any of them to Schulz if he thought they'd said something treasonous. A simple word could easily condemn them to a camp, or even death.

"Our orders are to rejoin our unit outside Caen, not engage in a stupid fight we must lose. Would you disobey those orders, Sturmann Lenz, and allow the Americans to destroy our Tiger?"

A pause. Lenz knew the penalty for disobeying an order. At best, transfer to a penal unit on the Eastern Front, at worse, death. He also knew his SD relative would not hesitate to pass sentence on a member of his own family.

"We must follow our orders."

"Yes. We'll leave when the engine is fixed, not before. As soon as we're clear of the flooded area, we'll turn east and do our best to reach Division in Caen. Schneider, contact Headquarters. Tell them we've had further engine trouble, but we'll be on the way shortly."

It may be enough to avoid a court martial. Unless Lenz's uncle, Standartenfuhrer Schulz takes an interest.

"Jawohl, Obersturmfuhrer."

After three hours, Franz declared he had it licked. They started up and rumbled on through the Normandy countryside, toward Caen and the other Tigers of 12th SS. By sheer luck, they seemed to have found a way through the invading armies. Perhaps it was the only clear route to Caen.

Once we arrive, link up with the other Tigers of the 12th SS Hitler Jugend and go into action, we can satisfy Siegfried Lenz's lust for glory.

He thought about that Sherman they'd hidden from at the farm outside. It was hard to bear, having to skulk inside the barn while they destroyed three valuable Panzers, yet they'd had no choice. Not on that occasion. It would all change, if and when they ever met Minnie Mouse on the battlefield. The Tiger's superior firepower would make short work of the medium American tank. Even so, something nagged at his subconscious. He had a strange feeling about that tank, a feeling he couldn't shake off. Was it to be his nemesis, a puny Sherman, named after a cartoon mouse? He chuckled to himself. It was impossible. Their popgun was barely capable of scratching his paintwork. So why was he so certain they'd meet again? And why did he feel so uneasy?

If I were religious, I'd see a priest and talk it out with him. The problem is, the new religion of Germany is the Nazi Party. To minister to the faithful the priests have been replaced by the Gestapo, and I'd sooner pull out a tooth than spill out my problems to those sadistic bastards.

CHAPTER FOUR

**SHAEF Headquarters, near London, England.
June 9, 1944**

General Sir Bernard Law Montgomery was his usual intractable self. Eisenhower sighed; he had other things on his mind than trying to pacify the irritable Brit. A good general, no question, and his men loved him. The problem was, the dapper Britisher had a fiery temperament, which made dealing with him a constant headache. He smiled to himself; these meetings at the Supreme Headquarters Allied Expeditionary Force had become little more than a trial by ordeal.

"Caen," Monty insisted, his voice imperious as he jabbed a finger at the huge map on the table, "We have to take the city, otherwise the entire invasion could fail."

"Of course, you're quite right, General," Ike acknowledged.

If I tell the prickly bastard he's one hundred percent wrong, it'll take me the rest of the day to calm him down.

"Of course I'm right. It's obvious to anyone but a fool."

He shuddered. When word of this got around, there'd be even more ruffled feathers to smooth.

He put on his famous, warm smile. "However, we do have one or two other tangles to resolve first."

Montgomery seemed to sniff the air for trouble. He reminded Ike of a Jack Russell Terrier looking for something to chase down.

"Tangles?"

"Uh, huh, just minor stuff. Like joining my armies on Omaha and Utah Beaches. They've been hit pretty hard, and if they don't link up soon, they'll be easy meat for the Germans to pick off once they bring up their reinforcements."

Monty was having none of it. "Caen must take precedence. There's no question." His voice was crisp and sharp, like he was lecturing students in a lecture theater, not talking to his senior officer, "We have to beat back the Germans now, so we're in a position to advance east."

"You'd leave an entire army of Germans, including heavy armor, in your rear?"

Monty shrugged. "We can handle it."

He kept the smile on his face. "Sure you can. In the meantime, I'm directing our boys to take Carentan. It's only a matter of time before Isigny falls. We have to link those two armies. It's more than vital; the Germans could punch through our center any time, and the entire invasion could fail. Isigny, then Carentan."

The Brit was already shaking his head. "We must take Caen first. I'm assigning the 7th Armored Division to advance east, cross the Odon River and capture Évrecy. They will then take and occupy the high ground around

Caen, while XXX Corps makes their advance to the east. I've planned it to the last detail. It can't possibly fail."

Eisenhower sighed. The Germans had already given the Brits a bloody nose outside Caen when the German 21st Panzers beat back the Third Infantry Division. It was evident Monty was champing at the bit for revenge, although Caen was an important and strategic crossroads, which meant it would have to be taken sooner rather than later.

"Do you have a plan, General?"

"Operation Perch," he snapped immediately, "We're ready to jump off at first light tomorrow morning."

Ike sighed again. It was like talking to a brick wall. He decided to hedge his bets.

"Then I wish you luck. The 101st Airborne is in position to punch up through the Cotentin Peninsula, so with luck, we'll achieve both objectives and link up ready for the breakout from Normandy."

"You said 101st Airborne?" Monty looked curious; "You don't have any armor available to support them, not in that region."

"We're working on it. As you know, our armor is spread thin, and we've already taken too many losses. More than anticipated, much more."

"In that case, you'd better pray the Germans don't bring up their armor. Airborne troops, as you know, are helpless in the face of armor. Talking of which, there's something I've been meaning to discuss, the heavy Panzer battalions. Do we have any idea where they are, or what they're doing?"

He nodded. It was the question that concerned him, the whereabouts of the heavy tanks. They knew now the invasion was not a feint, so why hadn't they brought up their ace in the hole, the heavy armor that could decimate the Allied forces battling to establish a foothold in Normandy?

"The Panthers and Tigers? We just don't know. It's something of a mystery. So far, they've brought a few of them up piecemeal, but there's been no mass attack, like that one at Kursk last year in the Soviet Union. Either the Germans are holding them in reserve for some reason, or they're making a big mistake. I hope it's the latter."

Monty nodded thoughtfully. "So do I, Ike. So do I."

* * *

Outskirts of Isigny, France, 00.15, June 9, 1944

"They're almost there, the infantry boys," Morgan exclaimed, "They say there're a few strongpoints inside the town, and they want us to shift them out of the way. It's just after midnight now. Our orders are to advance at 01.00 and overcome any defenders still inside the town."

They were parked in a wood outside Gruchy, where they'd fought yet another fierce battle to beat back a German counterattack. Each man was eating their meal, savoring every spoonful of the spicy, aromatic stew prepared by their new cook, a French girl, Margot Caron. She'd walked into the village, arriving just after the last German surrendered, threading her way past the bodies that still littered the ground. Most were German, but there were also a few Americans. She approached their encampment, brushed aside the sentry, and walked into Morgan's HQ, a bombed out bakery.

"Ma'am, you can't come in here!"

She'd stared him down. "Is that right? Where do you suggest I go?"

"Home, Ma'am, there's a battle going on here."

"I have no home, not since your men turned it into a battlefield."

"You can't stay here, Ma'am."

Morgan was unusually nonplussed, with no idea of how to deal with the feisty French girl.

"It is not Ma'am, it is Mam'selle." She glanced at the mess tin he'd put down while he talked to her, "Do you normally eat this pigswill? You need a cook here. That is obvious. "

"Well, er..." He looked down helplessly at the congealed mess he'd been trying to eat. They'd pooled their K Rations, and the result was a strange, gray concoction that was barely edible. Even so, "We don't have time to cook, Ma'am, er, Mam'selle. We're fighting a war. You see..."

"Exactly." Her chin jutted forward, like the prow of a sleek, graceful destroyer, "I will prepare your meals. Give me what food you have left. I need an hour to prepare."

"Er, er..."

"What are you waiting for, Major? Do you want a meal, or do you intend to die of food poisoning before you have time to beat the Germans?"

In the end, he raised the white flag of surrender, at least, halfway. Until the food arrived, then the flag went to the top of the flagpole.

"Oh, yeah, this is good," he grinned, enjoying the rare sensation of real food. Then his face darkened, "But this is only temporary. Until we leave the area."

She nodded and smiled. "But of course, Major,

whatever you say."

They finished their food in a hurry, and Morgan ordered them to prepare to leave. Grant checked his wristwatch. There was just enough time to reach Isigny, and pray the Panzers weren't waiting in ambush. They'd been lucky so far, but every man knew a well-placed ambush could wipe out the remainder of the Company.

Angel started the engine, and he dropped into the commander's seat, leaving the hatch open. In front of Minnie, Major Morgan was turning to survey the ground around them. Behind Grant, Daniel Karuk rode in Cochise, and bringing up the rear, Lieutenant Bligh in The Bounty. They were all that remained of an entire tank company. Morgan took a last look around and gave the order.

"Move out."

The drive to Isigny was easy at first. The only troops they encountered were American. The first houses came into sight, along with the first anti-tank shell. This time, the Germans were ready. The area crackled with gunfire where the infantry had been fighting a fierce battle for possession of the town. They'd advised the tankers there was no armor in the town, which was a plus. Although there was a unit of Panzergrenadiers, which meant anti-tank missiles, and maybe one or more STUG assault guns. It wouldn't be a walk in the park.

Morgan halted them before the town and surveyed the ground ahead. Then he glanced back at his company, as if one or more of his precious tanks may have got lost on the way. Four Shermans, some company.

"It looks okay. We'll go in fast and hard, and watch out for the panzerfausts. Company, advance!"

He roared away, and behind him, Grant gave the order

for Minnie Mouse to follow. It was quiet until they reached the outlying buildings, and the first missile flew, narrowly scraping past Morgan's vehicle. The flare of the launch had given away the enemy position, and they poured on heavy fire at the target, a corner turret in an ancient stone building. He heard Solly shout, "Load HE!" and the shell punched out, hit the turret, and exploded, leaving the structure a mass of stone fragments. Not for the first time, Grant felt sorry for the French, whose beautiful and ancient architecture was being systematically destroyed. But they had no choice.

The Krauts started it. We're just here to finish it.

Morgan charged ahead, his main gun fired shell after shell, and both his machine guns chattered their message of death to the German defenders. A flicker of light showed in the second floor of a large house, and Grant snapped out an order to Solly.

"Gunner, target eleven o'clock, second floor, fire."

The turret moved a fraction and aimed the main gun. It erupted in a fury of smoke and flame as the projectile hurtled toward the target. Lashed with shellfire and machine gun bullets, whoever had been trying to target them, disappeared in the ruin of broken masonry.

"Driver, keep up with the lead Sherman."

"You got it."

He forgot his fears, forgot his determination to seek vengeance, to kill Germans. This was thrilling, like an old time cavalry charge. Punching through an enemy held town and knocking out targets right and left, it was every boy's dream. Cowboys and Indians, or Cops and Robbers, but then he sobered. There was a difference. This was no game, and people were dying. A shell struck their frontal armor and glanced off, and he started searching for the source. Morgan's voice came over the radio.

"Grant, there's a German gun position ahead of us. It's well hidden. Come alongside me, and we'll charge him down together."

"Yes, Sir. Driver..."

"I'm on it."

They moved up and dropped alongside Morgan's vehicle. Another shell punched out from the hidden gun, and they were lucky when again the frontal armor took the brunt.

When we get back, I'm gonna look up the designer of the Sherman and treat him to a slap up dinner. If we get back.

"Driver, take a right, try and bring us up behind the Jerry gun."

"You got it."

He called Morgan to explain, but the Major was less than impressed.

"I told you to stay with me, Grant. Dammit, don't you know how to follow an order."

"I'm sorry, Major, but this is the only way we'll get him, Sir. Give us a chance."

A pause. "Very well. Call me when you're in position. We'll take him from both sides."

"I'll do that, Sir."

"And good luck."

Was it another STUG, he wondered, or an anti-tank gun? Panzergrenadier units had both, so there was no way of knowing which one lay ahead. If it was a STUG, it could already be moving away to change their position. That could make things tricky. If it were an anti-tank gun, he'd hit it from the flank before they could move the cumbersome artillery piece.

As they careered around the back alleys of Isigny, he wondered again about his thirst for vengeance. This was payback time for his brother, murdered by a marauding E-Boat at Slapton Sands. It was what he'd signed up for. Yet wasn't what he was doing the same as the Germans? Killing every enemy soldier he could place in the sights of Minnie Mouse's main gun, a blood-soaked quest to destroy as many enemy soldiers as possible.

Isn't that what the E-boat commander that killed David did?

Yet it was different. The Free World was on a quest to wrest the continent of Europe from the grip of the Nazi warlord, Adolf Hitler, and he was part of that quest.

The men who killed my brother are part of the criminal regime in Berlin. They were virtually guilty of murder, and it makes what they did wrong, and what I am doing right. Doesn't it? So why don't I feel so certain as I once did?

"Solly, three o'clock, Jesus! Hit him."

He'd snapped out of his reverie and glanced left. An anti-tank gun was in plain view, and the German crew had been caught unawares. They were frantically turning the gun to train the long barrel on Minnie, but Solly was ready, and he didn't wait for the order. The turret turned, the 75mm gun fired and hurled out an HE shell. It exploded next to the armored shield, showering the Germans with hot metal fragments. Angel barely slowed their pace as they neared the wreckage, and he drove over it.

When Grant looked back, all could see was the bloody, twisted remains of their foe. Torn metal, fragments of human tissue, bone, and blood. Parts of torn uniforms lay on the ground, like discarded rags. He realized there might have been body parts in some of those tunics and pants, helmets, and boots. Suddenly, he didn't feel quite so righteous. Death was death, no matter what the color of the uniform.

He shouted into his mike, "Solly, was that the gun that hit us?"

"No, no way. Wrong angle, the shot that struck our frontal armor came from further north. If we keep on this course, we should come across him."

"How's the HE holding out?"

"It's not good."

"Understood."

They reached the end of the lane with a suddenness that surprised them all. And there in front of them was a further enemy. This time it was a STUG III, the German assault gun. Along with the later STUG IV, they were the Germans' most successful tank destroyers, with their powerful and accurate 75mm StuK 40 main gun. This STUG was engaged in a duel with another tank; it could only be one of Company A's precious Shermans. A shell came from nowhere and hammered at the STUG's frontal armor, but the German vehicle seemed to shrug off the blow and kept firing. So far, they hadn't seen Minnie.

"Gunner, load AP, fire when ready. They're shooting at the Major."

Before he'd finished speaking, Dale was already swinging the heavy shell into the breech. Solly fired instantly. The shell traveled the short distance to the STUG and exploded on a stone monument several yards in front of the vehicle. Shards of shrapnel flew close to the German, but the hull was intact. The vehicle tracks began to turn as they swung around to face the new threat, and within seconds, the German would be in a position to shoot at them.

"Damn!" Solly cursed, furious for missing an easy shot.

"Gun loaded with AP," Dale announced.

"Fire."

This time the shell smash into the frontal armor of the STUG, and smoke began to pour out, but they weren't finished. The enemy gun fired, a shell glanced off the turret of the Sherman and exploded in a shower of steel fragments.

They fired HE, stupid bastards. If they'd fired AP, we'd probably be dead.

Even as he had that thought, the STUG gun moved a fraction to correct their aim. They weren't fools. The next shot would be AP, and they wouldn't screw it up.

"Driver, back up, back up. Get us out of here!"

"Shit, Sarge, I can nail the bastard," Solly shouted, his voice angry.

But Angel was already moving, and they screeched backward, tearing out great chunks of stone cobbles from the street. Another enemy shell narrowly missed the hull and impacted on a nearby building. When they were out of sight of the enemy gun, the driver began to slow, and Grant reached for the mike.

"Find another way to get us in, Angel. Another two or three streets, and we can get behind him."

"He'll be expecting us," he grumbled.

"He's too busy fighting Major Morgan, and maybe our other Shermans. He won't have time to think about what we're doing. Get going."

Angel savagely jerked the tracks around, and they turned into yet another darkened street. Grant saw a line of Germans running in front of them, a half-dozen men. One carried a machine gun on his shoulder, another had belts of ammunition draped over his back, and the rest were armed with rifles. Obviously, they were moving to fight off the attack of the 29th.

Grant squeezed the trigger of his .50 caliber almost without thinking and scythed down the group of running men. The heavy slugs took a terrible toll. As they rolled past the bodies two seconds later, he saw the awful damage the heavy lead had wreaked on flesh and bone.

"Nice shooting," Solly told him happily.

"Yeah. Heads up, people, and watch out for that STUG. He may get the same idea and change position to ambush us."

"There could even be a Tiger around the corner," Vern warned.

No one replied. For a fleeting moment, Grant thought about that Tiger he'd seen on the hillside. That almost superstitious feeling that somehow they'd meet him in battle, and their war would come down to a one on one. Minnie Mouse versus the Tiger. A David and Goliath combat.

No, there won't be a Tiger around that corner. Not unless it's that Tiger, the one we're fated to meet. The encounter that will decide everything, one way or the other. Whether we live to go home, or rot forever in some forgotten, muddy French field.

Angel threaded the tank through the narrow streets. He scraped around a tight corner and took the corner off a big house. The roof almost collapsed and tilted at a crazy angle. He hoped it wasn't the Mayor's house, but they were close to the Kraut, he could almost smell him.

"Driver, ease back. Gunner, stand by. If he hasn't moved, we're almost on him."

The Sherman slowed to a crawl, and they saw the

crossroads directly ahead of them. The roads weren't straight but wound in a series of tight curves, so they had no real idea of their exact position, only that somewhere ahead of them an enemy tank killer waited. As they neared the end of the street, Angel halted.

The crack of a gun sounded close, very close.

"He's still there, around the corner. Solly, stand by. Driver, advance."

They rounded the corner and there, right in front of them, laid out invitingly like a bride on her wedding night, was the STUG. Inside the enclosed casemate the crew was busy fighting off Morgan's Shermans, and they hadn't seen them yet. It was a golden opportunity, and he didn't need to give any order.

The main gun fired, and the 75mm AP shell sliced through the side armor of the STUG. They heard the warhead explode inside the hull, and the vehicle stopped moving.

"We got him!" Solly exalted, "Eat that, you fucking murderers."

"There could be someone alive inside the hull," Dale remarked, "Maybe we'd better check it out. We don't want Jerries running loose in our rear."

Grant knew it would be a gory task, but he wasn't prepared to delegate.

"You're right. Grab your carbine and come with me. The rest of you, stay sharp."

He cautiously opened the hatch and looked out. The streets were empty, and the only sounds were from the battle raging further to the northeast of the town. It meant the 29th Infantry was hitting the German defenders hard, fighting yard by yard, house by house, to dislodge them.

He drew his Colt automatic, climbed down from the hull, and Dale dropped down alongside him. He carried an M1.

"It looks pretty quiet, Josh."

"Yeah. I'll jump up on top, open the turret, and take a look inside. Cover me."

"I'll be right with you."

The dead assault gun looked huge from close up. Mounted on a Panzer III chassis, the absence of a rotating turret allowed for the installation of a more powerful gun. It was a tank killer with a record unsurpassed on any front, something to beware of. The hatch had partially opened with the force of the explosion, and he was able to fully open it and look inside.

He nearly retched. The shell had disintegrated inside the hull and into splinters that spun around the interior. They'd showered the crew with shards of hot metal, as they were designed to do, and some of the crew looked as if they'd been dragged through a giant mincing machine. They were all dead, no question. In the distance, an explosion lit up the sky. It also bathed the interior with light, displaying the gory remains in sharp detail. He glanced at Dale, who had looked away.

"That's it. They're finished."

He nodded. "Not a pleasant sight, even if they were Germans. You look as if you've seen a ghost."

"I have. Four of them."

"Payback for what they did to your brother? What the Germans did, I mean, not these particular guys."

He looked at Dale. "So why don't I feel good about it? How many do we have to kill to avenge the deaths of our loved ones, ten, a hundred, a thousand? Tell me, Dale, how many do we have to kill?"

He hadn't realized it, but in his passionate despair, he'd grabbed his friend's jacket and was pulling him closer, almost as if he was about to attack him. Dale stayed calm.

"Easy, Josh. You know I don't have those kinds of answers. Why don't you ask the Padre?"

"What for? What do you reckon the German Padres say to their own soldiers? Do they tell them killing Americans is God's will?"

Dale shrugged. "Beats me." He cocked his head, "Heads up, there's armor coming in."

Both men raced back to Minnie, and Grant slammed the hatch closed when they were inside. They waited tensely, but then the first vehicle nosed around the corner. It was Morgan. The Major popped his head out the turret and stared for a few moments at the wrecked STUG. Grant opened up the hatch, looked across at him, and waited.

"No prisoners?"

"No, Sir. All dead."

He grunted something inaudible, and then realizing it was hard to hear what they were saying, grabbed for his mike.

"Good work, Grant. We've got them on the run, no question. Battalion brought up some Company B reinforcements, and the Krauts are leaving town. Apart from a few infantry, probably Panzergrenadiers, the job's over."

"Did we lose any more vehicles, Sir?"

"We did not." He could hear the relief in his voice, "Company A still has a grand total of four Shermans. Lieutenant Bligh and Sergeant Kuruk are knocking out a machine gun nest in the southwest of the town. If we..."

He stopped as the sound of a burst of machine gunfire

sounded a short distance away. Not an American weapon. It was the peculiar tearing sound of the MG42, like cloth ripping. The MG42 was the feared German machine gun that had cost so many Russian lives on the Eastern Front. Belt fed, with quick-change barrels to cope with overheating, the weapon could punch out lead at the incredible rate of fifteen hundred per minute. The weapon was only capable of automatic fire, and the effect on troops caught out in the open was devastating. While they were training in England, they'd even attended a lecture on how to deal with the damaging psychological effects of the Nazi super weapon.

Except the machine guns were of little use against armor.

"Nail the bastard," Morgan shouted.

He gripped the butt of the gun, sighted on the target, and sent a stream of bullets into the night. The MG42 kept firing, and then the main guns hurled out HE shells. Explosions lit up the sky, and when the darkness had returned, the machine gun was silent.

"Form on me," Morgan ordered over the radio net, "We'll link up with infantry, in case they need our support. Watch the ground when we get out of town; parts of it are a quagmire after the flooding. Stay on the marked roads if at all possible. And remember, there may still be snipers, so stay buttoned up."

His Sherman swerved away and headed back down the main street. Angel fell in behind, and a hundred yards to the southeast, Bligh's and Kuruk's vehicles appeared and joined the rear of the column. They halted close to the 29th Battalion command post and were told to wait, so they made camp while they awaited orders. By some miracle, Margot Caron arrived shortly after they got there. She'd acquired a vehicle, an old van with the name of a local baker on the side. In response to his question about where she'd obtained it, she replied, 'The Boche murdered him, so he won't need it anymore."

The vehicle was a Citroen HY, with the peculiar corrugated metal bodywork so beloved of the French. She got to work with her cooking while Grant drove Bligh in a borrowed a Willys Jeep to go in search of their Battalion HQ, the 745th. They found them only a few hundred yards north of Omaha Beach, but Bligh's request for supplies was met with hard stares.

"You guys want fuel? The whole fucking Army wants fuel, what do you think we're running here, a gas station?"

Bligh stared at the Quartermaster Sergeant, his expression turning angry. Grant decided to try another tack.

"We need shells, Sarge. My Sherman is down to the last couple of HEs for the 75mm. I guess the others are running low as well."

"Shells! Everybody wants shells, what do they think this is?"

"A war zone?"

"Funnee. They ain't sending me anything across the Channel, so forget it. When I get what you want, you can have it. Until then, you'll have to manage. Go kill some Germans, take their gas."

Bligh fixed the Sergeant with a hard gaze. "If you don't have any stores, Sergeant, you'll be needed at the front. You can make yourself useful. There's no point in your being here with nothing to do. I'll give you a lift, and you can join up with the 29th. They're fighting a hard battle right now, and they've taken plenty of casualties. Come with me."

"Er, I, er..." They stared at each other for long moments. He knew he was beaten, and his shoulders slumped, "Look, I do have a few crates of shells. They told me to keep them in reserve. As for fuel," he sucked in his breath between his teeth, "How about four drums of gas. That's it. After that, the pump's dry."

Bligh gave him a curt nod. "You're all heart, Sergeant. We can't manage all that stuff in the Willys. You'll have to lend us a vehicle."

"Sure, sure. Anything."

Fifteen minutes later, they were driving back to Isigny. Behind them, a frightened PFC drove a Dodge Weapons Carrier, with the bed loaded with fuel drums and wooden crates of shells.

By the time they returned, Margot had a hot meal prepared. Grant sniffed at the stew streaming in the pot on the portable paraffin stove she'd found, enjoying the delicious odors that surrounded him.

She smiled when she saw him. "I kept some for you. Otherwise your men would have eaten the lot. Sit down, Sergeant Josh."

"Grant."

"Whatever." The mess table was a door ripped out of a destroyed building, supported on two piles of salvaged stone blocks. It wobbled, and it definitely stank of soot, gasoline, and smoke. It could have been a length of barbed wire for all they cared. The food was all that mattered. She served them the meal in aluminum mess tins filled with the stew, and they ate in silence, wolfing down the culinary miracle.

Margot sat on an upturned ammunition box and watched them eat, almost like a doting mother. Grant half expected her to chide him to finish up and clear the plate. When they were halfway through, she left them to brew fresh coffee. Bligh and Grant regarded each other, not quite certain what they'd done to warrant such wonders.

Bligh looked puzzled. "Didn't you destroy her farm?"

"That was the Jerries."

"Right. But it was your battle. Most people would have taken a shotgun to you."

He shrugged. "It's just my natural charm, Lt."

He grinned. "Sure it is. Tell me, why did you turn down a commission? You're a lawyer, and you have a college degree, so you could have done real well."

"They offered me JAG or nothing. I told them I wanted to fight, and when they dug their heels in, I enlisted. Simple as that."

"I see. And what about this French girl, Margot? She seems struck on you."

"I hadn't noticed."

"Hmm, is there anything going on there? I mean; I wouldn't want to tread on your toes, so to speak."

Grant was startled for a few moments. It hadn't occurred to him that they were anything more than two people who'd met in a war zone and quickly formed a friendship. He thought about her pretty face, her calm resolve, and her French confidence.

What do they call it? 'Sangfroid.' A kind of poise and composure under strain, you don't get much more strain than armored units pounding each other to scrap inside your farmyard.

She was more than merely confident. Clever, tough, and not a little feisty, so what was she doing running a farm, apparently all on her own? There was a story there, and he made a decision to find out more when there was a lull in the fighting.

She was clearing away the remains of the meal, and as she leaned over his shoulder, she gave him a smile that was at once warm, friendly, saucy, and unless he misunderstood, inviting. All at once, he wanted her for himself. He looked back at Bligh, who was waiting for his reply.

"Lt, don't get this wrong, but I aim to get to know her a whole lot better."

Bligh nodded. "I don't blame you, Sergeant." He climbed to his feet, thanked Margot for the food, and announced he was about to hit the sack. "You, too, Sergeant Grant. You'll need a rest. Chances are we'll be back in action early tomorrow."

As if to illustrate the point, an artillery battery opened up several miles away, and the sky was lit up as they fired, and multiple flashes hitting whatever they were shooting at. Bligh had a point; they'd all need to get some rest, although he had something to attend to first. He went over to Margot, who was clearing away the pots and dishes. She stopped, looked at him, and waited as he approached.

"I wanted to thank you for the food. It was wonderful."

She gave a small nod. "You are more than welcome, Sergeant Grant."

"Josh."

She grinned. "You looked so serious and warlike. Not at all like a Josh. Is it true what I overheard, you were a lawyer before all this?"

She waved her hand around, indicating the tank park, the jeeps, the guns, the ammo and stores, the bustle of soldiers preparing for a coming battle.

"I'm afraid so."

She looked puzzled. "Is that not a good thing in America, being a lawyer?"

He grimaced. "Some think so. Others would like to see us all rounded up and shot."

She giggled, and he was enchanted by the musical tinkle of her voice. "I think they do not appreciate you, Josh. And here you are, fighting to free us French from the Boche." Her dark brown eyes shone, "You are my white knight, come to France to save me from the evil Nazis."

"It's not just you. I mean, I'm sorry about your farm, Margot. You see, if you..."

Her smile was huge as she listened to his faltering protest. She put a finger to his lips to silence him, "I know the reasons, Josh."

She put her face to his and kissed him lightly on the lips. "I don't care about why you came. You're here, and I care about you. And that's my way of saying thank you."

She skipped away, leaving him feeling like a love-struck twelve-year-old standing in the school playground. He was still standing on the same spot when Solly arrived.

"Major Morgan wants a word, Sarge. And we all need some sack time. It's been rough today, and it looks like we'll need to do it all again tomorrow."

"I'll be right there."

He followed the gunner, aware his legs felt like rubber after the encounter with Margot. He stumbled once, and Solly grabbed him to prevent him falling.

"You okay? Did you take a bump to your head or something?"

He found his footing again. "I'm okay. I must have banged it on something hard."

* * *

Three kilometers outside Caen, France, June 9, 1944

It took them the rest of the night and part of the next day to arrive at their destination. The constant threat of aerial attacks forced them to thread their way through thick woods and endless bocage. When they sighted aircraft in the vicinity, they sought the nearest cover and hid from the menace of the fighters until they'd disappeared. Finally, they rejoined their unit, the 12th SS Hitler Jugend.

There were Panzers from other units gathered in the assembly area, Panzer Vs, known as Panthers, further Tiger Is, and a couple of the new, much vaunted Tiger IIs. There was also a motley selection of lesser armor, including a battalion of the useful Panzer IVs from the 21st Panzer Division. Even a squadron of French Renaults made an appearance, little more than cannon fodder against the armored might pouring ashore. Also present was Standartenfuhrer Meyer.

"The Reich is faced with its biggest crisis, Manhausen, and you go waltzing around the French countryside looking for God knows what. Were you drunk, or was it a woman?"

He patiently explained about the mechanical problems, but Meyer was unimpressed.

"I don't give a shit about your excuses. I needed you here, not playing touchy feely with some fucking American Sherman. The Allies are building up their forces for an attack on the city of Caen. Our orders are to make sure it doesn't succeed. I've received word the enemy has taken the village of Rots, so our first task is to throw them out. Clear?"

"Jawohl, Standartenfuhrer. I take it you mean a night attack?"

"Yes. At night we are able to maneuver without interference from enemy aircraft. We leave shortly. Make sure your vehicle is ready for battle. "

With what? We're low on gasoline, low on shells, and low on spare parts. What does he expect, a miracle? He probably does.

"Yes, Sir."

"Good. See to it."

He saluted and returned to his tank. Another officer was chatting to his crew, an SS Obersturmfuhrer like himself. The man turned, and Rolf felt a lurch in his guts. He'd seen the man before in Russia, on the Eastern Front, where this tanker was something of a legend. A Knight's Cross with oak leaves testified to his prowess on the battlefield. He held out a hand.

"Michael Wittmann, Obersturmfuhrer. 101st SS Heavy Panzer Battalion."

They shook, and he introduced himself. "Manhausen, 12th SS Hitler Jugend. You don't need any introduction, Michael. I was in Russia, too."

"Kursk?"

"Yes, I was there."

Wittmann grinned. "We gave Ivan a good pounding on that occasion, my friend. They'll think twice before they throw so many tanks against our Panzers."

Manhausen nodded, although privately, he didn't agree. They'd come out on top at Kursk, no question. The problem was they'd lost most of their armor, Panzers the Reich couldn't replace, whereas the Russians appeared to have unending supplies of new weapons. Knock down a T-34 and the next day three would appear in its place.

"Why are you here?"

He wiped a greasy hand over his forehead. Rolf could see Wittmann looked tired, very tired. Yet the blaze of fanaticism still shone in the other man's eyes.

"We were stationed in Beauvais when the Allies landed, and we've been ordered to Villers-Bocage. The idea is to prevent a British armored breakthrough. We'll be in support of your 12th SS and Panzer Lehr, so no doubt we'll see each other on the battlefield. Now I must leave. We still have some distance to travel, and we've been on the road for three days already. My crew is anxious to arrive."

He was aghast. "Three days, to get this far from Beauvais? How so?"

"Aircraft," Wittmann spat out the single word with contempt, "Every time we move, at least during the day, they come at us. We've lost half our Panzers already, and we still haven't reached our objective." He stared at Rolf. "Be wary of aircraft. They're death to our Tigers."

"At least the Allies haven't any armor we need to worry about."

Wittmann slowly shook his head. "Don't you believe it! You've met the American Shermans?"

He thought of the enigmatic Minnie Mouse, and something felt cold against his spine.

"Yes, but surely..."

"Our intelligence reports the British have a modified Sherman. They call it the Firefly. Some of our armored units have come across them, and they're a problem."

"A Sherman? But..."

"A Sherman with a more powerful main gun, a specially designed 76mm. It's easy to spot; the barrel is much longer than the normal Sherman M4 with the 75mm gun. They say this new gun can penetrate the frontal armor of a Tiger, maybe even a Tiger II. We're not certain yet. If you come up against a Firefly, make sure you shoot first. If they get in a shot, you're dead."

"You're that worried about these new Shermans, Wittmann? I can hardly believe it. How could any gun they fit to a Sherman be that powerful? It's just a medium tank, not a heavy like our Tigers and Panthers."

He grimaced. "If you tangle with a Firefly, be afraid, my friend. Be very afraid."

The ace tanker nodded a farewell and left to continue his long, slow journey to the Normandy Front. Manhausen returned to his Tiger and supervised his young crew while they frantically worked to prepare for the coming attack. Franz Schelling was nowhere to be seen, until he crawled out from underneath the engine compartment.

"Obersturmfuhrer."

He sighed. "Franz, don't tell me we have another problem with the engine."

The young driver looked concerned. "Not exactly a problem, Sir. It's just these valves. I can't guarantee they won't let us down at a critical moment. Then there're the gearboxes."

"What's up with the gearboxes?"

"They're crap, Obersturmfuhrer. You know they use foreign workers, many of them prisoners from the Eastern Front, to work in the factories that make them. They're almost slaves, so what incentive do they have to do a decent job?"

"I agree, but our skilled men are all in the Wehrmacht or the SS. We have to use foreign labor, otherwise we'd have no one to operate the machines in the factories."

Unterscharfuhrer Heinrich Boll had been listening, and he joined in. "That's the Fuhrer's master plan, you see. He demands that we Germans fight and die, while enemy captives are kept safe inside cozy factories back in the Reich. They then turn out sub-standard spare parts to make our job even harder. The way things are going; the only men left alive will be the prisoners working in our factories inside the Reich. Some of us find it difficult to understand how we will achieve victory in this way, but of course, the Fuhrer cannot be wrong."

"What you say is tantamount to treason," Sturmann Siegfried Lenz snarled, "Only a madman would send good Germans to die in battle while the subhuman scum we take prisoner are kept safe. Why..."

He stopped. They were staring at him, and none dared speak. Even Meyer, the Battalion commander, had overheard his comment and was walking over. They were acutely aware of the Knight's Cross with oak leaves and swords casually displayed around his neck, a higher award even than Wittmann's. He stared at Lenz, who shivered slightly, aware he'd said the wrong thing, but not quite sure why.

"You're suggesting the Fuhrer is crazy, Sturmann Lenz?"

He shook his head violently side to side. "No, Sir, of course not. Everything that happens in Germany is because of the genius of Adolf Hitler. He is the sanest man on the planet. "

Meyer cocked an eyebrow. "So you're saying it is

the strategy of a sane man? Sending us out to die and protecting the Poles and the Slavs."

"Yes, Sir. I mean, no, Sir. I, er, don't know, Sir." He reddened and looked around for a way out.

Meyer glared at him. "Which is it, Lenz? Either it is his plan, or it isn't."

Manhausen felt sorry for the fourteen-year old. "Standartenfuhrer, the boy is tired and confused. I will talk to him later."

Meyer swung around and gave him a hard look. "Rolf, come with me."

They went out of earshot of the rest of the men.

"Manhausen, tell that young fool of yours to keep quiet. If the Gestapo or the SD gets wind of what he says, they'll put him in Dachau."

"Of course, Sir. His uncle is an SD Standartenfuhrer."

"That won't help him. He's right, of course."

"Right?"

"Hitler's dropped us in the shit, and we're right up to our necks in it." Rolf stayed silent and waited. This was dangerous ground, "You know we can't win," Meyer continued in a low voice.

"Sir?"

"The Fuhrer thinks his new wonder weapons will tilt the balance in our favor. They won't. We've already lost."

He felt the ground moving beneath his feet. "I can hardly believe it."

"You'd better believe it. You know the 101st lost half its armor moving up from Beauvais, and they haven't fired a shot."

"I spoke to Wittmann."

He grimaced. "Yes, the daring Panzer hero. He's a good

tank commander, one of the best, but he tends to go out on his own, thinks he's a one-man band. One day he'll meet one of those new Sherman Fireflies, and they'll fry his ass, which is all academic; Wittmann or no Wittmann, they're pouring men and materiel onto the beaches at a crazy rate."

"What do we do, Sir?"

"Do?" Meyer grinned ferociously, "We obey our orders, Manhausen. We keep fighting, and pray they give us the chance to group all of our heavy Panzers into a single fighting unit. We'd be unstoppable. We could divide the enemy, roll them up from the center, and make them wish they'd never come."

"Can we do it?"

"I doubt it. If we hadn't lost so many Panzers already, it may have been possible. And if we weren't led by complete fools."

"So it's true we're finished."

He shook his head. "Not if we can regroup. It's our only chance to beat them. Remember, we're Waffen-SS, the elite, and the best in the business. However, right now, our orders are to proceed to the village of Rots and kick the Allies out. I came here on my motorcycle. I lost my Tiger during an air raid. If Headquarters doesn't find me a replacement, I shall have no choice but to ride it into battle, leading the Division from the saddle, like the knights of old."

He grinned, but Rolf wasn't fooled. Beneath the cheery expression, his face looked gray and lined. Meyer was thirty-three years old, yet he looked more like fifty-three. He went to walk away, but he stopped him.

"Standartenfuhrer, surely that was a joke, about losing

the war. When we've thrown the Allies back into the sea, they won't dare to attack us again."

"Is what you think?" Meyer nodded absently to himself, obviously thinking, "Tell me, Rolf, how do you plan to defeat the fighters and bombers that have freedom of the skies, now that our Luftwaffe is nowhere to be seen?"

"The Luftwaffe will come, Sir. They just need more time to transfer their aircraft from the Eastern Front."

"Maybe. So who will fight back the Reds? You know that even now their hordes threaten the borders of the Reich? They have vast armadas of aircraft, new fighters, and bombers. Who will defend Germany when they come?"

"I don't know," he replied lamely.

"No. The war is lost, Rolf. If we assemble a strong enough force, we can win the battle here in Normandy. But they will keep coming, and we will lose sooner or later. All that remains is for us to do our duty, and if necessary, die like heroes. No doubt Wittmann is counting the days before he enters his own fiery Valhalla. Stay away from him, and try to keep out of trouble. Watch out for aircraft, and remember, the dead hero is of no use to the Fatherland."

"No, Sir."

"Get going, Obersturmfuhrer. And good luck."

Manhausen saluted smartly, and it was returned. Meyer strode away, and he returned to their Tiger.

"Franz, are we ready to move?"

The boy grinned. "The engine is purring like a cat, Sir."

"Good. Unterscharfuhrer Boll, do we have enough ammunition?"

"It's tight, but we can fight, Sir."

"Excellent. It's time to show these Allies how to fight a

war. Let's go."

They sat waiting; twelve massive Tiger Is with their huge Maybach engines ticking over, using up precious fuel. Meyer still hadn't arrived at the head of the column. In fact, he'd disappeared. And then a motorcycle roared past the line of tanks and took its place at their head. Manhausen grinned.

It's Meyer, the mad bastard.

He held up his arm like an American nineteenth century cavalry commander, and waved it forward for them to follow. He roared away into the night, and Franz gunned the engine to follow. It was time to hit the enemy.

They charged forward, and Rolf felt a thrill as they raced behind their charismatic commander. Behind them, elements of the Panzer-Grenadier-Regiment 26 followed in their SDK-251 half-track transports. A single STUG III assault gun trailed them. The narrow road ran straight like an arrow to the nearby village. When the clouds cleared the night sky, the farms and houses were bathed in bright moonlight.

There was no sign of the enemy, only Mad Meyer thundering ahead on his motorbike. They were close, very close, and yet there was still no sign of the enemy.

Have they abandoned the village?

Even as he had that thought, the first gun fired from deep concealment on the right flank. All doubts were dispelled. Every man in that column knew battle had been joined, and they began seeking targets for their 88mm guns.

The Panzer in front of him took a direct hit on the engine compartment from an enemy shell, and smoke and flames poured out of the hull. Franz swerved to avoid the wreck, and as they drove past, he noticed the escape hatches were still closed.

Poor bastards.

A shell slammed into their frontal armor but did little damage, and they charged down the enemy in an insane race to kill them all, except they couldn't see them. Only the muzzle flashes when they fired lit up their positions, and Heinrich Boll returned fire repeatedly, to little effect. The enemy guns continued shooting at them, and another Tiger exploded. This time, it was a frontal shot. The shell threw up sparks and flames at the point of impact, penetrating the thick steel of the hull. It had to be anti-tank artillery working with the howitzers. Rolf pressed the transmit button.

"Panzergrenadiers, you must go forward and deal with those anti-tank guns. They're murdering us!"

"This is Untersturmfuhrer Grenz, commanding the STUG III. We're moving up now on the left flank. Some of the men have panzerfausts and anti-tank rifles, so we'll do our best for you."

"You'd better make it quick, while we still have a few Tigers left with which to fight."

"Jawohl, the SS Panzergrenadiers are moving forward now."

Rolf watched the shadowy figures go ahead at a crouching run. An enemy machine gun opened up, and several troopers fell, scythed down by the heavy bursts.

"Heinrich, that enemy machine gun, can you see it?"

"Jawohl, but there are more guns I'm trying to hit on the right of the village. There must be a half-dozen of them, and they're well dug in."

"Understood. Stay on it." He grabbed for the butt of

the MG-34 machine gun and searched the gloom for the gun. The bullets were little pinpricks of light, like fireflies, and he was able to trace them to their source. The enemy fired again. He sighted along the barrel and pulled the trigger. A stream of 7.92mm tracer bullets sped toward the target and missed by only a couple of meters.

He corrected his aim and poured hundreds more rounds into the unsuspecting men. The enemy gun went silent, and then Boll fired their main gun. He looked for the fall of shot and saw an explosion light up the sky, and then a secondary explosion. Good, a hit on their ammunition store. But there was much more to do. Another machine gun fired from only a few hundred meters away, and bullets pinged off the steel turret, forcing him to drop inside and slam the hatch closed.

"Driver, advance. Go left, we need to flank those guns."

"Jawohl, Obersturmfuhrer."

Franz gunned the engine, and they drove so fast he had to grip a stanchion for support. Another Tiger was alongside them, attacking the same target. A third came in behind them, and the three iron monsters hurtled forward. The enemy fired a salvo, and several shells impacted the ground around them, but they weren't hit. Boll was firing on the move, and Lenz was hastily feeding shells into the hungry breech of the big gun. The interior was filled with smoke, and although the fans were working at maximum speed, the fumes were choking all of them.

The Tiger tilted at a crazy angle as they climbed a low hill, and then the tank beside them almost stopped dead, hit by a heavy caliber anti-tank shell. A second massive shell struck the mantlet next to the barrel, penetrating the heavy armor. The Tiger slewed around and came to a stop, pouring smoke. He stabbed the transmit button.

"Grenz, where the hell are you? We just lost another tank."

The reply came a few seconds later over the radio, and he could hear the rattle of machine guns blazing like fury.

"We're bogged down, Sir. The enemy ambushed us. They were dug in on the side of the village. I've already lost eleven men."

He sighed.

The poor bastards are getting creamed. We'll have to manage without them.

"Do your best."

"Yes, Sir."

They still had their formidable firepower and heavy armor to destroy the enemy. All they needed now was to get near enough to locate them. That was the trick, to get close up and open fire, before the enemy destroyed them. He looked back. The second Tiger was right behind him. He grimaced; there was no way they could use their firepower from back there. They were just using his tank as a shield, which meant until they reached the guns ahead of them, and fanned out for the attack, he was on his own.

An artillery piece fired from a small wood to his left, and he shouted for Boll to engage. But even as their turret was turning, a weird-looking machine emerged. A strange beast, it looked like a Sherman chassis with a howitzer mounted on top. The crew was virtually unprotected in the open cupola.

Boll fired, and the 88mm slammed into the trees, missing the target by less than a meter. The enemy fired, and their huge shell arced into the night and fell fifty meters short. Boll fired again, and this time the big shell slammed into the enemy. The mobile gun exploded, and then the ammunition detonated. He watched open mouthed as the detached howitzer sailed through the air to land on a dark patch of ground some distance away. It was a small victory. The enemy artillery was firing again from further away, and shells were bracketing their vehicle.

The entire area was shrouded in smoke, and when he looked for friendlies, he couldn't see any German armor. There were only the flashes of big guns as they flung shell after shell at the enemy in a duel to the death, and then came the explosions when some of them found their target. The approach to Rots had become an inferno of exploding ordnance, and he knew if he continued the attack, they wouldn't make it through the anti-tank fire that had turned the village into a death trap. He looked to the left and had an idea.

"Franz, drive us into the wood. We'll come out the other side and flank them."

"If we can get through, Sir."

"The Sherman with the howitzer got through, so we can. Hurry, man," he shouted.

"Zum befehl, Obersturmfuhrer!"

They punched through the leafy trees, and visibility was almost zero in the dark forest. He ducked inside the turret when an overhanging tree branch nearly took off his head, looking out through his periscope at the foliage as they careered through the trees. They emerged the other side, but he realized he'd made a mistake. Instead of open tank country, he was on the opposite end of the village, and with no sign of the enemy gun positions. Franz started to slow, but he shouted at him to pick up speed.

"Drive straight into the village, Franz. We'll come at

them from behind! Gunner, stand by."

"Yes, Sir."

Instead of trees and leaves, they raced past houses, cottages, and wood and iron fences. They reached an intersection, and once again Franz started to slow. He stabbed the transmit button.

"Take a right. We have to get behind them."

"But, Sir, it's too tight. The houses..."

"Fuck the houses! Do it!"

"Jawohl!"

He moved the levers, stopped the right track, and the left track drove them around in a tight turn. They tore away half of the facade of a big, stately French town house, and then plunged on. The enemy gun positions loomed in front of them, only two hundred meters ahead. They were three big 30-pounder guns, death to Tigers. Rolf's vehicle had maneuvered behind them, and already the startled gunners were turning to face the new threat. Some ran, some tried to lever the big guns around, a few froze. They were all too late.

"Fire! Keep firing."

Boll fired, again and again. The 88mm shells smashed into the enemy. He was firing HE, and the massive explosions tore apart both men and guns. It took less than a minute. The three guns were a mass of mangled scrap, intermingled with the remains of their crews. He was looking for the next target when a shell slammed into the side of their tank. He looked around and saw yet another of those strange Sherman mobile artillery pieces, with the huge howitzer mounted on the top.

"Heinrich, left flank, enemy armor. Engage!"

Another American shell slammed into them just below

the turret, but still they weren't powerful enough to penetrate the thick armor. Boll rotated the turret; the long barrel struck a lamp standard and stopped. Two more shells slammed into them, and in that instant, Rolf knew they had to get out fast. Their side armor was good, but a lucky hit could destroy them before they had a chance to bring their gun to bear.

"Franz, reverse, go back!"

The Tiger jerked to a stop, just as a well-aimed shell punched across their front, aimed to offset their forward motion. Franz backed into a narrow street and started retracing their path. They had to find another way through if they were to destroy the rest of the enemy guns. He was about to give orders to cut through a gap between two houses when the radio came alive.

"This is Meyer. All units withdraw. I repeat, withdraw!"

What the hell is going on? We're winning.

He hit the transmit button with fury. "This is Manhausen, Sir. We can't withdraw, not now. We're inside the village. Give us another half hour and we can wipe them all out."

Meyer's tone was icy. "I doubt that. We had twelve Tigers when we started the attack. I'm left with six. There are too many of them, and I don't want to lose any more armor. Get out now and return to base. Meyer out!"

He felt numbed. Six Tigers destroyed was a high price, and for what? They were retreating.

"Franz, did you get that?"

"I did, Sir, but..."

"Get us out of here."

"Yes, Sir."

As they left the village, he worked to control his anger.

These piecemeal attacks are useless. The enemy is too numerous.

Until we can use all of our heavy armor to deal them a single, knockout punch, we're allowing them to pick us off, tank by tank. When will the High Command learn?

He thought of the Fuhrer and his tardy response to the invasion.

When will our High Command get out of bed?

CHAPTER FIVE

SHAEF Headquarters Camp Griffiss, London, England, June 13, 1944

Eisenhower waited while the new arrival, General Omar Bradley, shook the rain off his wet coat and took the indicated chair. The weather for the invasion had been bad; only a small window allowing them to get the first troops ashore. Since then, it had got worse. He put on his customary smile.

"How was the trip, General?"

"It was fast. That's all I can say about it. We were lucky to land my C-47 on the beach, and I had a fighter umbrella all the way back."

Eisenhower nodded. "I know; I ordered it. How's it going over there, any problems I need to know about?"

Bradley looked thoughtful. "Sir, we're making progress. That's about the best I can say. The armor is short on gas and ammunition. We have to get more of everything ashore. Fortunately, the Mulberry Harbors were completed on the

June 9. That means the materiel is starting to come ashore a bit quicker, but it's still a long, slow process. Christ, at one time, we didn't even have enough food, let alone fuel and ammo. As long as both those harbors keep working, we're good. I guess you know we've taken Carentan."

"Yes, the news just came in. What about enemy aircraft, any trouble there?"

For the first time, he smiled. "You jest. The Luftwaffe flew a few sorties, but every time they take off, our guys shoot them out of the sky. They don't cause too much of a problem."

Ike smiled. "We have the Russians to thank for some of that. The best Kraut pilots are in Russia fighting on the Eastern Front; those that are left, that is. The Luftwaffe had taken quite a pounding, so I'm told, and they're a shadow of what they once were. Still, they may transfer fighters west to attack us, so keep your AA batteries sharp."

"No sweat, every man with a gun pointed skyward is waiting for a chance to shoot down one of those Messerschmitts."

"I guess so. They'll come, sooner or later. The Germans have a huge shortage of fuel. That's not helping them much. The Brits hit their main oilfields at Ploiesti with a saturation-bombing raid, and the pumps have started to run dry. Our intelligence suggests their aircraft are dangerously low on gas. I guess that goes for their Panzers as well. Any sign of them coming out in force?"

He saw Bradley wince. "None, and that's what worries me. They're too quiet. We've had a few brushes with armored units, but they haven't attacked yet in any kind of strength. We don't know why."

"Can you hold them if they do hit hard?"

"Against several divisions of heavy armor, Tiger Is, Panthers, even the new Tiger IIs? I don't know. If they'd done it a couple of days ago, I'd say no, we couldn't hold. However, as long as the Mulberry Harbors keep bringing our equipment ashore, and we get the air support we need, yes, we can hold them. Just."

"You're not too confident, are you, General?"

"I'd be stupid if I were. You know what a Tiger tank can do to a Sherman?"

"I know, but we have air support."

"Not when the weather is this lousy. If they hit us with an entire Panzer army, they could punch through."

"How can I help?"

Omar Bradley grimaced. "Pray that the weather breaks so the fighters can fly, and we keep those Mulberry Harbors operating. Also, that the Jerries don't group their heavy Panzers into a single unit."

Ike didn't answer for a few moments, and then he stared back at Bradley.

"When are you going back?"

"First thing in the morning. They're timing it for when the tide is out and there's a wide strip of beach to land on."

He nodded. "Then I wish you luck. I guess our best move would be to step up attacks on their armor and fuel dumps."

"Yes, Sir, especially the heavy armor. The men are scared shitless of those Tigers. Just the name is enough to worry them."

"I'll advise our air controllers accordingly. With Carentan in our hands, maybe things will be easier for you."

"Unless they take it back from us. You know the Germans are past masters at the art of counterattack. Sure, we've taken Carentan, and we're about to link the American landing beaches, and then roll up the Cotentin Peninsula. But tomorrow may be a different story."

"I hear you. You know that some people say if we keep hitting them hard enough, they'll break and start running back to Berlin."

Bradley looked skeptical. "I doubt it. They're more likely to hit us with their heavy armor and try to wipe us out. If that attack comes, and they have enough Tigers, it's anyone's guess."

Ike grimaced. "Just keep hitting them, and I'll do what I can from here. Good luck on the flight back."

Bradley saluted and left for the return flight to Normandy, leaving Ike to his own thoughts.

The Tigers, always the Tigers, Hitler's bogeymen, always lurking in the background, and a story to frighten my troops! But if they do come, my fighters and bombers will slaughter them, bogeymen or no bogeymen, provided the weather clears, and if it doesn't clear? I don't want to think about that.

He was still thinking of the fearsome enemy armor when he picked up the phone and asked to be connected with Air Chief Marshal Arthur Tedder, Deputy Supreme Commander Allied Expeditionary Force. It took less than twenty seconds for Tedder to answer.

"Arthur, you'll have to get your aircraft up, and locate their heavy armor. We must destroy it now."

"General Eisenhower, you know how bad the weather is. Most times they can't get off the ground."

The English voice was calm, filled with patient reason. He didn't give a damn.

"Get 'em up, Arthur. I don't care how you do it. Right now we're winning, but if we give them a chance to use their armor, we could lose everything."

He heard Tedder say he'd do his best, and he put down the phone. It was the dark threat that loomed over the entire invasion. The Tigers.

* * *

The attack on Carentan the day before had been a fierce and bloody action, part of Bradley's strategy to link the American invasion beaches, Omaha and Utah. After the 101st Airborne fought their way into to the town, the Germans finally withdrew, and the generals breathed a sigh of relief. For the 745th Battalion, it had been a bloody, grueling nightmare. Grant was drinking the first decent coffee he'd enjoyed in several days, courtesy of Margot Caron, when the messenger found him.

"The Major wants you, Sarge. Right away."

He tossed the remains of the coffee into the mud, gave Margot a rueful glance, and ran after the man. Battalion Headquarters building was in chaos, and he found Morgan standing outside with Lieutenant Bligh. Morgan's Sherman was parked only a few yards away.

"Sergeant Grant, we're moving out shortly. Get aboard your vehicle and join me back here!"

"What's up, Major?"

"The Germans have counterattacked at Carentan. Intelligence says they brought up two regiments, and one of them is some kind of elite unit, the 17th SS Panzergrenadier Division. They're all over our boys; so we need to get in there fast and push them back before the invasion strategy goes down the toilet. They'll have anti-tank missiles, and maybe even a STUG or two, as well as the usual anti-tank artillery."

He stopped and looked around as a corporal dashed out of the Headquarters building, a semi-ruined Normandy farmhouse, and handed Morgan a message. He glanced at it quickly.

"The two companies on the left flank are falling back, so we need to get in there fast. Move it, guys."

He sprinted back to Minnie Mouse. Angel had the engine ticking over. He vaulted onto the hull, climbed into the turret, and gave the order.

"Move out! The Jerries are attacking Carentan."

"Tigers?" Vernon called out. The question was not unexpected.

"Nope, Panzergrenadiers."

Angel slammed the vehicle forward, and they raced to join Morgan, who was already four hundred yards away. Bligh was in his wake, and Daniel Kuruk's Cochise brought up the rear. They were heading for Carentan, and after the bloody action the day before, every man knew the importance of the town. Behind them, swarms of Shermans were forming up. Mechanized infantry kept pace riding in half-tracked White M3s. Purple Heart Boxes they'd nicknamed them, due to their abysmal armor plating.

Further back, a company of self-propelled howitzers pulled out to join them. Whoever was running this show was serious, no question. Ahead of them, the town was already in flames, lit up by artillery strikes, decorated with crisscrossing lines of tracer fire, and garlanded by lines of vehicles rushing to join the battle.

He heard the sound of explosions behind him.

"The Jerries just hit our HQ with artillery," Morgan announced over the radio net, "They're calling up a company from Second Division to take care of it."

Margot!

He strained to look back at HQ, but all he could see was a patchwork of smoke and flames roiling into the sky, as yet more shells hit. The Headquarters building was ablaze, and he could see the shadows of vehicles moving around, weaving an intricate dance as they attempted to escape the onslaught.

Please, God, don't let anything happen to her!

Shells hammered toward them from the German lines, and he automatically began assessing what lay in front of them. Another shell landed and detonated with a blast that tore down several trees. PAK 40, no question, capable of turning a Sherman into scrap. Then he saw it, the long barrel poking out from behind camouflage.

"Solly, anti-tank gun dead ahead, twelve o'clock, open fire."

There was no shortage of shells, not since the Mulberry Harbor had arrived, allowing streams of replacement to come ashore. Solly fired HE, and the other tanks around them found targets. The night became a cacophony of exploding ordnance. He missed. The enemy gun fired again, and the shell smashed into a Sherman that was racing alongside to keep pace.

"Solly, hit the bastard."

"I'm trying, but we're running over rough ground. It's like trying to shoot from a fairground ride."

"I don't give a shit. They're creaming us. We need to finish them."

Dale shouted, "HE loaded."

"Fire."

This time the shell hit its target and plastered the German crew over the French soil. Another gun cracked out and then from much nearer, a panzerfaust missile came toward them. He grabbed for the machine gun, stitching a line of shells into the shooter who was stupid enough to stand watching for the hit. The missile struck the right side track, and their vehicle slewed to a stop, but Grant had killed the shooter, and the danger had receded, for the moment.

A recovery crew came up from the rear. An engineer ducked over to them and inspected the damage with a shielded flashlight.

"It's just the track. You need a couple of new links, but you're out of action for tonight. We'll tow her back in, and you can borrow a spare vehicle while we fix her up."

"I'd sooner ride in Minnie Mouse. Can't you fix it sooner?"

He stared at Grant. "Yeah, I know the way it is. We'll have her repaired by tomorrow. It's just for one night."

The crew climbed out and watched the engineers hitch up the tow chain, and they rode their vehicle backward all the way back to the camp. On the journey, he called Morgan and reported in. The sounds of battle were loud in his headset.

"Understood, Sergeant Grant. If there's any way you can get back into the battle, we could do with more armor. These Krauts are putting up one hell of a fight."

"Any losses, Sir?"

They knew he meant Company A.

"Not yet, thank God." He glanced around them and

flinched, "Jesus Christ, Jankowski, over there, kill the bastard, three o'clock. Yeah, him, you crazy Polack!"

Grant stared at the destruction. Tents, vehicles, and a couple of Shermans, part destroyed during the attack. He turned to a soldier who was leafing through a thick military manual.

"What happened here?"

"Bunch of Krauts hit us. That's what happened. After Division pulled out toward Carentan, they hit us like a tornado. Machine-gunned everything they could find, dynamited our equipment, and then left. I mean, jeez, it was all over so quick."

He nodded his thanks and went looking for Margot. He found her vehicle, or what was left of it, a tangle of twisted metal. The paraffin stove was nearby, ruined and bent. There was no sign of Margot. He ran around, looking at the heaps of bodies, staring at the faces, but there was no sign of her. Perhaps there never would be.

He knew she was dead. They'd killed his brother in the icy seas off Slapton Sands in Devon, and when he'd found someone special amidst the carnage of Normandy, they'd killed her, too. He felt his anger grow in intensity until he was ready to explode. There was only one way to go, so he found the engineer who'd towed in Minnie Mouse.

"You said there was a spare Sherman around here. How is it for stores?"

The guy nodded and pointed to a solitary tank parked nearby.

"She's ready to go, fueled up, full stock of shells; you can just drive her away."

"What's the story, where's the crew?"

The engineer looked around, and when he spoke, his

voice was low, "This is just for your ears, right?"

Grant shrugged. "Sure."

"They were taking five, brewing up a can of Java next to a clump of trees. Problem was, they were too far from the rest of the Battalion, so I guess they wanted some peace and quiet, probably a high stakes poker game. An Allied fighter came over and mistook them for Krauts. Shot the shit out of them. When he went away, they were dead, every last man."

Grant felt a chill at the useless waste, the terrifying irony of death at the hands of your own side. They'd trained on the M4s, traveled thousands of miles across the Atlantic to Britain to fight Hitler, then that last, perilous crossing of the English Channel to attack the French coast, and all for nothing.

"It was one of ours?"

"A Brit, so someone said who saw it fly away. What does it matter? Brit, American, French, Polish, whatever, they're dead just the same."

"Yeah."

He went across to their new tank. The rest of his crew followed him, and they climbed aboard. Once he had the headphones and mike adjusted, he fed in the frequency for the Company A net and reported to Major Morgan.

"Sir, we have a replacement vehicle. We're ready to rejoin the Company."

Morgan chuckled. It was a company in name only.

"We need you back here ASAP, Sergeant Grant. They're hitting us real hard. If we don't push them back soon, we'll have to withdraw."

"Withdraw! We only just took the damn place."

He could hear in the distance, explosions, shellfire, and

the sound of men fighting a desperate battle to survive.

"Tell that to the Krauts. Get back here, Grant. We need you."

"I hear you, Sir. We're on the way."

He switched to the crew net. "Driver, advance. Hit the gas. Our guys are in trouble."

"You got it."

The race back to Carentan was like driving into hell. A storm of gunfire came from both sides, artillery, tanks, anti-tank guns, machine guns, and all backed by the faint pop, pop of semi-automatic weapons as men fought to stem the tide. Away from the immediate battle zone, the countryside was dark, shadowed by the distant conflagration, which is why they almost failed to see the enemy assault gun.

"STUG!" Vernon shouted from his position next to Angel.

Grant hunted for the enemy armor and found it, lurking in a thicket of small trees that camouflaged its bulky outline. The assault gun was not quick to deploy. With no moving turret, the vehicle had to be moved to make anything other than a small change to the aiming point. Not so the Sherman. The turret rotated as Solly tracked their 75mm main gun onto the target.

"Load AP!"

"Shit! I have HE loaded," Dale shouted.

"Leave it. Make the next one AP. We'll use what we have."

The turret stopped moving as he acquired the target, and the gun fired. The shell smashed into the side of the STUG, and a wisp of smoke appeared from the hull where the projectile hit. It wasn't enough, not nearly enough.

"We just scratched the paintwork, and she's about to fire!" Vernon shouted, "For fuck's sake, you stupid kike, kill him!"

The enemy shell was aimed in haste and whistled past the turret.

"AP loaded."

"Fire."

This time the shell pierced the steel hull, and smoke poured out as it exploded, sending hot shards of steel around the interior. The German crew would be sliced to ribbons, and every one of Minnie's crew knew their job was done.

"Driver advance."

They pushed on to Morgan and linked up with him at the edge of town. He'd located a good position in a narrow defile, a natural feature of the landscape. They were hull down and pouring fire onto the advancing Germans. Angel halted alongside Daniel Kuruk's Cochise, and they went to work.

Bodies of German Panzergrenadiers were strewn all over the approaches to the town, together with burned out assault guns and wrecked artillery pieces. Yet still they came, advancing in short rushes, hardened professionals who'd learned their bloody trade on the Eastern Front. Another STUG appeared on their right flank and fired two shells in quick succession. The second round impacted only yards away before they realized they were under fire.

"Gunner, target four o'clock, assault gun. Nail the bastard. Christ, Solly, he's real close."

"AP loaded!"

"Target acquired."

"Fire!"

The enemy machine was already moving away from the battle, and the shell smashed into the earth where only a second before the assault gun had been standing. Grant searched for more targets and found infantry, a bunch of helmeted German Panzergrenadiers racing toward them, covered by machine guns pouring out fire on either flank.

"Target one o'clock, Panzergrenadiers coming in. They have panzerfausts, Solly.

"Yeah, I see them. Load HE."

The breech clanged open as Dale extracted the AP shell he'd just loaded, but before they could load a high explosive shell, several Shermans raced in and fired a hail of HE on top of the Germans. The multiple blasts tossed more bloodied bodies to the ground to join the earlier casualties, and he was reminded of a quote he'd learned a long time ago. The Duke of Wellington, the nineteenth century general, when surveying the carnage after the Battle of Waterloo, stated;

'Nothing save a battle lost is so terrible as a battle won.'

The enemy losses were fearful. Grant searched the shadows, waiting for the attack to continue after the terrible slaughter, but Solly shouted, "They're running. The yellow bastards are running!"

They were indeed running. Most abandoned their heavy weapons; a few even tossed away their helmets and rifles in their desperate need to flee the butcher shop carnage.

"They're not yellow," Grant sighed, "Flesh and blood can't fight armor, you know that, Solly. They've lost most of their troops already. If they keep coming, we'll wipe out the rest."

"Fucking Krauts," he snarled in reply, "They deserve everything they get."

"Maybe."

I know why Solly is sore. It's because of the way they treat the Jews in Germany, but all of them? They can't all be bad, can they? Those bodies lying there, bloody and broken, are they all rabid anti-Semites? The Germans are known as a civilized race. A race that produced giants like Bach, Beethoven, and Brahms. Bismarck, Goethe, Gottlieb Daimler and Karl Benz, inventors of the internal combustion engine. Mass murderers? That takes some believing. I guess time will tell.

An argument was brewing inside the tank, and he listened to the angry voices of his crew. He heard Solly first, his voice laden with bitter venom.

"What the fuck was that, Vern? Calling me a kike?"

"That's what you are," Vernon Franklin's treacly southern tones answered him, "A kike, a Yid, you know what I mean. Everyone knows that's what Jews are."

Solly's voice was cold, "Southern crackers screw their younger sisters, everyone knows that."

"Fuck you," he snapped back, "You come down here and say that, and I'll punch your teeth down your Yid throat."

"Save it for your sister, white trash."

Grant swarmed down into the hull. Both men had left their positions and were squaring up to each other in the dark, cramped interior. Dale was trying to force them apart, but Vernon was spitting insults at him, too. "Get off me, you damned nigger. I'll deal with you later!"

The loader stepped out of the way. Vernon swung a punch, and Solly avoided it. He connected with a hard left to the Southerner's kidneys. Vern grunted in pain and reached out to take a hold of the gunner, but Grant had had enough. He grabbed both struggling men and held them apart. Their faces were red with fury, and they snorted with anger as they tried to pull away from him.

"Cut it out, both of you." His voice was hard and cold, "Either you stop this, or I'll replace you with two crewmen who don't act like total assholes. You'll both be in the stockade, and they tell me it's mighty uncomfortable."

They eased back.

"You wouldn't do it," Vernon panted, his voice hoarse with anger, "You wouldn't dare. Besides, you can't do it. You're not an officer. You're just a grunt, like us. And you're under arrest. Chances are they'll put you against a wall and shoot you."

"He did it for me!" Solly snarled, lashing out again.

"Leave it out, Solly. He's right; I'm not an officer. I'm a lawyer, and if I report what you're doing in the middle of a battle, they could put you against a wall and shoot both of you along with me. Think about it. I have nothing to lose. Do you want to die?"

They both shut up, although the air inside the Sherman crackled with tension.

Angel shouted, "Enemy armor coming in! Heads up, you guys."

Grant climbed up to commander's seat, shouting orders.

"Gunner, load AP. Angel, prepare to move out, only on my order. Where are the rest of our tanks?"

"They could be Tigers," Vernon Franklin almost whispered, watching through the vision slot.

"Movement on the left flank, distance about a thousand yards. They're not Tigers. They look more like Panzer IVs."

"I see them," Solly shouted.

Dale was ready. "AP loaded."

Grant was studying the new arrivals. Something about them looked... "No, wait. They're ours."

"You sure?"

"Yes. They're 75mm howitzers, M8s. I saw them earlier. They're the 14th Armored Field Artillery Battalion. They must be going after the retreating Jerries. Jesus Christ, we've won! They're falling back. It's over."

Except the war raging inside Minnie Mouse wasn't over. Vernon was a problem, a serious problem, with his grating racist views. Not untypical given his Southern origins, but in the middle of a war wasn't the time to ass around. Grant looked down at them and realized they were waiting for him.

"Stand down, we'll wait for orders. But well done, it looks like we beat them."

They cheered, all prejudices forgotten in the elation of victory. He grinned to himself as Vernon even patted Solly on the back, and Dale shook hands with every man in the crew. He let them enjoy the moment and waited until they quietened down. It was time to lay down the law.

I'm a lawyer, aren't I? He smiled to himself, *Grant's law. It sounds good, anyway.*

"All of you; listen up. We're here to fight a war. These Krauts are killing our people, and we want to make them pay." He thought about David, his body lying somewhere on the bottom of the sea. Of Margot, did she suffer when they killed her, or was it quick? "We're here to kill Krauts, and anyone who wants to waste time fighting amongst ourselves is in deep shit. So cut it out, all of you."

They were silent. Only Dale met his eye, and the black crewman understood. The rest of them looked away, their expressions guilty.

"Is that clear?"

A few mumbled, yeah and okays, and then there was silence.

"Good. If I hear someone call my crew a yid, a spic, a kike, a cracker, or anything else, he's finished. Period." He glared at them; "I might even take it into my head to shoot you. I'm already looking at a murder charge, so I haven't got a single thing to lose."

It was a forceful argument, and they were silent. He smiled as he climbed back into the turret. He was fighting hard to stop himself from laughing aloud, which would ruin it all. He was a killer, a murderer, a condemned man, so they'd believed it and swallowed the lie. Maybe it was the way he framed it, using all of his legal knowledge and experience. No wonder people hated lawyers. But he had to have a crew who would fight the enemy, who would hack into the enemy and not themselves. Maybe he had it.

"Sarge?"

He looked at Solly. "What is it?"

"How're you going to deal with that murder charge?"

He obviously felt guilty about Grant taking the rap for what he did. He stared back at the shamefaced gunner.

"Solly, sooner or later we're going to tangle with a Tiger, right?"

"Well, yeah."

"How do you think it'll end?"

He grimaced. "Bad. He'll shoot the crap out of us."

"Right. So why should I worry about Lindbergh and his stupid court martial? We're up against superior armor, so the chances are I won't survive long enough to be around for it."

He looked dubious. "I get it. At least, I think I do."

"Good, now forget about it."

"Okay, and thanks again, Sarge."

"Sergeant Grant," a voice called out to them.

Morgan was climbing out of his Sherman, and he jumped to the ground. Grant joined him.

"Sir."

"You did well. We all did well. The plan now is to push forward and complete the linkup with Utah Beach. It's a good time for us, daylight hours. If the Krauts come out to fight, out aircraft will crap all over them."

"Yes, Sir. We need to collect our tank, Minnie Mouse. The engineer said they'd have it ready. It was just the track."

"There's no time, Grant. We're moving shortly."

He shook his head. "Sir, it'd mean a lot to the men. You know, they feel better in their own vehicle. They fight better, too."

Morgan considered for a moment and nodded his head. There was little of the academic inside the Major. He looked more like a member of a barbarian tribe. Like those who'd rampaged out of the dark German forests to savage the Roman Legions, two thousand years before. His face was covered in soot and grease, and the serious, academic man had disappeared. He'd become a savage. He'd become war.

"Go get it, but if it isn't ready, you take the vehicle you have."

"Yes, Sir."

The replacement vehicle had served them well, but it wasn't Minnie. Solly swore he wouldn't have missed that shot if they'd been in their own Sherman. Almost an hour later they reported back with Minnie Mouse. Morgan looked hard at the newly repaired M4. The engineers had done a good job, but the new steel track gleamed in the harsh light of dawn. They'd also welded plates over several shrapnel holes. He pointed it out.

"Get some paint and cover it all up. You may as well put a target on the side."

"Yes, Sir."

"When you're done, I have a couple of matters to discuss with Division, so we'll be delayed. I'm hoping for some replacements before Company A becomes a single tank outfit. As soon as I'm back, we move out."

The Major went away, and Grant looked around them. The stink of the battlefield savaged his nostrils, rank and putrid. He'd been in several actions since they'd landed, but the slaughter of the Panzergrenadiers beat everything that had gone before. It wasn't all bad. Somewhere, a clump of trees had caught fire, evoking memories of childhood, campfires, bush cooking, companionship, and stupid songs.

Dead bodies still lay where they'd fallen. Like abandoned garbage-filled rags on a landfill, yet these rags contained men, or what had once been men. Each of those men had a wife or mother. A father, a brother, drinking buddies, workmates, from a life before the military. He felt a wave of melancholy come over him. This was the reality of war, death for some, and for the rest, death was only delayed until the next time, or the time after. He looked up, and as Morgan's tank started up, the Major returned. He vaulted onto the hull of the Sherman and climbed into the turret.

Minnie lurched, bumping over an obstacle as they rode out after Morgan. When he looked back, they'd driven over a small heap of bodies, an entire squad of Germans who'd been struck down by an HE shell. The bodies were imprinted with the pattern of a steel track pressed into the corpses.

Is Margot lying like this, the victim of a sudden and vicious attack, her body trampled by rampaging armor?

He felt numb, unable to put to rest his grief over the knowledge he'd lost so much. First David, and now Margot. He would also have to live with the knowledge that their bodies may not even avoid hideous desecration in death.

There was just one way to help heal his pain.

Kill Germans.

* * *

She opened her eyes and found she was staring up at the sky. Her memory was only hazy, the wild flight from the bloody battle that engulfed the camp when the Germans made a lightning attack, and as she ran, she'd looked back to see her vehicle overturn in a mountain of smoke and flame. She raced away from the devastation with the others, escaping the streams of machine gunfire and the explosions from artillery shells and mortars. The Allies had pushed back the Germans, and now they were triumphant in their unexpected victory.

She'd made it a kilometer away from the blazing action. Ahead of her, soldiers, American soldiers, were still racing for the illusory safety of Omaha Beach. Suddenly, she tripped and banged her head when she hit the ground. When she came to, she opened her eyes and saw movement nearby. A man came toward her.

"Hey, little lady, what's up? You running from the Jerries?"

He was huge, a great, hulking brute of a man. His uniform was tight over his broad chest, and his pants were too short for his long legs. She didn't reply.

"I can help you, Missy. Help you escape. You stick with me and Joe, and we'll see you okay. Ain't that right?"

"Sure is, Benny."

The voice came out of the darkness, and a man walked out into the open. Where the first man was huge, a looming menace, a walking nightmare; the other man was short and weasely. His thin face wore a sour expression, yet like his partner, his eyes gleamed with an expression she was familiar with. There was something off about them, and she realized they were the first foot soldiers she'd seen without rifles. It came to her suddenly.

Deserters, subject to no laws, no morality, and with nothing to lose only their lives if they're caught!

She was aware she was at a disadvantage, lying on her back on the ground. She forced her dazed mind to think clearly and climbed unsteadily to her feet. The big man came forward to help her, but she backed away.

"I, I must go now. I have some distance to travel."

She was aware her voice was shaky, and she resolved to appear confident. These people would sense fear and be on her like a pack of wolves. She turned to walk away, but the thin man, Joe, blocked her path.

"There ain't no rush, Missy. Take a rest. It looks like you took a tumble."

The big man came up behind her, and she could hear his hoarse breathing. Then he moved closer, and his hot breath was on her neck.

"Please, I need to..."

The big, meaty paw was on her shoulder, as he came

even closer, his breath stank as if he'd been living on a diet of rotted flesh. Perhaps he had. Her heart fluttered as she tried to control the growing terror inside her. Then a huge arm came around her and held her tightly. The hand was fondling her breast.

"You're not very friendly, Missy," the small man, Joe, muttered, "Benny is only trying to help. Why don't you relax and sit on the ground? Get yourself rested before you go on your way."

The pressure on her breast was greater, and pain shot through her as the man gripped her nipple and squeezed hard. She screamed, and the man laughed.

"Yeah, you get it all out. There's half the fucking world screaming and dying around here. It won't make any difference if you sing out." Joe suddenly stepped forward and wrenched at the front of her thin cotton dress. The ten-year-old cotton tore as if it was no more than paper, and the material hung around her body, leaving her covered only by her brassiere and panties.

The men were gulping in huge quantities of air, the sight of a semi-naked young woman pitching them into new heights of arousal. She struggled, but Benny held her in a grip of steal as Joe wrenched away the last of her underwear. She stood, shivering with terror and cold, wearing only her patched cotton stockings and rubber boots on her feet. She blocked another scream from emerging and began planning how to escape the two beasts that would rape her.

What can I do, can I reason with them? Offer them money? What?

A huge hand moved down and fondled her vagina. A small squeal left her lips, and Joe sniggered.

"That's right, Missy. You like it, don't you? Give her some more, Benny. She's falling for you."

The fingers felt around her labia, and then they were inside her. She felt repulsed as the dirty, rough hand explored her, and then the big man dragged her down backward until she was prone on the grass. With a miserable feeling, she knew it was over. There was no escape. These men were going to abuse her, rape her. Probably they'd explore as many ways as possible to inflict pain and humiliation on her. They were those kinds of men. Brutes. It was their aphrodisiac to have a squirming, terrified woman at their mercy and abuse her body with callous disregard for any common humanity.

As if to confirm her thoughts, the hand slid round, felt her rear, and then a finger pushed inside her ass. At the same time, the man in front of her, Joe, unbuttoned his pants and brought out his engorged cock.

"Push her down, Benny. She'll know what to do, French whores always know how to please a man."

I'm not a whore, and you're not a man!

They slammed her to her knees, and the big penis came nearer, nearer, until its tip touched the lips of her closed mouth. There was no escape; the big man had her locked in one strong arm while the other continued to explore her breasts.

"Open wide for Uncle Joe, Missy. You know you want it."

She kept her mouth tightly closed. It was only delaying the inevitable.

I can't just give in. Can't!

"Open your fucking mouth!" he snarled, "I'll bust your fucking teeth if you don't do it now!"

She felt the wetness as tears streamed down her face. To give in to these animals was inconceivable, yet not to meant they would hurt her even worse. Something inside her, a strong, iron streak of pride refused. She shook her head.

Do what you want with me, but I'll fight you every inch of the way!

"Hit the fucking whore, Joe," the big man shouted, his voice slurred, a man possessed by base lust, "Bust her face, show her you mean business!"

"Damn right. She'll do as she'd told, so help me, or we can fuck her corpse. It's all the same to me."

He took a huge combat knife from his pocket and held it in front of her.

"Say hello to my little friend, whore. He knows how to open a girl's mouth. You don't open it, I'll cut it open."

The blade looked razor sharp, and Joe held it sideways to swipe across her mouth. He grinned at her. "Say goodbye to the pretty face, Missy."

The explosion was so loud it was deafening, close to her ears. Dimly, she realized it was the noise of a shot. Then there was another. The arm that gripped her slackened, and she turned to look at the source of the shot; A German, wearing the familiar coalscuttle helmet and clutching a still smoking, Luger pistol. She fainted.

CHAPTER SIX

Chateau La Roche Guyon, Normandy, France - Rommel's Headquarters, 05.15, June 19, 1944

The famous face wore a grim expression. "What the hell is going on? I have spoken to the Fuhrer, and he demands immediate action. Now!"

As he spoke, he banged the map table, and the staff officers around him flinched. Most were damp from the heavy rain that had lashed Normandy for the past few days. They'd mostly traveled in open staff cars, some in Kubelwagen jeeps, which was fine on a warm summer's day. Not like now, the journeys had been sheer bloody misery in such stormy, wet weather the entire region had experienced, and now this. Erwin Rommel, no less, adding to their misery with the fury of his anger.

The setting was incongruous, a French chateau, luxuriously furnished in Louis Quinze furniture, gilt mirrors, and a huge Ormelieu clock on the mantel. Rommel had complained it was more like a whorehouse than Army Headquarters. He stared at his Chief of Staff.

"Ernst, do you want to know what action the Fuhrer authorized me to take for officers who appear to fail in their duty?"

"No, Herr Feldmarschal."

"A firing squad! No court hearing, no defense, he told me to just take out the offender and shoot him. And that's what I intend to do, unless you light a fire under our troops."

He stared around the room, and a junior officer glared back at him.

"Well?"

"It's not all our fault, Sir. Headquarters failed to release the heavy Panzer battalions! We could have beaten the Allies back if we'd had the tools to do the job."

"Perhaps you'd better take your objections to the Fuhrer!" The man looked away, "I thought not. It's no use crying over it now. We have the Panzer Lehr Division fully engaged, and they're hitting the enemy hard at Tilly-sur-Seulle. If they win, we shall be in a position to retake Carentan. It is as you know is the key to the entire Cotentin Peninsula, to Normandy itself."

"Panzer Lehr will not fail," a Panzer liaison officer, a Wehrmacht Major insisted, "Herr Feldmarschal, you know those crews are the best we have, and their armor is second to none. Tigers, King Tigers, Panthers."

"Panzer IVs as well," another officer muttered drily.

The Major flushed. "Panzer IVs, yes, but they're still better than anything the Allies can throw at us. However, the Tigers and Panthers will carry the day, Sir. They're unbeatable."

"Yet we're still falling back, still losing tanks and men,"

Rommel countered, his voice low, "You've heard of these new Shermans, the Fireflies?"

The Major turned a deep shade of purple. "We've heard of them, of course. They carry a 17-pounder gun, which I admit can penetrate and destroy our heavy armor. We've begged the Luftwaffe repeatedly to overfly the battlefield and destroy them. Where are they? Perhaps Reichsmarshall Goering can tell us."

"The Eastern Front," Rommel said casually.

Every man shuddered at the phrase that conjured up so much blood and suffering. It was their perpetual nightmare, a transfer to the fighting in Russia, slowly moving eastward, nearer to the Reich.

"However, Goering informs me that aircraft have been reassigned to this theater of operations, and they are already on the way. In the meantime, we have to deal with the Fireflies as best we can. When we destroy them, we can push the Allies back into the sea. The Panzer Lehr must not fail if we are to defeat this invasion."

"Tilly-sur-Seulle will..."

"It is not Tilly-sur-Seulle that concerns me! We must reinforce our defenses at Saint-Lo. That town is our Achilles heel, Gentlemen. If they break through at Saint-Lo, all France will be theirs for the taking. No matter what happens, Saint-Lo is where we must stop them, and it is there our heavy Panzers must fall back and dig in. If the Allies break through, we will lose France, perhaps the entire war. Get back to your units, and prepare to fight the battle of your lives."

They clicked their heels and saluted. One by one they left, until he was alone in the map room, once the ballroom of the chateau. He looked down at the map again, and then checked through the unit returns, to consider what he had left to fight with. The losses had been enormous. Could they defeat this mighty invasion? Not if the enemy kept pouring materiel ashore from their temporary harbors at such an unbelievable rate. His thoughts were interrupted as an aide knocked and entered.

"Sir, a communication from Luftwaffe Headquarters. One of their reconnaissance flights has just returned from the beach areas."

"Yes, what of it?"

The man smiled. "The Allied harbor to the west of Port-en-Bessin, this thing they call the Mulberry, has been destroyed in the recent storm!"

"You are certain?"

"It is definite, Sir. They are sending photographs as soon as they have been processed."

"Good, good. And their other harbor, to the east?"

The smile faded. "It is still intact, Herr Feldmarschal. But if this weather continues..."

"Yes, yes, maybe it will suffer the same fate, or maybe not. Dismissed."

Once again he was on his own, left to go over and over the plans to defeat the landing.

Could the destruction of that harbor mean we have a chance? No, of course not. The war is lost, only a fool would deny what is staring us in the face. The transfer of aircraft from the East would be helpful, but at the cost of weakening our defenses against the Soviet hordes. A few months, no more, and they could be knocking at the doors of Berlin itself. There is only one solution; we have to replace Hitler and negotiate for peace. The Fuhrer will never stand down, of course, but there are officers on the General Staff who plan a more direct approach to get rid of the maniac who's brought

Germany to her knees. God help us all if von Stauffenberg fails.

* * *

They'd set up a makeshift camp in the rubble of what had once been a French village. No one knew the name. It had been blasted into an amorphous collection of smashed buildings and heaps of rubble over the past few days. At least it hid them from the marauding Germans, who were increasingly hitting back over the battlefront. Someone had brewed a can of fresh coffee, and they sat on blocks of stone enjoying the respite. They were sheltering beneath a half ruined cottage roof that kept them out of the driving rain while they enjoyed the break from the sour, stale stench of oil and fumes inside the vehicles. Morgan sat alone and gestured for Grant to join him. He got to his feet and walked over.

"How can I help you, Major?"

"What happened to that girl of yours, the one who did the cooking?"

"She was in the headquarters area when the Germans overran it and destroyed it."

"She's dead?"

He told the officer what he'd found, the destroyed vehicle and equipment, the heaps of destruction and bodies piled everywhere. Morgan looked thoughtful.

"So you haven't seen the body?"

"No, Sir, but it seems pretty conclusive."

"Does it? I don't agree. She could have been taken prisoner, or run away, or even wounded and be lying in a hospital. I wouldn't give up, Grant, not yet." He lit his pipe and puffed away, "You know Saint-Lo is the key to breaking out from Normandy?"

"No, Sir."

He nodded. "After we've broken through at Saint-Lo, you should make some inquiries about what happened. You never know."

"Thank you, Sir. You're sure we'll fight a battle at Saint-Lo?"

"Yes. Napoleon certainly would have."

"Napoleon?"

"Yep. He lost the war, but he won a great many battles before the end. The application of maximum force to the weakest point, I believe that was his maxim. That's Saint-Lo, in our case. We'll be there sooner than later."

"Yes, Sir."

He left the officer enjoying his pipe and returned to his crew, just in time to intercept another problem between Vernon and Solly. The Southerner had a cut to his eye and was about to land a haymaker on Solly before Grant managed to grab his arm. He held the two struggling men apart.

"I told you to cut it out. What's the problem now?"

Neither man spoke, so he looked across at Dale. "You gonna tell me what happened?"

He shrugged. "Just the usual. Calling each other names, you know how it is."

Which meant Vern was on his anti-Semitic kick again.

"I've had about enough," he hissed. He wanted to kick Vernon out of the unit, but that wouldn't be fair without finding out who started it. He looked at Dale.

"Who was it this time?"

Dale stared back, his face blank, unwilling to rat either man out. This was more than Vern deserved after his

196

'nigger' taunts at Dale. Grant was still wondering when everything happened at once. Kuruk came running toward them.

"Jerries have broken through. We're moving out!"

Morgan and Bligh were already on the move, racing to their vehicles. Grant and his crew leapt aboard Minnie Mouse, and while Angel started the engine, he fastened his headset in place and listened for orders. Three seconds later, the headphones burst into life.

"This is the Company Commander. The Germans are trying to break through our front lines, three miles south of Isigny and close to a village called Rupalley. We're heading there now, but be warned, it's tough going. The area is partially flooded, and the roads we need to follow are bordered by..."

"Bocage. I fucking knew it," Angel Montalban muttered.

"Shut up and drive!"

Angel muttered something, but Grant ignored it, and he fell in after Bligh's Sherman. Kuruk came last, and they followed a narrow farm track that led south. The sounds of battle were already loud in the cold dawn, and it occurred to Grant the Germans were making good use of the weather, which prevented air attacks. Within yards, the high walls closed in. They were inside the Normandy bocage, and every man knew fear. Who was waiting behind the thick, opaque walls? Anti tank guns maybe, STUG assault guns, Panzer Grenadiers, even entire Panzer companies. There was no way to know.

"Sarge," Vern called over the internal net, "I don't like what I'm seeing."

"You think anyone else does?"

"Well, no. But there could be..."

"A Tiger, yeah, I know. Then again, there may not be. So shut up."

"Bird-brained cracker," Solly muttered angrily. He was still sore about the last confrontation, although he'd come off best.

"Tell that fucking kike to button it, or I'll knock his teeth down his yid throat."

"That's enough! We're going into battle. I'll transfer out the next man who says another word."

They shut up. Minutes later, a shell came from nowhere and hit The Bounty. Bligh and his crew had no chance. The vehicle exploded, and incredibly, Grant watched the turret fly into the air as the ammunition stores exploded. Bligh was still inside the turret as it sailed into the air and descended into a nearby field. At least, the top half of him was. The rest of him, his legs, was incinerated inside The Bounty.

He worked to control the churning in his guts and find a way out of the bocage shooting gallery. Another shell fired and glanced off the frontal armor of Cochise. They were next, no question. Morgan's Sherman had gone to full speed, and he was bouncing over the rutted lane, seeking a way out of the trap. Grant saw a gap in the hedge, a narrow gap, little more than large enough to drive a motorcycle through.

"Angel, hard left. Now!"

He held on as they smashed into the thick foliage, and for a sickening moment Minnie hesitated, and he thought they weren't going to make it. Then they picked up speed, and they were through. The enemy gun was in front of him, one of the bastardized Pak 38s fitted with the French 75mm field gun; a powerful weapon that had destroyed more than its fair share of Shermans, and now they were levering the carriage around to take on the new threat.

"Angel, nail the bastard."

"HE loaded."

"Fire!"

The projectile left the barrel at the exact moment they ran into a deep ditch that cut the field, and the shell exploded harmlessly thirty yards short.

"Fire again!"

"Loading HE."

"Angel, forget that, ram the bastard. He'll hit us before we're ready to fire."

"I'm on it."

He hit the gas and they surged closer. It was a tossup as to who would get there first. He saw the sweating German crew, their faces white beneath the iconic steel helmets, struggling to get a fresh shell into the breech of the Pak 38. All the while, Minnie was surging toward them, an iron monster come from their nightmares to bring down death and ruin on their heads.

The German breech clanged shut, and the gunner looked down the sight to make certain of the shot. It was too late. Minnie hit the gun like an avalanche, and thirty tons of tracked steel rolled over the gun and crew, turning them into so much twisted scrap metal, flesh, blood, and bone. He looked back, but they were finished, pulverized into the rich Normandy soil.

"Nice job, Angel. They're done for. We need to...Oh, Shit!"

"What do I do, Sarge?" Angel screamed.

"Gunner, load AP," Solly intoned, "We'll nail ourselves a few more Krauts."

Dale removed the HE and began to slam in the AP. Ahead of them, a line of three STUG IIIS were deployed, hull down, waiting to catch a few unwary Shermans. He searched around and saw a sunken lane, only twenty yards north. He screamed out the order to Solly to get them away.

The German guns crashed out; two missed, and one hit on their turret armor. They were lucky, the shell struck at an oblique angle and spun away. Then they were dropping into the sunken lane and only showing their upperworks to the enemy. In the distance, perhaps a half-mile away, five German tanks were moving in a parallel direction. It looked as if the single Pak 38 had been the rearguard for an intending ambush, perhaps of a larger formation that was heading toward them. Morgan's voice came into his headphones.

"Company A report in. Grant, Kuruk, what is your status?"

Dan replied first, a hurried confirmation that they were only a few hundred yards behind Morgan.

"Sergeant Grant, where are you?"

He rapidly gave their location. "You have German armor to your right flank, three STUGs and four Panzers, they look like IVs."

"Can you rejoin us?"

He looked around at the enemy armor. Morgan and Kuruk were in sight now; somehow they'd found a way through and were the other side of the Krauts.

"That's a negative, Sir. Only way is to attack, and I don't fancy our chances."

"Me neither. Very well, you'll have to turn north and see if you can work your way around from the flank. Call me when you're nearing Rupalley."

"Roger that."

Grant suddenly felt very alone. They were gaining on the Panzers, but every yard was a yard further away from his unit.

He smiled to himself, *my unit, three Shermans, some company!*

Angel steered them along further sunken lands, cutting through the bocage when he could find a gap, and each time, they held their breath until they came out the other side and found it clear.

They were all alone in a maze of high hedges, the occasional ruined farmhouse and burned out vehicle. Nothing moved, neither friend nor foe. The sky was still thick with heavy cloud, and the rain fell incessantly so that no aircraft could overfly the battlefield. They pushed through one high hedge, and every man tensed as they emerged in a tangle of equipment, guns, tanks, artillery, and men. Yet still nothing moved, it was the detritus of a recent battle, too soon for the grave units to come in and bury the corpses.

They were like fallen logs, brown with mud, unmoving, strewn carelessly amongst the steel and iron that had so recently been used against them, and was now their only grave marker.

"Jesus!" Vernon exclaimed, popping his head out of the escape hatch to take a look, "This was some battle. I wonder who won."

"They did," Solly replied.

"How do you know that? You some fucking psychic?"

"I counted the wrecked equipment. Most of it is ours. Was ours."

No one commented as they drove past the carnage. By

some instinct, Angel had slowed as if to pay homage to the fallen. Then he picked up speed, and soon it was behind them. They drove for two hours, attempting to rejoin Morgan and stem the German attempt at a breakthrough. Another hour went by, and Grant suddenly realized they were lost.

* * *

"Firefly!"

Rolf jerked his head around as the shell punched past them and buried itself in a Panther of Panzer Lehr, running a few meters on their left flank. There was nothing, just wrecked and burning vehicles, trucks, bodies, and in between, heavy and medium tanks weaving an intricate ballet as they tried to kill the enemy before they were killed themselves.

"Heinrich, do you see him?"

"Nein, not yet. Verdammt, where is the bastard! Fucking Fireflies, they're murdering us. What's the use of the Fuhrer's super tanks if the enemy can blow holes in them with those converted tin cans? Where is he?"

"Franz, turn ninety degrees right, and take cover behind the wrecked Tiger one hundred meters to the northeast. If we stay out here, we're going to end up like him."

"Zum befehl!"

They slewed around as he worked the levers to stop one track and apply maximum power to the other, and the huge Tiger swung onto the new course. Another shell whistled past them and buried itself in an old Panzer IV, totally outclassed on the battlefield. Newer models of the veteran Panzer had side armor fitted and additional armor plate, but this early model had none. The big 17-pounder shell exploded inside the hull close to the gas tank, and the vehicle blew apart, as if it was made of tin.

That could have been us. Dammit, our Tigers were supposed to better than this!

Even the King Tigers were not invulnerable to the devastating Allied gun. The High Command was already worried about the effects of the new weapon and had issued instructions to all Panzer crews to deal with the Fireflies first. Problem was, they looked like Shermans. They were Shermans! Only the gun was different, with a longer barrel that the Allies had camouflaged so they looked no different to standard Shermans.

Another shell pursued them and smacked into the wreckage of the Tiger, and then they were behind the thick steel of the burned out hull. Franz brought them to a halt and waited for orders.

Where can I go?

The enemy was everywhere; yet the seemingly advantage of lack of enemy air cover was negated by the devastating Fireflies.

"Driver, go south."

"But, Obersturmfuhrer," Franz objected, "The enemy is to the north."

"The Fuhrer would want us to engage the enemy at all costs," Lenz added.

It was too much, and he snapped at the stupid little HJ loader.

"Fuck the Fuhrer! He's not in command of this fucking Tiger, is he, Lenz?"

There was no reply, and Rolf cursed himself for losing his temper. It was stupid; making a statement that could be construed as treason, was treason.

"I take that back. Allow me to explain. The Allied advance on Normandy is all pointing in one direction, Saint-Lo. Panzer Lehr will have no choice but to fall back on our defenses in that area, and the 12th SS Hitler Jugend has standing orders to link up with them. I am merely anticipating their withdrawal to the south."

"The battle here is not finished" Lenz almost screamed.

Manhausen glanced through the vision port and the wreckage of German armor that littered the battlefield. Every vehicle a grave for those brave men who were trapped inside.

"It is, Junge. Believe me, it is. Driver, take us out of here. Head south, and stay off the roads. As soon as this cloud clears, they'll put aircraft up, and we won't last more than a couple of hours."

Two hours later, he told the driver Franz Schelling to halt. They'd taken a broad sweep around the area of battle, hugging the wooded areas, except where they'd had to dart along narrow causeways between the flooded areas. They climbed out of the Tiger to stretch their legs and take a break from the noise and the stink of fumes. Rolf spent the time poring over a map. After a half hour of checking and calculating, he realized they were totally and hopelessly lost.

* * *

"Where are we? Still in France?"

He grinned at Dale. "Just about. I think we're close to some village called Tribehou. It's about ten miles north of Saint-Lo. That's just a guess, and we could be anywhere.

This map's useless."

"What about the radio? Any chance we could talk to Morgan?"

"And tell him what? We haven't got a clue where we are? How could he help us?"

Dale shrugged. "No idea. I'll grab some coffee."

Grant surveyed the surrounding countryside, as if some feature, a tree, a building, or a low hill could tell him where they were. He took the offered tin mug and appreciated the steaming java trickling down his throat. It helped him come to a decision.

"We'll head north and try to intersect the Battalion somewhere in the area of Isigny. Mount up, we need to link up with the others before the Krauts counterattack and we find ourselves behind their lines."

"We could already be behind the lines," Solly said, walking over and tossing out grounds from the bottom of his mug, "Maybe Vern will meet his Tiger sooner rather than later."

"Fuck you!" Vernon Franklin snarled, "You think you're so fucking clever. I tell you, when we do meet up with a Tiger, it ain't gonna seem so funny." His face twisted into an evil expression, "Besides, there's always a chance you could become a prisoner. Those Nazis, they're not too friendly with Jewboys, are they?"

Grant readied himself to stop them. If there was one thing calculated to throw Solly into a murderous frenzy, it was talk of the Nazi treatment of the Jews. This time, the gunner managed to control himself. Instead, he rammed a fixed smile on his face.

"Tell you what, Vern. If we're taken prisoner, I'll them you're the Rabbi of an obscure Jewish tribe, one that hates

Germans and has sworn to kill Adolf Hitler. They'll string you up from the nearest lamppost."

Franklin looked uncertain, but he tried to bluster. "You're talking a crock of shit, Rothstein. Everyone knows Jews are circumscribed. One look at my cock and they'd know you were lying."

"It's circumcised, you dumb cracker, not circumscribed," he laughed, "I said an obscure Jewish tribe, didn't I? That means one that doesn't go in for circumcision."

"There's no such thing."

Solly had the upper hand, and he knew it. "How would you know, Rabbi Franklin?"

Vernon for once had no reply. He even looked frightened. Finally, he said, "You wouldn't do that to me, would you?"

"Maybe, maybe not. We need to get rolling. Rabbi Franklin."

Vern scowled but climbed up onto the hull and dropped inside. Grant checked Solly before they followed and kept his voice low.

"This thing about Jews, a tribe that doesn't believe in circumcision. You serious or winding him up?"

"It's a wind up, but don't tell him. If he believes it, it'll give him the incentive to kill more Germans."

His voice was bitter, charged with malice and hate.

"That's why you're here, Solly? Just to kill Germans. Nothing else, not to win battles, win a war?"

"Kill the fuckers, Sarge. That's it. No other reason to be here. Many truths are going to come out when this war is over, and one of 'em is they've murdered a lot of Jewish people. They're calling it war crimes, and there's talk about putting some of the leading Nazis on trial."

"That's the right way to do it, Solly. Due process of law."

He grimaced. "You can say that. You're a lawyer. These Nazi bastards will tie up the courts for years, you'll see. There won't be any justice for what they've done. They'll get off scot-free. No, the best thing to do right now is to kill as many as possible. If they're dead, they're not killing Jews."

"I hear you. Time to move, we'll head north, and who knows, you might get a few more Nazis in your sights."

His eyes glinted. "Bring 'em on. Even the Tiger Vern's so shit scared about."

"We're all shit scared of a Tiger. You know we're as helpless as a baby if we run into one of those monsters."

"Unless we can get a shot at the rear."

Grant laughed. "Sure, when they see us, they'll be so terrified of a Sherman they'll run like hell, and give us the shot of their rear. In your dreams, buddy. Let's go."

They rumbled north, and the low cloud seemed to shut off the noises of the battle, so they were alone in the open French countryside. It seemed impossible that battles were raging around them, battles that would decide the fate of the Free World. Birds sang, and once when Angel stopped the engine to check a possible fuel leak, the buzz of crickets sounded from the grass verges. Water birds took off and landed from the areas of flooded land. It was an idyllic scene that could have formed the subject of a French Impressionist painting.

Angel resolved the fuel leak quickly with the help of Vernon. He was brought up on a farm and understood how to make running repairs to heavy machinery. It was almost a disappointment when they started the engine again. The bellow of the big Continental gas engine caused the birds to take flight, and the crickets to fall silent. The war had to go on. Solly had plenty of Nazis to kill, and Vern had to remain on watch for his nemesis, the Tiger tank.

"Move out. Let's go find our people and do some fighting."

They trundled forward at half speed. Gas was starting to run low, and running flat out ate it up so fast they'd run out of fuel before they reached HQ. He had the hatch open, and he kept a wary eye out for German aircraft. Although the cloud ceiling was so low, it'd be a brave man who flew in that murk. While he was looking up, a movement in the corner of his eyes distracted him. A speck of dirt, maybe, he wiped his eyes and looked again, and now he could see it was still there.

A vehicle, moving on a parallel course to their own, except this one was coming toward them, maybe three miles to the east. When they past each other, they'd be about a mile apart, near enough to do damage; especially if the oncoming vehicle was a Jerry and mounted an 88mm gun, like the Tigers.

I'm becoming as nervous as Vern. And yet...

He took out his binoculars and focused on the distant vehicle. It was a German, no question.

It could even be... yes, a distinct possibility. What is it doing out here, so far from the battle? Are we behind the lines, or is there something going on I don't know about? Or are we hopelessly lost, doomed to tour the French countryside until such time as we come up on our own unit, or the enemy?

He bent his head inside the turret, tapped Solly on the shoulder, and beckoned him to come up top, handing him the binoculars.

"What do you think?"

At first he didn't answer. He just kept his body tense and propped his elbows against the edge of the hatch for stability. Finally, he turned to Grant, his eyes glinting with the fury of righteous determination.

"Tiger. No question. Let's go nail the bastard."

Grant stopped him before he could climb down inside. "No! We fight that bastard and we die. Our only chance is to run; you know that. A Sherman against a Tiger, it's no contest."

But Solly was staring back out at the distant tank.

"It's not going to work that way, Sarge."

"Damn right it is. I command this tank, not you."

He stared at Grant, and his lips twisted in an ironic smile. "That's not what I mean. He's seen us, and he's changed direction to head us off. Either we turn south and head for the German lines, or we fight. There ain't no third option."

He looked across. The Tiger was driving down a long flat slope, as Solly had said, and coming at them across their front. Their intention was obvious, to engage. As Solly dived inside the hull, he shouted down to the crew.

"Tiger!"

* * *

"Sherman!"

"I see him," Rolf grunted. Franz Schelling had spotted the enemy first; he must have been daydreaming when he should have been watching.

"Load AP, button up, prepare to engage. Driver, full speed."

Which is all of forty-five kilometers an hour on a good day. And that's assuming the defective valves don't crack up after a few minutes use. We'll also be burning fuel faster than we can replace it. What a way to fight a war!

"Target in range."

"Open fire!"

The 88mm shell slammed into the earth a few meters past the Sherman, and Heinrich Boll hurried to correct. But even as they fired again, he knew they'd missed. The target was veering away, heading for a dark lane he could see at the side of the field, and then the Sherman almost disappeared.

Sunken road, damn!

"Driver, try and head him off. He's going north. There's only one road he can take."

"Yes, Sir."

And then the Sherman disappeared completely, as if the earth had swallowed it up.

What the hell?

"Franz, head to where you saw him last, along that sunken lane. Be careful, I think this is a tricky one."

"Jawohl, Obersturmfuhrer."

Should I tell them what I saw on the side of the tank? Minnie Mouse, the same picture I've seen twice before? How can our fates be tied together, and we seem doomed to confront each other, time after time.

There had to be a final reckoning, and he wondered how it would end. The German Tiger should smash the Sherman to pieces. It was no Firefly, and its puny gun could barely scratch their paintwork. Even so, he decided to keep quiet. Warriors were a suspicious breed, and his boys no less so than older, more experienced soldiers.

"Gunner, stand by to fire the moment that Sherman is in your sights."

"Yes, Sir!"

* * *

"We're screwed! Oh, Jesus, we're well and truly fucked!"

He almost smiled to himself at Vern's panic, the realization of his nightmares. He'd already seen the sunken lane and reckoned they could get out of a confrontation with the German. The truth was, Vern was spot on. If they tangled with the Tiger, they were dead. No question.

"Angel, you see that dark lane at the side of the field? Go there, now. Make it snappy!"

"You got it."

His normal laconic tone had risen almost an octave, and the laconic acknowledgement came out as little more than a squeak. But he swerved the tank over in the right direction, bumped out of the field, and they rolled down the steep bank until they were in the lane.

"I can't get a shot," Solly shouted, "Not from this angle."

"That's okay. You'd be wasting your time. We're going to work around behind him."

"If you say so."

"I do."

He watched the German storming toward them, and then he was out of sight as the lane dropped lower and they were away from his line of fire, just in time. A massive 88mm shell chewed a huge crater in the field right next to where they'd been a second before. The Kraut had to be shooting almost blind; they were impossible for him to see. Time to see if those theories were right. What was it Major Morgan said?

'Speed and surprise, appear where they least expected it. Maneuverability. The tools of war.'

Time to give this mother a taste of history.

"What're we gonna do?" Solly shouted, "You're not going to let him get away?"

"It's more a question of whether he'll let us get away, my friend. But no, we have a chance to roast his ass. We need Napoleon."

"You what? Who the fuck is Napoleon, he on our side or theirs?"

"Ours. Now shut up and wait for my order. We'll get one shot if we're lucky, then we're away from here. Angel, halt the vehicle. Reverse back along the lane."

"You're not serious! Sarge, there's one big mother waiting for us back there. We need to get out of here as fast as this baby will carry us."

"Negative. That's exactly what he'll be thinking. The moment we show our turret out of this lane, I guarantee we'll find him there waiting for us. We're heading back, and let him vector across country to where he thinks we are. As soon as he shows, nail the fucker."

A pause. "Well..."

"Do it, Angel. There isn't time to mess around. He won't give us a second chance."

"Bastard won't give us a first chance," Vern cut in.

But Angel had already put the vehicle in reverse, and they were going backward. It was difficult without using the vision slot. Except he knew there was nothing in the lane behind them, unless the Tiger came down for a look-see. In which case, the first they'd know would be when the shell slammed into them. He was able to line up on the sides of the track and keep the Sherman moving in reverse without hitting the sides too many times. They reached the point just where the lane had dipped down below the level of the field, and Grant called a halt.

"I'm going out to see where he is. The rest of you stay inside and wait for my order. Solly, you get a chance to put one in him, do it."

"Damn right I will. Nazi fucker, we'll make it one less SS murderer for the Fatherland."

"Just sit tight and wait. Be ready to take the shot. If we need to move, I'll signal."

He climbed out of the turret and jumped down to the muddy track. The rain had stopped, but the water had settled in pools in the deep ruts, and he landed almost up to his knees. He scrambled up the bank, with his head kept low and peered over the top. The Tiger was charging toward the position five hundred yards away where they expected them to emerge.

Stupid bastards fell for it.

He raced back to Minnie Mouse, climbed into the turret, closed the hatch, and waited. Just a few seconds more, and scratch one Tiger.

* * *

He should be in sight by now. Where is he?

Rolf found he was almost holding his breath as his iron monster stormed down the shallow slope, the wide tracks throwing up sheets of water from the sodden field. He'd pinpointed the precise position where they'd intersect the Sherman's course, and unless he'd got it all wrong and forgotten everything he'd learned about trigonometry, gunnery, and target acquisition, he had to be there. Had to be there, except he wasn't.

Verdammnt! A Sherman can't just disappear, thirty tons of steel, a crew of five men. So where is he?

Something nudged at the corners of his mind. This was no ordinary tank. This was Minnie Mouse. The vehicle he kept having nightmares about for some strange reason. It wasn't logical; there was no reason for concern. Their puny 75mm popgun couldn't touch them, could barely put a dent in their thick frontal armor. He laughed, there was no cause for concern. The only way that tiny gun could hurt them was from...

Oh shit!

"Driver halt! Back up, now, reverse course and get us out of here!"

Obediently, Franz jerked the Tiger to a halt, flung the gearbox into reverse with a grinding, grating noise, and they started to go backward. The shell rocketed past their engine compartment, missing them by less than a meter, to bury itself in the Normandy mud, without exploding.

"Gunner, he's behind us. Swing the turret around. He's right behind. Get..."

The second shot slammed into the side of the turret just as it had started to turn. The Tiger turret was slow to rotate, much too slow, but it took the explosion on the curved section where it was strongest. At the rear, where the horseshoe shaped thick steel plate welded to the rear section, it could probably penetrate.

He realized Franz had slowed.

"Keep moving. Keep moving. We're not out of trouble yet!"

"But Obersturmfuhrer..."

Lenz's sniveling voice, and another report for his cousin, the SD Standartenfuhrer.

"Shut up. Franz, get us out of here. He's too damn clever, that American. We'll pick him off when we can expose our frontal armor. Not before."

Another shell slammed into them. This time it hit them on the corner of their frontal armor, just over the drive wheels. He felt the slew as the heavy iron disks that propelled the tracks buckled under the force of the explosion. He was about to shout to Franz and ask him for a damage report, when the engine stuttered.

"Franz!"

"It's the damn valves. I keep telling you. They're crap, foreign labor, that's the problem."

"The problem is we'll be dead if you don't get us out of here. Move it, go as fast as you can."

"Sir, I have to stop, just for a moment. The valve timing, I need two seconds. I can reset it from here."

"Very well. Gunner, watch for the Sherman. And man the machine guns. We need to hold him off."

Shit! It's all we need, a clever Ami in a Sherman that seems to have a charmed life, and we have mechanical problems.

He grasped the stock of the 7.92mm machine gun and looked forward for the enemy.

Nothing. Damn these vision slots! They're useless.

The rain had started again, and he could hardly see more than fifty meters. There was no infantry around, as far as he knew, no snipers, so he flung the turret open and popped his head out. There he was, no more than five hundred meters away. He thumbed his mike.

"Heinrich, you see him? Shoot the bastard."

"I can't, Sir."

"You what! I don't give a shit for can't, get him."

"The turret's out, Sir. I can't bring the gun to bear, not until the engine starts."

"Franz, how long?"

"A couple of minutes, Sir. It's tricky. The adjuster broke off in my hand. Fucking foreign..."

"Shut up and fix it."

He knew it was too late. The Sherman was already reversing away, keeping their frontal armor toward the Tiger. They rounded a bend in the sunken lane, and then they disappeared. He knew they wouldn't find him, not again. That commander was clever. No, more than clever, he was cunning. He reminded Rolf of a friend of his who'd become a lawyer after attending university. They were keen swordsmen, and he had that same kind of cunning on the fencing mat. Just when you thought you were about to plunge your blade into the area of his heart, he seemed to shift his body slightly, and he was in another position, while his blade came from nowhere to deliver the coup-de-grace.

Is he a lawyer in civilian life, that Sherman commander? He acts like one. But we'll meet again, and next time, I'll be ready for you.

CHAPTER SEVEN

Gestapo Headquarters, Isigny, 21.40, July 2, 1944

"Where am I?"

She'd regained consciousness in a strange place, with the stink of disinfectant in her nostrils, as well as feces and decay.

Some kind of hospital, obviously.

Every bone in her body ached, and she knew instinctively she'd been out for some time, hours, maybe even an entire day. She looked for a window, but there was just a small barred opening high on the bare brick wall. It was like a prison cell, except for the pieces of rusting and dusty medical equipment littering the room. It was dark through the tiny window, which meant she'd been in this place for a whole day. A nun stood over her, looking down with a face that was both kindly and concerned.

"You are in the town of Isigny. Do you know what happened to you?"

She had to think hard. "I was caught up in an attack.

The Nazis..."

The nun inclined her head, her expression said, 'They killed many people. War is evil.'

"How long have I been unconscious? Has it been all day?"

The woman looked puzzled. "All day? My child, they brought you here almost three weeks ago. You have been unconscious ever since. We were concerned you would never awake. They called me in to look at you, and when I realized the severity of your injuries, I persuaded them to allow me to visit you each day."

Three weeks! Josh, where is he? Did he survive that terrible attack?

"The war, how does it go? Are we winning?"

The nun shrugged. "We get little news in here. If people know anything, they are afraid to say."

It was all hazy. She seemed to remember there was an attack, and Americans, but they were trying to rape her. It was hard to believe, but she was sure a German soldier rescued her.

How could that be? Everyone knows the Germans are evil.

"What is this place? I need to leave. I must go home."

The gentle smile faded. "Home? No one goes home from here."

"Why not? What kind of hospital is this?"

"Hospital? My dear, this is a prison, part of Gestapo Headquarters, Isigny."

She felt herself going dizzy. "The Gestapo?"

"This place serves the Gestapo and SS. A German brought you here, an Army captain; you'd been wounded. They put you down here in a basement storeroom that used to be an interrogation cell. Perhaps you would like to speak to Father Bouchet. He may be able to explain things better."

"Who is he, something to do with the Gestapo?"

The nun struggled to keep her expression neutral. "He is a prisoner like you, but he is also a doctor. Sometimes they use him to treat the prisoners. Their interrogation methods are..." she grimaced, "They are very harsh. I will call him, and you can speak to him yourself."

The nun left to find the priest, and Margot was left in turmoil.

Josh, is he alive or dead? Will this priest have any answers? How can a priest work in a Gestapo hospital?

The door opened, and she saw for the first time a sentry was standing outside the cell. He wore a steel helmet and held a machine pistol. So the nun spoke the truth, there would be no escape. A priest entered the room and greeted her with a kindly smile. She noted his face was covered in bruises, and one eye was almost shut. Even so, he looked cheerful enough. An Army captain followed him.

"My dear, I am Father Vincent Bouchet, the parish priest and doctor. I have been treating you since they brought you here. This is Captain Gunter Sturm."

She felt sick. "A Nazi! Get him out of here! Please!"

The priest looked embarrassed, but he nodded at the German who left. The priest was short and stocky, heavily muscled despite his obvious age. He had a straggling, gray beard and long, gray, hair that curled over his shoulders. His face was dominated by his remaining blue eye, which had the effect of seeming to look right through you. He wore a classic, long, ankle length black cassock with a tiny 'SJ' lapel pin, and on his head a black biretta, the square-sided hat favored by French priests. She afterward found out he was sixty years old, and before he joined the Society of Jesus, he was a soldier of the French Foreign Legion. She was immediately reassured by his presence.

"I...I'm not too sure. The Sister told me you might be able to help me fill in some of the gaps. Have you heard anything about the attack on Isigny?"

"Perhaps," he looked carefully around, "How may I help you?"

"I imagine some of those who died were Catholic, and you would have said the last rites over them."

"Last rites? You misunderstand; I fought in the battle, my dear. Some of those dead Germans were men I killed. A pity I couldn't kill any more. That's where they captured me. They were going to kill me straight away, but the officer in charge of the unit which captured me was a Catholic." He gave her an ironic smile, "In any case, when they found out I was also a doctor, they brought me here."

She was shocked by his vehemence. "But, you're a priest. How could you..."

"Kill Germans?" He shrugged, "They were killing Frenchmen, my parishioners. Was I supposed to stand by and do nothing while these thugs murdered my congregation?"

He waved a hand at the German sentry outside the door, and she saw to her horror the palm bore a huge, dark red wound. She grabbed for his other hand, and saw the twin of the wound, even worse than the first.

"Your legs, too?"

"Yes."

The Gestapo had crucified him. She slumped back on the bed, speechless. The priest left the room before she could question him more and returned a few minutes later.

She almost fainted. He was with an armed German soldier, clutching his steel helmet and rifle. The soldier spoke to the sentry, who allowed them in, and Father Bouchet did the introductions.

"This is Captain Gunter Sturm. He is the man who brought you here."

The German nodded and smiled. "I'm pleased to see you looking better, Mam'selle."

He spoke French but with the thick guttural accent of a Berliner.

"You're German."

"I am."

"But why?"

"Why did I rescue you from those thugs? Why are you a prisoner? Or why did we imprison and crucify a priest?"

She shook her head in confusion. "All of the above."

"I rescued you, Mam'selle, because you were a lady in trouble. Even Germans have a sense of honor."

"But, you're a Nazi."

"I am no Nazi."

"So you're a deserter?"

He looked amused. "In a way. I prefer to say objector to the whole, sick Nazi apparatus. To the murders committed in the name of the German people. I object to the Nazis and the SS, because I've seen their cruelty and had enough."

"I owe you my thanks for saving me from those men."

He shrugged. "It is not necessary."

There was an awkward silence, and Bouchet began to fill in the gaps.

"Gunter is a Wehrmacht liaison officer attached to an SS unit outside Caen. The local SS commander, Kurt Meyer, established his headquarters in the Ardenne Abbey.

During the fighting, the SS took a number of Canadians as prisoners. I believe it was twenty in all. When they decided the prisoners were an inconvenience to them, they put them against a wall and shot them. Executed them. Of course, Gunter protested to the squad leader, Scharfuhrer Bernd Bachmann, and told him it was a war crime. To no avail, the SS are a law unto themselves. He saw those men shot down in cold blood."

She closed her eyes, thinking of the cruelty of the Nazis in executing those men.

"As for why you are a prisoner," the priest went on, "you were seen aiding the enemy."

"I cooked some hot food, that's all!" she objected.

"Whatever. It seems what you did is a capital crime in the Third Reich."

"A capital crime?" she whispered, "You mean..."

"You are under sentence of death, Mam'selle Caron. The trial was held while you were unconscious." He glanced at the priest, "They sentenced Father Bouchet to death as well."

"How..."

"Both sentences are due to be carried out in two days' time, a firing squad. At dawn."

She closed her eyes as she felt herself falling into a deep fog, but she opened them again when she heard a commotion outside her room.

My room? My cell.

A man swept into the room, an SS officer. No, there was something different; his cuff band carried the initials SD.

What does that mean?

A soldier came in behind him, with the twin lightnings

of the SS on his collar, and she shuddered when she saw his face. Some men are cruel but manage to look innocent. This was not one of those men. His face was twisted in a cruel parody of a smile, like a hungry predator about to devour its prey.

The SD officer snapped at Sturm and Father Bouchet to get out of his way, and stood over her bed. He stared at her for a few moments, and then opened his rattrap of a mouth.

"I am SD Standartenfuhrer Schulz. I am here to ask you some questions. Tell the truth, and it will be quick and painless. Otherwise, I will be forced to use," he paused, and gave a significant look at the Scharfuhrer. Bachmann's crazed, brutal stare gazed at her and lingered on her body. "Different methods. Do you understand?"

"Yes."

"Good. You were seen sheltering the enemy on your farm. Who are you spying for, Caron?"

She looked back at him in bewilderment. "On my farm? I'm sorry, I..."

His hand flashed out and slapped her hard on the face. "I warned you to tell the truth. Who do you work for?"

She saw stars for several seconds, and when she recovered, the German Captain was holding her head in his hands. She realized he was speaking to her.

"Are you okay?"

She touched her face and knew there would be a severe bruise, maybe even permanent damage. The SD officer hovered over her.

"I can manage."

The man nodded and turned to stare at the SD man. "You cannot treat her like this. She is wounded already. It is inhumane."

"Is that so? Get out, Captain. This is Sicherheitsdienst business, Gestapo business. State Security. Leave, before I have you arrested."

Sturm hesitated but finally turned on his heel and left. Schulz nodded.

"Excellent. Now, who do you work for?"

"I don't..."

The hand snaked out and collided with the other side of her face. She felt something break.

"Last time, and then I hand you over to the Scharfuhrer here. Who do you work for?"

"Standartenfuhrer, please." The priest interrupted. For his pains, Scharfuhrer Bachmann smashed the butt of his machine pistol on his head, and he collapsed in a heap. Schulz looked at the unconscious body for a few moments, and then turned back to Margot.

"Now, you were telling me who you work for."

She shook her head. "I cooked food for a few soldiers, that's all."

He was thoughtful for a few moments. Then he glanced at Bachmann. "I will leave it to you, Scharf. I want a result. We need to know what she's up to, what the Allies are planning. Don't kill her. In fact, I don't want anything broken. Apart from that, do anything you like. Just find out what she knows."

"Yes, Sir. And the priest?"

"Leave him on the floor. When he comes round, you may be able to use him to gain some leverage. You know how it goes, torture one to get the other to see what will happen to them if they fail to cooperate."

The noncom grinned, showing a row of blackened

teeth. Schulz winced as he caught a whiff of the man's breath. "I know how it goes, Sir. Leave it to me."

"Excellent. I have business elsewhere. I will return tomorrow."

The Scharfuhrer saluted, and Schulz left. Margot had listened to the exchange, and her heart sank as the door slammed shut. Bachmann advanced on her.

"Now, my little French flower. Let's have a pleasant conversation."

He reached up and ripped of her blouse to expose her bra. Another wrench, and it came off. He reached for her nipple, gripped it hard, squeezed and twisted. She couldn't help the scream that erupted from her mouth.

"Who do you work for?"

He squeezed and twisted even harder, and white-hot pain engulfed her entire body. She passed out.

* * *

Five miles Northwest of Isigny, 21.50, July 2, 1944

Josh waited a few more minutes, and then he began to understand the other commander had outwitted him. He wasn't about to fall for it, so he climbed back out and surveyed the surrounding countryside. The ground seemed to have swallowed up the German heavy tank.

Shit!

Solly was standing on the hull looking around for his hated foe, but eventually he had to admit he'd gone.

"We had him, bang to rights," he snarled, "Maybe if we'd..."

"If we'd done anything different, we'd have been dead."

"We have to go after him."

"A fucking Tiger? Are you out of your mind?"

Vern climbed out of the hatch to stretch his muscles, and he overheard the last comment.

"Course he's out of his mind. You want to tangle with a Tiger; you deserve everything you get. What've you Jews got inside your heads, shit for brains?"

Solly stared at him for a long moment, and Grant could see he was struggling to control himself. After several seconds, he seemed to calm, and he smiled at Vern.

"Not shit for brains, no. We have real brains. Shit for brains is what you get when cracker men screw their sisters, and they give birth to imbeciles. Like you."

"You motherfucker, I'll break your fucking neck!" he roared as he charged forward, his hands reaching for Solly.

He almost missed him, although he'd been waiting for something like it. He stepped between the two men, but Vern twisted around him and kept going. He was within inches of Solly when Grant connected with a hard, left hook. He felt the power of the blow jar all the way up his arm, and he knew he'd suffer for it later. But it was enough. Vern went down like a sack of potatoes and lay stunned on the steel deck of the Sherman.

"You hit him!" Solly was incredulous.

"Damn right I hit him. What else am I supposed to do? He was about to start a brawl. I warned him."

"I could have handled him, Sarge."

"No one brawls on my tank. Not Vern, not you, not anyone. When he wakes up, I'm going to tell him he's gone too far. I'll file a report when we get back to the Battalion. He's been spoiling for that ever since he joined the crew of Minnie Mouse. Help me get him inside the hull. We've been here too long. It's time we headed north and found our own people."

They maneuvered the unconscious man inside, and Dale helped to put him on the co-driver's seat. Angel stared at his unconscious co-driver, but said nothing. Dale fastened spare webbing around him, to stop him falling out of the seat. When Grant was satisfied, he made sure Angel could manage without Vern.

"Sure, Sarge, no problem. He was getting on my nerves anyway. Always complaining about blacks, Jews, Hispanics, you name it. I mean; we're a mixed crew. He should knuckle under and get on with fighting the war. I was finding it hard to concentrate with all the carping and whining. You gonna transfer him out?"

"Probably. I'll decide later. If he comes to, let me know."

"Sure."

"Right. Move out."

"Which direction?"

"North. Keep driving until you see someone who speaks American."

"You got it."

The Sherman lurched forward. Grant returned to the turret and poked his head through the hatch. He was on the lookout for Tigers, or anything else that tried to shoot holes in Minnie. The rain had stopped, and he even started to enjoy being in the open without water trickling down his collar and inside his shirt. The landscape was vibrant, bright with the sparkle of leaves, trees, and wet grass decorated with raindrops, which caused them to glisten in the sunlight.

He looked up, and it seemed the cloud ceiling was higher, so maybe USAF and the RAF could fly off a few of their fighters and bombers.

Good, those flyboys could clear a few Tigers and Panthers out of our way, and maybe give us a chance to get home in one piece.

A short time later he did see movement in the sky, a distant speck that resolved into an Allied fighter. It closed on them with the screaming roar of the single piston engine, and he smiled as the fighter jock flung his aircraft over into a steep dive as he came in for the attack. Closer, closer, and he felt an icy feeling in his spine. Almost as he recognized a Republic P47 Thunderbolt, he saw sparks on the wings.

The bastard is shooting at us. We're on your side, you moron!

He slid down into the turret and slammed the hatch closed.

"Air attack, Angel, take evasive action. Find some cover, fast."

"Do we shoot back at him?" Solly asked.

"He's one of ours, don't be crazy. If we're lucky, he'll see we're American and stop the attack. You start shooting and he'll murder us."

Angel had gunned the engine up to full speed, and he tried to zigzag toward a stone barn a couple of hundred yards from the track. The Thunderbolt bored in, remorseless, uncaring, and they heard the hammering of the eight heavy caliber machine guns as it opened fire.

The burst of lead chewed up the rich Normandy soil and threw up clods of muddy earth. They were only halfway to the doubtful protection of the barn when the fighter plane soared into the air, looped the loop, and swung around to a new attack path. They waited for the hammering of armor-piercing incendiary .50 caliber bullets on the hull. Not sufficient to penetrate their main armor, maybe, but there was always a chance of serious damage, enough to disable their vehicle.

The roar of the engine was louder and louder, and every crewman inside Minnie tensed for the impact.

Our own side shooting us up, don't those fighter jocks know the difference between a Sherman and a Panzer? Stupid, testosterone fueled shit-eating bastards!

Nothing happened. The Thunderbolt roared overhead and kept going. The guns remained silent. Four men let out their breath in a huge sigh of relief. Vern was still unconscious, unaware of how close they'd come. A minute later, Grant's thudding heart slowed to something like a normal rate. He slowly opened the hatch and looked up at the sky. A black speck was heading north.

"Angel, drive back on the road."

"Has he gone?"

"He's gone."

"Jesus. One of our own."

"We're behind enemy lines. You can hardly blame him."

"What, is he fucking blind? We're American, a Sherman. What's the matter with him?"

Grant didn't reply, but he understood something of the problems a fighter pilot faced over the Normandy battlefield. Diving on a target at speeds of up to four hundred miles per hour in poor visibility and a low cloud base, with the constant threat of enemy aircraft and flak from the ground. Pilots should check their targets to make sure, but factoring it all in, when flying over enemy territory, a 'shoot everything that moves' philosophy was understandable.

They trundled on, traversing vast areas of fields, some flooded, and they all had one thing in common. They were empty. No farmers, no armies of soldiers marauding through the mud, nothing. He knew the battle still raged, somewhere. Yet, once again, he had the impression they were on some unending Kafkaesque landscape when he saw the village in front of them. In the distance, a small town, it had to be Isigny. Yet who was in control? He called Morgan on the Company net, but the hiss of static mocked him as he tried again and again.

There was only one possibility. They'd have to go forward and check out the small village before they drove into Isigny. They'd know, one way or the other. And if the Krauts met them when they went in, well, they'd give them a taste of American munitions. A 75mm shell, or a burst of machine gun bullets had a tendency to resolve most arguments, unless they shot first, or they met a Tiger.

"We're going into that village. Solly, load HE. If you're not certain about anything, shoot. The place could still be occupied by the Germans."

"Roger that, Sarge. Vern has come round. You want him to man the machine gun?"

"That's affirmative. If we run into trouble, we need all the firepower we can get. Vern, how is the head?"

A pause. Then he heard the Southerner's slurred tones.

"You do that again, and I don't give a fuck who you are…"

"That's enough! Do your job, and the next time I think you're trying to start a fight in my crew you're out. Last warning, got that?"

He mumbled an inaudible reply, but it was enough. He had more to concern himself with than a fracas between a racist and a Jewish zealot.

"Driver, advance."

He grabbed the handles of his .50 caliber and began looking for a target. He checked every opening, window, and gap between the buildings for a sign of trouble. Angel slowed down, but Grant ordered him to speed up. If they clipped some housewife's front garden wall, it was too bad. But there was no way he was prepared to make it easy for some Kraut sniper.

They entered the main street of the village. He saw a large building ahead of them, something like a convent or even a hospital, but he ignored it. He'd seen the shape of a German steel helmet glance around the side of a building, and then the barrel of a gun poke out, either a rifle or a light machine gun.

"Driver, halt."

Stupid bastards, this is a Sherman tank.

And then a note of caution entered his head; the Jerries were anything but stupid.

"Gunner, target hundred and fifty yards ahead, the house on the right with the iron fence in the front garden."

"Blue front door?"

"That's the one. Saw signs of activity on the far side. There could be Panzergrenadiers hiding in ambush waiting for us to get closer. Bury them."

"With pleasure. Load HE."

"Already loaded," Dale sang out.

"Fire!"

The shell smashed into the front of the house at an angle to destroy most of the interior and the far wall, but it wasn't enough. There was a chance they could have survived.

"Give it a few more, Solly. Don't stop until you can see daylight the other side."

"Roger that. Fire."

The second shell smashed into the house, and then another. After the fourth shell, the remaining walls of the house tumbled to the ground so that there was only a mound of bricks and broken furniture where once stood someone's home.

Too bad, we didn't start this war, and we didn't want to come here.

"Driver, advance."

Angel drove cautiously forward until they were level with the destruction they'd wrought. In the middle of the broken bricks, Grant could see fragments of the field gray uniform poking out and a corrugated gas mask case a few yards away. Chances are they were dead. He looked ahead at the large building and wondered if it was a German strong point.

"Gunner, watch that big building ahead. It may be trouble. It's a likely spot for a German headquarters. Driver, go forward, but take it slow. It may be a trap."

They advanced slowly toward the building, watching for any sign of the enemy. They almost missed the sniper, but at the last moment, Grant glimpsed a slight movement opposite the building. It was almost nothing. It could have been a small domestic animal, even a rat. But something told him it was more than a rat, or maybe a Nazi rat. There was no time to direct a shell at the enemy position, so he grabbed the butt of his .50 caliber, aimed quickly, and pulled the trigger.

The heavy caliber shells smashed into the ground ten yards to the right of the target. He cursed and began to walk the fire into the enemy position. And then the gun jammed. It was as if the German sensed his helplessness, and the odd shaped steel helmet appeared a few inches out of the ground where the sniper had taken cover, and the barrel of his rifle became still as he took aim.

Grant could still have ducked inside the turret, but something stopped him, some strange feeling that he needed to watch it happening. See the bullet that was to kill him fly through the air until it struck him square in the face, and he would know no more. He could never explain afterward what strange emotion had gone through his head, but it meant he could see what happened next.

Another German appeared from the big building and ran toward the sniper. He had an MP38 machine pistol clutched in his hands. The sniper's rifle abruptly angled down to the ground as a burst drilled into him, and the still helmeted head flopped sideways. A moment later, the body came into view. The dead German wore Leopard pattern camouflage uniform, Waffen-SS Panzergrenadiers, probably.

What the fuck!

The village street was a frozen tableau. The German stood still, with his weapon pointed harmlessly down at the ground. He stared at Grant, as waiting for something to happen.

"It's short range, but I can splatter him all over the street. I'm loaded with HE," Solly said. But despite his bloodthirsty intention to slaughter every German soldier he encountered, there was little bellicose intention in his voice. The man clearly did not intend to attack them, even if it were possible with a puny 9mm machine pistol. And Solly was no butcher.

"I'm going out to talk to him," he announced to the crew.

"That's crazy. I can bust his ass with the Browning."

"Save it, Vern. Everyone, hold your fire."

He drew his Colt .45 automatic, put the slide to put a round into the chamber, and climbed out of the turret. He started walking toward the German, feeling once again the incongruity of the situation that faced them. They'd wiped out the Kraut Panzer Grenadiers by dropping the building on their heads, and the guy in front of him was on the same side as the men buried under the rubble. It could even be a trap, yet he didn't think so. There was something odd here, something about that enemy soldier.

Since when did Krauts go around killing each other? It'd certain shorten the war if a few more killed their buddies.

He walked toward the stone building. It was big enough to hold a company or even a battalion headquarters. There was no movement, although that didn't mean there was no one inside. They could be waiting for him, waiting to put an anti-tank rocket into the guts of Minnie Mouse. And yet...

He stopped six feet away and kept his pistol pointed toward the ground. He was confident he could put a bullet in the German if he showed any sign of hostile intent.

How do I handle a situation like this? Offer the guy a smoke while we talk about it, or hit him with a hard left, put him down, and place a boot on his back until he's explained himself?

He decided to try a civil approach, although the man looked wild and disheveled.

"The name's Grant. Sergeant Josh Grant, 745th Battalion, US Army."

"Sturmann Ivan Bolkovich. SS Panzergrenadiers, Hitler Jugend."

Bolkovich? Sounds like a Russian name.

He nodded. "What's the story, Bolkovich? Why did you shoot that guy? You're on the same side."

"I wish to surrender. I am Russian, not German. They made me join their army."

"I thought Germany was the enemy of Russia."

"It's a long story, Sergeant."

"Just give me the bare bones, Sturmann Bolkovich. The war ain't gonna wait for us."

"They forced us, me and my comrades. We were in a prison camp, starving to death. They said either we volunteer to fight for them, or we would be left to die of hunger."

"Comrades? Where are the rest of them?"

"In that big building. There are twenty-three of us in all, Panzergrenadiers. The man I shot, he was our Sergeant. He would not have allowed us to surrender, so I killed him."

No shit.

The Russian's statement reminded him of the camp guard Solly killed, and the shitstorm that still hung over his head. Then it hit him, forget the trouble with Lindbergh. There were twenty-three armed Panzergrenadiers inside that building. He turned to Solly, who was watching from the turret.

"There're Krauts inside that building. Load HE, and wait for my order."

"We're loaded and ready. I can hit 'em right now, Sarge."

"Not yet, hold your fire!"

He looked back at the Russian. "Can you get them to come out and put down their weapons?"

"I think so, yes. They were frightened when they saw your tank. If they tried to surrender, they knew our Scharfuhrer would have killed them. And if they fought, your tank would have killed them. I said I would come out here and try to reason with you."

Grant smothered a smile.

The situation is absurd. A bunch of SS men desperate to surrender, so much for the image of the Aryan Superman.

"Tell them to drop their weapons and come out, Sturmann Bolkovich. They won't get hurt. But only if all of them come out, you hear me? If a single soldier remains inside that building, we'll kill all of you, in case it's a trick."

"I will tell them. Do not kill us."

Several minutes later, the SS 'volunteers' were clustered in a group in front of Minnie Mouse. Solly had them covered with the turret machine gun. He glanced down at Grant.

"What do we do with this lot?"

"We take 'em back to Battalion. A present for Lindbergh, maybe it'll win him some Brownie points with the brass."

He shouted to the prisoners, "March, double time! I'll call directions from the tank, and don't forget, we'll be watching every move you make."

Bolkovich started to click his heels, and then thought better of it. He said something to the men, and they doubled away, with Minnie following them. When they came to an intersection, Grant shouted directions to them, and the unconventional column made its slow way back to Battalion HQ.

* * *

Eight kilometers East of Isigny, 21.50, July 2, 1944

It had been a long drive, but finally they linked up with the remains of 12th SS Panzers, Hitler Jugend. Meyer greeted him warmly.

"Rolf, we thought you'd gone for good."

"So did we, Sir. We had a few run-ins. An American Sherman almost got us."

Meyer's eyebrows rose. "A Sherman? One of these verdammt Fireflies?"

"No, Sir. Just an ordinary Sherman, but this one was clever, very clever."

Meyer grunted. "Next time you meet him, roast his ass with that 88mm gun of yours. Although I doubt you'll recognize him, sometimes I think Normandy has become one huge garage for American and British Sherman tanks."

"I'll recognize him. What are our orders, Sir?"

"Apart from survive for long enough to return to the Fatherland?" Meyer murmured with a small smile. His voice was low. In spite of his Knight's Cross with Oak Leaves and Swords, he had to be careful. They all had to be careful of the Gestapo. No one knew who was listening. Manhausen thought of Lentz's cousin, SD Standartenfuhrer Werner Schulz. If he overheard Meyer make a defeatist comment, he would be more than prepared to haul him off to a concentration camp. Hero or not, Knights Cross or not, it would make no difference to the Gestapo.

Rolf waited him out. Finally, Meyer sighed and went on, "We're in the shit, Obersturmfuhrer. It's no secret. The two American beachheads have almost linked, and by now they may already be joined. The British are in an even stronger position. If they break out and link up with the

Americans, they'll push toward Saint-Lo, and I doubt we'll be able to stop them taking the whole of France."

He whistled. "That bad?"

Meyer grimaced. "Worse. They lost one of their artificial harbors, the one in the west, but they're still landing armor and equipment at an incredible rate. Now they've taken Cherbourg, they can reinforce and resupply at a rate we could only dream of. God only knows how we'll manage."

"What about the Luftwaffe?"

"The what?"

He said nothing. He could only speculate about the absence of German aircraft, despite the rantings of Reichsmarshall Goering and the promises of the Fuhrer.

"It's all up to us, Rolf. We're joining forces with another unit of heavy Panzers, the SS Heavy Panzer Battalion 101. Our plan is to crush the British attack at Caen. We have a major advantage, the Normandy hedgerows. The bocage. They will allow us to conceal our defenses, even our armor and assault guns from the enemy. When they are in our sights, we can fall on them like wolves and inflict heavy casualties. It is essential that we contain them in a small area and not allow them to break out with the Americans to Saint-Lo. If we're successful, we can drive them back into the sea, just like we did at Dunkirk."

"That was a long time ago, Sir."

"Along time ago, yes. Come with me, I'll introduce you to Obersturmfuhrer Wittmann."

"Michael Wittmann?"

"The same, our top scoring Panzer ace. There he is. It's time for you to meet him."

They walked across to where an officer was giving orders to his crew, who were loading ammunition and stores into the hull of a Tiger I, almost identical to Rolf's own machine. Meyer grabbed his attention and did the introductions.

"Obersturmfuhrer Wittmann, this is Obersturmfuhrer Manhausen, of the 12th SS Hitler Jugend."

He was of medium height and build, a good-looking man in his black tanker's uniform with the wide lapelled, short, double-breasted jacket.

"Manhausen."

"Wittmann, it's an honor. I heard about the Battle of Villers-Bocage. They say your unit, Heavy SS-Panzer Battalion 101, destroyed fourteen enemy tanks, two anti-tank guns, and fifteen transport vehicles. And that most of them fell to your Tiger."

His face struggled, and failed, to contain his pride. "We all fight for the Fuhrer and the Fatherland, individual scores make little difference. I understand you will be joining us. How many vehicles do you have in your Company?"

The Panzer ace spoke with a rolling Bavarian accent, sounding not unlike the Fuhrer who'd spent so much time in the region; especially before and after his service in the First World War, in the List Regiment. Although Wittmann was an officer in the Waffen-SS, everyone knew he'd begun his military career as an NCO. Just like the Fuhrer.

"I've no idea. We only just got in." He looked at Meyer. "Sir, what kind of strength do we have left?"

"A single Panzergrenadier battalion, and I believe the 12th SS can field at least seven Tigers."

"Seven! Is at all?"

"Between the barrages from the ships in the Channel, and attacks from enemy bombers and ground attack fighters as well as their Fireflies, we're lucky to have that many. Fuel is another problem."

"Fuel?"

"The Allies have hit our stocks hard. Every time we move our fuel dump to a secret location, they seem to locate it and send in squadrons of aircraft to destroy it. I believe we have enough for the coming action, and of course, if we are successful, we will be able to commandeer stocks of captured fuel."

And if we're not? What do we do, harness teams of horses to drag our Tigers into battle?

"We will be successful," Wittmann said firmly, "When the battle is over, we will have regained much of the territory we've lost over the past weeks." He grinned. "Who knows, in the next few weeks you could be the owner of one of these." He grinned as he held up his Knight's Cross, "Isn't that worth fighting and dying for?"

At that moment, Rolf realized he was a true believer, a Hitlerkind; one of the new breed of Germans who believed the myths the Nazis had spun about the Third Reich. He was about to reply when Meyer gave him a warning glance, and he kept silent.

When he didn't get a reply, Wittmann went on, "You haven't tangled with the Fireflies, Manhausen? We're bound to run into them sooner or later."

"Not yet. Anything I need to worry about?"

The Bavarian grimaced. "Just the main gun. It's a piece of heavy artillery; the British call it the 17-pounder. The shell is quite capable of penetrating the frontal armor of a Tiger. In fact, we've lost Panthers and even Tigers IIs to the Fireflies, and the damn Sherman hull makes them more maneuverable than our heavy tanks. In short, they're bastards. When I come across a Firefly, it's time to find a nice spot to go hull down and hit them when they're not expecting it."

"I'll keep in mind," he replied.

Something about Michael Wittmann left him less than impressed. It was whispered he'd left his own men in the lurch while he went looking for targets of opportunity. His loader, Siegfried Lenz, would undoubtedly hero-worship such a high-scoring ace, until a British shell blew his fool head off.

"I served in Russia, too," he pointed out to the tanker, "Like you, I learned a thing or two on the Eastern Front."

"We all did," Wittmann replied, "But this is different. The Americans and British are better armed and better equipped. Besides, their Air Force is deadly."

"I know. That's why the 12th SS is so short on Tigers. Most of them were lost to air attacks. Anything else?"

He thought for a few moments. "That about covers it. As if we haven't enough to worry about," he grinned, "There is something else, the Achilles. It's a tank destroyer. It carries a 17-pounder gun the same as they mount in the Firefly, but this one is configured as a tank destroyer. I tell you, if you see one of those long barreled guns in the vicinity, watch yourself."

He stared at Wittmann. "What do you do when you come up against these things?"

The reply was spoken in a voice that crackled with iron fanaticism. "Check the rings on my gun barrel, Manhausen. That's what I do, I kill the bastards."

He turned on his heel and returned to his crew. Meyer was about to say something when an SS Scharfuhrer rushed up to him.

"Sir, a message from intelligence. They say if we mount an attack as soon as the light starts to go, we will have the enemy at a disadvantage. If we do our job properly, a big push now could turn the tide of the war."

Rolf heard Meyer mutter, but not audible to the NCO, "We'd better inform both the Allies and the Russians of that interesting fact."

"Very well, Scharfuhrer. This is Obersturmfuhrer Manhausen, commander of one of the 12th SS Tigers. Manhausen, this is Scharfuhrer Bernd Bachmann, he served with me on the Eastern Front. Bernd is a Panzergrenadier attached to my headquarters.

Rolf gave him a friendly nod, but the man merely scowled, his eyes displaying an inner brutality. He was young for the rank of Scharfuhrer, blonde hair and blue eyes. A Nazi icon, probably no more than eighteen or nineteen years old and already a natural born killer. He wondered what the NCO had done to gain promotion so early. Then again, on the Eastern Front, it was often just to slaughter enough Russians, civilians, or soldiers, it made little difference.

There was an embarrassing pause for a few seconds, and then Meyer sent the young Panzergrenadier on his way. He smiled at Rolf.

"You'd better make your vehicle ready. We will leave shortly, and when the battle is over, we shall be in a better position to give these invaders a bloody nose. We'll turn the tide, eh, Manhausen."

"Yes, Sir."

He walked away, thinking about the cockeyed world of the SS. The constant assertions from the Reichsfuhrer, Heinrich Himmler, that one more big battle would 'turn the tide.' He'd heard it all in Russia before almost every battle. The tide never turned, and the men at the front all knew it never would. Of one thing he was certain, he would stay the hell away from Michael Wittmann. If the man wanted fame and glory, good luck to him. All he wanted was to go home and get his crew back to their families. Give them a chance to grow up to be men, instead of the ferocious, juvenile killers the war and the SS had made them.

He reached his crew. "Men, we're going into battle tomorrow, with the rest of the 12th SS and the 101st Heavy Panzers."

Linz, the Nazi fanatic stared at him. "You mean Wittmann's unit?"

"The same. Refuel, replenish our ammunition, and make certain we're ready to move out. If fortune favors us, tomorrow we'll see a great victory. We go to fight in the hedgerows. The Normandy bocage."

He'd intended his words to encourage them, but Linz leapt to attention, clicked his heels, raised his arm and shouted, "Heil Hitler!"

Most ignored him. Someone, he didn't see who, murmured, "Asshole."

"The battle of the hedgerows," Heinrich Boll commented to break the awkward silence, "it sounds like a child's game."

"Not a child's game, Heinrich. Tomorrow will be a bloody game of warriors. A tough and grueling test of strength."

"Can we win, Obersturmfuhrer?"

It was the driver, Franz Schelling, who asked the question.

Should I tell them the truth, these boys who are too young to have had a woman, even to grow a beard? No, let them enjoy their illusions for a little longer. Tomorrow will be terrible. At least give them the rest of today.

He smiled. "If we don't, I'll kick your ass, Franz. Especially if your fucking engine breaks down again, and a Firefly puts a 17-pounder shell in our bellies."

No one laughed.

CHAPTER EIGHT

SHAEF Headquarters, near London, England, 05.00, July 3, 1944

"It's time we made our move," Monty said, his face earnest, as if to convey the accuracy of his statement. Ike thought he made it sound like they were playing a game of chess, "We must take Caen. No question."

"Bradley wants Saint-Lo. I spoke to him on the radio yesterday; he said it's the only way out of the peninsula. Now that our campaign in the Cotentin is almost complete, it's time we looked to the future. We need maneuvering room, and that means a breakout into France. We can't stay in Normandy forever."

General Montgomery made a gesture with his hand, as if sweeping away Ike's statement. "And leave Caen in our rear, occupied by German units, including their heavy armor? No, it has to be Caen, General. No question."

He folded his arms to underline there was no point in continuing the discussion.

"May I interrupt?"

Both men looked at the rotund figure of Winston Churchill as he entered the room, wearing the one-piece siren suit that had become part of his public image. Like the large cigar and the booming voice, which always seemed to strike the right jingoistic note.

"Of course, Prime Minister," Ike acknowledged.

"Our campaign in Normandy has succeeded in most of our objectives, and we're in a strong position. You're making telling points, and I believe you're both right. We should target both objectives. General Montgomery's forces can hit Caen like a sledgehammer and drive the wretched Germans out of that benighted city. He has the resources to deal with the kinds of heavy tanks we know the Germans have in the vicinity. At the same time, The American forces can take Saint-Lo and open up the gateway to the rest of France."

Montgomery pursed his lips. "We should consolidate our resources on Caen. It's vital we make sure we have no serious German resistance left in our rear. Especially the Tigers and Panthers."

Ike, forever the diplomat, smiled and put his hand on his arm, a gesture of affection. "You're absolutely right, General. You have the men and the equipment, so go to it."

The Brit General looked surprised. "So you'll concentrate all our forces on Caen?"

"Absolutely, all our British and Canadian forces. The American Army will strike out for Saint-Lo."

Churchill did his best to hide a grin. Eisenhower had outmaneuvered the prickly British General, and he had to hand it to him, he'd done a neat job. All that remained now was to fight the battles. And win. He'd visited the area of Saint-Lo on a painting vacation and produced a couple of pleasant watercolors, which still hung in his home.

An image flashed through his mind, and his mood darkened. The high and impenetrable Normandy hedges before Saint-Lo were a gift to the defenders.

Enough for them to win the battle and defeat the Americans? Maybe Monty's right, except the Germans are reeling from the overwhelming Allied forces. It's time to hit them hard, a devastating and final blow from which they'll never recover. If it works, the path to the River Rhine will be wide open to us. If it works!

* * *

Four miles North of Isigny, 09.20, July 3, 1944

They thundered along the narrow French farm tracks chewing up the soggy ground, a vast armada of armor, mostly Shermans, company after company, tank after tank. Many showed the scars of the recent fighting, with patches hastily welded over battle damage and painted in varying shades of drab green. Behind them, the support vehicles, M10 tank destroyers, equipped with a 3-inch gun in a sloped, circular open-topped turret. Unpopular with their crews because the gun was less than effective against its prey, the heavy Panzers which they would face. Equally, the open gun platforms left them vulnerable to high explosive shellfire and mortars.

In the rear, a multitude of support vehicles followed. An engineer company, with their winch-equipped armored recovery vehicles, a host of armored trucks carrying spares, and the headquarters support company. Some of the vehicles towed fuel bowsers, enough to make the crews nervous of enemy attacks.

They passed lines and lines of troops, most from the 29th Infantry Division, who'd pushed up to within only two miles of the town. A heavy weapons company carried 81mm mortars to give them more powerful, longer range hitting power. At every junction, even at every farm gate, MPs directed the solid mass of traffic, all of it heading in one direction, southeast toward Saint-Lo.

At the head of the 745th, Colonel Martin Lindbergh III cut a dashing figure, standing in the turret so most of his trim figure was on view to the men. His Sherman was festooned with aerials, some with gaudy pennants on them, just in case anyone had any doubt about the importance of the man in charge. A long way back, eating the dust of the Battalion, Grant rode in the turret of Minnie Mouse. He'd been assigned the position of back marker. Ahead of him Daniel Kuruk's Cochise spat dust and pebbles into his face so that he needed to wear goggles.

In front of Cochise rode Major Grenville Morgan. At least he'd greeted them with some warmth when they rejoined the unit, in contrast to the chilly greeting from Lindbergh. Grant grinned to himself as he recalled the irate Colonel.

"Where the fuck have you been, Sergeant? Your orders were to stay close to the Battalion."

Grant sighed inwardly. After fighting across Normandy, they now had to endure this asshole, the Battalion commander, Colonel Martin Lindbergh III. Grant started to explain, but the dapper, gung-ho Colonel was in no mood to listen.

"In case you don't know, Sergeant, we've been fighting

a war while you sauntered around the countryside. What were you looking for, French girls or French wine? No, don't answer that. I suspect you've been cowering in some ditch while we've been doing all the fighting. Dammit, I can't abide that kind of behavior. You're already under open arrest, and I intend to add this to the charges."

He stared the elegant officer in the eye.

"What exactly is the charge, Colonel? Killing the enemy?"

"Damn you, Grant, I'm talking about a court martial here. The charge will be cowardice, or maybe desertion in the face of the enemy. I'll let you know when I've made my decision. Clear?"

Grant stared at the angry officer for a few seconds, and then gave him a curt nod. "Oh, yeah, it's very clear, Sir."

"In that case, you can report to Major Morgan. Now you've finally decided to return, he'll have a grand total of three tanks, until he's careless enough to lose another. Jesus Christ, who the fuck are they? What the hell are they doing in my headquarters?"

The Russian SS men had lagged behind, and Dale had shepherded them along with an M1 carbine to cover them. Not that they had any interest in escape. They staggered into camp in a long, straggling bunch, looking around curiously, probably for something to eat. All of them were covered in mud, dirt, dust, and everything else the Normandy countryside could throw at them. But they were still SS, no question.

He explained how they'd surrendered to Minnie. Lindbergh snorted.

"Surrendered, this pathetic bunch? I thought for a moment they were SS."

"They are SS, Sir."

He regarded the prisoners more closely, seeing the twin lightning flashes on the collar tabs. "Damn, so they are. What's the story? They don't exactly look like Hitler's elite stormtroopers."

He explained how the surrender had come about, and Lindbergh looked thoughtful.

"Russians, uh? Still, they're SS, no matter where they were born. This'll look good when I report it to HQ, Sergeant, real good."

Good for Martin Lindbergh III is what he means.

He examined them for a few minutes, as if he was looking for something more.

Horns growing out of their heads, maybe, Grant thought.

Finally, he nodded in satisfaction.

"Ike may hear of this, a whole unit of SS prisoners. Pass them over to the MPs. Don't forget, you're still under open arrest. If you think bringing in this sorry lot is going to save your ass, you can forget it. When you've done some real fighting, maybe you can call yourself a soldier. In the meantime, watch your step, Sergeant, and don't go wandering off again. Don't fuck with me, Sergeant. You savvy?"

"Yes, Sir."

He saluted and climbed back aboard Minnie Mouse, while Dale pushed the SS men toward the MPs tent. Major Morgan at least gave Grant's crew something of a welcome, his relief they were still alive was heartening after Lindbergh's bitter recriminations. The news of his bitter diatribe spread like wildfire, even in the few minutes it took them to reach Morgan's depleted Company.

"Is it true? You just had another dust up with the CO?"

he asked.

"Kind of."

"I'll try and take care of it, Sergeant. It's absurd. I guess you know why he's doing it?"

"No, Sir."

"There's been a blast from Ike. Apparently, he's not happy with the performance of the Battalion, or of Lindbergh himself. He wants an example made, so the Colonel hit on blaming you to demonstrate it's not his fault." He sighed, "Leave it with me. What have you been up to?"

Grant gave him a rundown of their movements and put the question for which they all wanted the answer.

"Where do we go next, Sir? Unless you think they'll stand us down for a few days for R&R."

Morgan chuckled. "You're kidding me, Sergeant. We're getting ready to kick open the door to the rest of France."

"Saint-Lo?"

He nodded. "Saint-Lo. We attack tomorrow morning, so get yourself some chow, and make sure your vehicle is fuel and armed. I don't suppose there's any sign of that French girl who cooked for us?"

"No, Sir." He was silent for a few moments, and his expression was bleak, "She disappeared when the Germans counterattacked. I believe she's dead."

He recognized Grant's grief. "I remember now, I'm sorry, real sorry. She seemed a nice girl."

"She was."

"I'm afraid it's back to K Rations. Some of the men came down with dysentery. I'm not sure how they got it, but I'd go easy on the Army chow."

Grant smiled. "Maybe we should shoot the K rations at

the Krauts. That'd be enough to send them packing."

"Too true."

They were interrupted by a shout, and a corporal was walking through the assembly area, carrying a leather satchel. "Mail! I'm looking for Company A."

"That's us, Corporal," Morgan smiled, "Don't that beat all! Mail in this place."

There was only one letter, for the Major. He casually opened it while they swapped jokes about inedible rations. He stood to one side and read it through, and then he read it again, and again. He looked like a man who'd seen the writing on his tomb.

The sight of a farm half a mile away jerked him back to the present and made him think of the feisty French girl, Margot Caron. He felt a deep sadness he would never see her again. In the short time he'd known her, something had changed inside him, and now he recognized what it had been. After he met her, he no longer wanted the war to continue until he'd wreaked his vengeance on the Germans. Instead, he wanted it to end, so he could work things out with her.

He warmed as he thought of her smile, and then her more serious expression when she defended her point of view. She'd gone, and the prospect of a wonderful future with her had vanished. He wanted vengeance, more than ever. No, that wasn't entirely true. He wanted her. Yet he couldn't have her. So he'd have to settle for revenge on the Nazi fuckers who'd taken her from him. Yet even killing the enemy didn't seem quite so important. Something inside him had changed.

Too many dead bodies, many of them children and civilians, shit, I don't know what I do want, not anymore.

They were grinding along a narrow track, a huge column of American armor, with a division of infantry in trucks following close behind. The Colonel's hand went up to signal a halt. The column came to a ragged stop, and Lindbergh beckoned to his Company commanders to join him. After ten minutes discussion, they returned to their vehicles, and Morgan came through on the Company net.

"Hill 192, men, that's our first objective. It's about five miles to the east of the town. Take a look. The Krauts are dug in, and the Colonel wants us to support the infantry when they take it."

Grant shuddered. The approaches were the worst kind. This was bocage with a capital B. The entire area was a maze of narrow lanes and high, thick impenetrable hedgerows. It was going to be a bastard. He watched as the motorized infantry units accompanying them halted, waiting for the armor to push a way through.

He stared at Morgan. "Sir, if we attack this position head on, they'll slaughter us. The Germans are not stupid. They'll have strong points set up behind almost every hedgerow, and it's almost impossible to get through them."

Morgan chuckled. "Since you've been on your travels, things have changed. You haven't heard of the Culin Hedgerow Cutter?"

"No, Sir."

"Sgt Curtis Grubb Culin III, one of our tankers, a guy with the 102nd Cavalry Reconnaissance Squadron attached to 2nd Armored Division came up with a way through the Bocage. He invented a four-pronged device built from scrap steel he took from a German roadblock. Sergeant Culin attached this contraption to the front of his tank, and it plowed gaps in the hedgerows like you wouldn't believe. As soon as we hit the hedgerows, we're going straight through them and come at the German defensive positions from behind."

"You're sure it'll work, Major?"

"You haven't seen the device fitted to my tank. I tried it a couple of days ago, and it works; believe me. Works like a charm. More than half of our Battalion vehicles are fitted with the Culin device, and we're going to hack through the Jerry defenses like they were made of paper."

"That's good news, Sir."

It sounded unlikely, but when a half hour later they entered the tortuous area of high hedgerows, they drove straight through a gap, courtesy of the Culin device, and into the fields behind. Grant heard a sudden eruption of machine gunfire, and then a German anti-tank rocket exploded on one of Lindbergh's Shermans. There was no doubt they'd taken them by surprise, and although the enemy hit back fast, it only took a couple of minutes for Lindbergh's headquarters Company to flatten the enemy position and drive on. Which meant now they were coming at the Germans from behind them. Already, the 29th had deployed their mortars, and the 81mm shells whistled overhead to land amongst the waiting enemy.

"Follow me!" Morgan radioed on the net, "We're going straight through. Watch out for anti-tank fire."

The Major's Sherman smashed through into the field behind. Cochise and Minnie Mouse followed, and at first there was little sign of the enemy. Until Morgan reached the south edge of the field and smashed through the next hedgerow, crossed the track, and penetrated the bocage the other side. A pair of STUG III assault guns confronted them, one on each side of the field, tucked in beneath layers of leafy foliage. The Germans were as astonished as they were, and they hightailed back through the tall hedge, looking like small, mobile forests with the branches fastened to their hulls.

The infantry battalions had halted at the first sign of trouble, and they waited for the Shermans to punch a hole in the enemy defenses. A couple of infantry platoons set up a machine gun to cover the field, just in case the Panzergrenadiers showed their faces, but wisely, they stayed back behind cover. A heavy weapons platoon dragged in their mortar and sat down to wait, when Lindbergh's Sherman rolled up to them and he leaned out the turret.

"You men, I want you in that damn field. If I send my tanks in there, they're liable to get shot to pieces by Kraut anti-tank fire. Move your asses, all of you!"

A young captain walked across to him and looked up.

"Colonel, if we go in there, we're liable to get our asses shot to shit. We need your armor to flatten Jerry before we can show our faces."

"Damn you, Captain." Lindbergh stared at him for a few seconds, his face reddening with anger, "I want your men deployed in there on the double. You're holding up the war, Mister, so move it."

With a contemptuous glance at Lindbergh, the Captain passed on the order. Men shuffled up to the thick hedgerow, and a few brave souls went through the gap the tanks had made. The rest found other tiny gaps to squeeze through. There was still no shooting; it was as if the Germans were waiting, which of course they were. The Colonel finally nodded and shouted. "Move out!"

The Major's tank charged through the gap, and he opened fire at the enemy armor. His gunner had loaded

HE, probably thinking of anti-tank gunners. He'd clean forgotten the STUGs, and his shell exploded harmlessly on the armored cupola of one of the assault guns.

Cochise and Minnie Mouse moved up in support and fanned out on either side of the CO to face down the STUGs, not a moment too soon. A German shell glanced off the turret of Morgan's Sherman. Another missed him by inches, and then the American armor went into action. Solly was already taking aim, and with good anticipation, Dale had already loaded AP. Daniel Kuruk fired next, then Grant and Morgan's gunners, but both had targeted the same STUG.

The German assault gun exploded in a sheet of fire, but the second gun was still unscathed. If the commander had stayed cool, he could have destroyed at least two of the American tanks. Instead, he tried to make a run for it. The vehicle began backing out at an awkward angle through the gap in the bocage. The heavy vehicle jammed as the thick, tangled branches clutched at the hull, holding it with the strength of sprung steel.

"Fire!" Grant shouted.

Cochise's gun spat smoke and flame at the same moment, and their shell hit the thick armored mantlet of the gun, to zoom harmlessly off into the hedge. Solly fired next, but the range was too short, too confusing, and his shell smashed into the iron drive wheels inside the track. The STUG couldn't maneuver, but it could still fire.

Grant saw the vehicle move slightly as they took aim. It was pointed at him, and all he could see was a round, black 'O' shape the end of the barrel.

"Solly, hit the fucker. Incoming!"

The enemy 75mm shell smashed into their frontal

armor, three and a half inches of solid steel mantlet. It was the best-protected area of the tank, but it was still vulnerable. Incredibly, the warhead failed to explode.

Some munitions work, and some don't to their job right. Thank Christ for whoever it was in some distant German factory that screwed up that fuse.

This time Solly made no mistake. The STUG had slewed part sideways in the mud and branches during their panicked attempt to escape. His AP shell slammed into the center of the German armor, and a volcano of fire leapt out of the wrecked fighting compartment. It wasn't over, and the field started to come alive with other threats. They'd stumbled onto a main German defensive position, and the fight was by no means finished. Panzergrenadiers appeared as if from nowhere, coming out from behind heavily camouflaged positions.

Grant watched as their infantry did their best to flatten the Panzergrenadiers, but the enemy had it down to a fine art. They'd positioned their guns to give overlapping fields of fire, and the field became a death trap. A light machine gun opened up, and scythed several of the infantrymen to the muddy ground, while the rest ducked back into cover. More machine guns opened up at the back of the field, and their fire swept across the muddy field like a hurricane.

"Solly, load HE, wipe those fuckers off the face of the earth before they kill any more of our boys."

"Roger that."

He fired a snap shot that tore into the thick branches and missed the machine guns by several yards.

"Solly!"

"Sorry. Dale..."

"HE loaded."

"Fire!"

This time there was no mistake, and Grant watched a large chunk of hedgerow blown apart by the shell, together with men who'd been hiding inside it. Fragments of field gray uniforms and shattered steel soar into the air, mingling with the leaves and broken branches. More field gray uniforms appeared, soldiers frantically pushing out a PAK 40 anti-tank gun from behind its camouflaged concealment. Morgan shouted a warning on the Company net, but they were already on it. And then another PAK 40 began to show its ugly snout from the other side.

At the far end of the field, the German machine guns were still firing, pinning down the infantry with their all-important machine guns, which would have made short work of the guns. It was a well-planned and timed ambush, and it would have succeeded if they hadn't hit the STUGs so fast.

"Charlie Company, follow me," Morgan shouted.

Angel went to full speed, and he ducked inside the turret to escape the fury of the machine gunners, doing their best to target him. Solly fired HE that narrowly missed one PAK 40, and the shell exploded harmlessly inside the thick bocage. Morgan fired, and the other gun disappeared in a fury of smoke and flame. But the remaining gun was still firing, and they managed to score a hit on Cochise.

Kuruk and his crew bailed out of the burning tank, and Grant realized he was counting them, even as he was directing Minnie to attack the enemy gun.

Four men, five, yes, they're all out.

Solly fired, and the back pressure from the propellant charge filled the tank with choking fumes even as the extractors fought to clear the air. There was no explosion.

He heard Solly's roar of anger.

"It's a fucking dud! Dale, load another, fast."

They were nearing the enemy gun, and Grant watched as the gunners laid the barrel of their piece to face Minnie. There wasn't time for another shot. They'd be dead long before Dale extracted the dud and slammed in another HE round. There was only one thing they could do.

"Angel, ram the bastard."

"You got it," came the laconic reply. He smiled, somehow the driver managed to remain calm when everyone was panicking. Probably thinking about his pizza shop.

The Germans fired, and the shell slammed into Minnie's 76mm frontal armor. The steel held, although the enormous vibration of the blast sent their ears ringing, like they were standing in the bell tower of a Gothic cathedral during bell-ringing practice. He watched the Germans hasten to reload. They were SS Panzergrenadiers he noted, with the distinctive leopard-pattern camouflage.

Like those poor Russians we captured, except the Russians will live.

Two seconds later, Minnie smashed into the gun. The Sherman reared up on the broken remains of Krupp steel and gray clad bodies, and Angel drove straight through and into the next field. Two hundred yards away a new enemy waited for them. More Krupp steel, fifty-four tons of it. Vernon shouted the warning, the one word they'd been dreading, and this time no one contradicted him.

"Tiger!"

* * *

Three kilometers outside Saint-Lo, 16.22, July 3, 1944

It was glorious to be part of such a mighty armored force. It was true he'd been at Kursk, and there were more tanks on that battlefield than in the entire history of armored warfare. But this was different. Tiger Is were at Kursk, but the much vaunted Panthers had performed badly, and most limped off the battlefield with mechanical problems. Those problems were now resolved, and in addition, they had a couple of the new Tiger IIs. The mighty King Tigers.

They had even more reason to feel confident. The 12th SS Panzers Hitler Jugend was today a support unit to the awesome power of Panzer Lehr, the so-called 'Schoolmasters.' The tankers who'd trained the best tank crews in the Third Reich. These men knew every trick in the book, and then some. The 101st SS Heavy Panzers was part of their force, the unit that included SS Obersturmfuhrer Michael Wittmann's Tiger. Even though their numbers were less than they'd hoped, due to losses from Allied bombing raids, salvos of shells from warships off the French Coast, and the Fireflies.

Even so, today will be different. Today we will tear into the Allies and rip them to shreds. We are unbeatable! Providing our engine keeps running, the engagement doesn't go on so long we run out of precious fuel, and we have enough shells.

He thumbed the mike switch.

"Franz, how is the engine? Any problems?"

"None, Obersturmfuhrer. She's running as sweet as a prostitute's smile."

He smiled.

At the age of seventeen, it's unlikely he's ever been with a prostitute. If things go badly over the next few days, the chances are he never will.

"Keep it like that, driver. We don't want to make fools of ourselves in front of Panzer Lehr, even less with Obersturmfuhrer Wittman. How about gasoline?"

A pause. "The tanks are half full. That was all they'd give us."

"Understood."

He switched to the command net and almost immediately heard the Standartenfuhrer's voice in his headphones.

"This is Meyer. You know what we're up against. The Allies are heading for Saint-Lo. Without doubt they intend to take the town and open the door to the rest of France. Our job is to stop them, our 12th SS HJ with 101st SS Heavy Panzers and Panzer Lehr. We also have units of Panzergrenadiers to strengthen our battle group, so we should make mincemeat of the enemy. Do your duty, men, and we'll send these so-called Allies back into the sea. The Fuhrer has every confidence in us and expects a historic victory. Hals und Beinbruch!"

Incredibly, he'd placed a gramophone close to the mike, and they heard the strains of the Panzer Lied across the radio net. It was crackly, the quality poor, but it nonetheless made him feel proud.

When before us a hostile tank appears,
Full throttle is given and we close with the enemy.
What does our life matter but for the Reich's army? Yes, Reich's army.
To die for Germany is our highest honor.'

"I don't want to die," he heard Lenz complain.

"Not for the Fuhrer, Siegfried?" Heinrich Boll taunted him, "We thought that was the peak of your ambition, to die for the Fuhrer, and for Germany."

"I want to live for the Fuhrer, and for Germany," he whined.

"Too bad. You'd better give Adolf a call. I reckon the enemy intends to kill us all."

Lenz snorted in derision. "You're just joking, Heinrich. You don't seriously believe the Allies can beat such an armored battlegroup as we have here?"

"The Soviets managed quite well at Kursk, so I understand. And the British and the Amis have given us a damn good kicking in Normandy. How many Tiger and Panthers have we seen destroyed? Scores of them."

"We won a mighty victory at Kursk," he objected, "You were there, isn't that so, Obersturmfuhrer?" Lenz asked. He sounded even younger than usual. Pleading for reassurance.

Rolf thought about how he could phrase his reply.

It's true; this battlegroup is impressive, but so was it at Kursk. Did they win there? Berlin says yes, but they left a lot of good men and tanks on the battlefield. Who are the current owners of Kursk and the land for hundreds of miles around? It isn't the Third Reich. Will it be any different here?

"Kursk was...complicated," he replied carefully. The specter of Lenz's cousin, SD Standartenfuhrer Schulz, was always hovering in the background, "But you can be certain today we'll hit the Allies hard." He attempted to inject some humor into the conversation. "Perhaps we should consider going into the scrap business. There'll be plenty of metal to trade after today."

"There you are," he told Boll, "We're going to kick their asses today. Obersturmfuhrer Manhausen said so."

"He said nothing of the sort!" Boll snapped back.

"He did..."

"Cut it out, all of you. We're about to move out, so attend to your duties."

In the event, it was almost an hour before they were ready, after last minute delays and breakdowns. He saw the lead tanks of Panzer Lehr heading out toward Saint-Lo. They were not all Panthers and Tigers; many were the older Panzer IVs. Updated and modified from the early days, to be sure. But still, they were terribly vulnerable even to medium tanks, like the Shermans and British Cromwells. The Tigers of the 101st followed, and then Meyer gave the order.

"12th SS, advance!"

He called Franz, "Driver, advance." Then he thought of Lenz's relative, the SD man. It wouldn't do any harm to spout some propaganda, and it might even keep him off their backs, "Today, we will give the Fuhrer and Germany an epic victory. Sieg Heil!"

The shout echoed through the interior of the Tiger. Boll managed to make it sound mocking, but what the hell. Lenz wasn't subtle enough to pick it up.

They deployed before Saint-Lo, using the vast swathes of bocage to hide them from enemy aircraft. Manhausen's Tiger was assigned to wait in ambush with a screen of STUGs and Panzergrenadiers in the next field. When the shooting started, he gave the order to load AP, and they waited as smoke and flames erupted into the sky on the other side of the thick hedgerow.

He ached to go through and engage the enemy, but his orders were to wait in ambush. The Maybach engine was ticking over, and after the exchange of shots, he heard the roar of a tank engine going to maximum revolutions, and then a main gun appeared in the gap in the hedgerow. A second later the familiar high sloped deck appeared. He grabbed for the microphone.

"Sherman!"

* * *

Three miles North of Saint-Lo, 17.55, July 3, 1944

"Driver, back up, back up!"

Angel stopped the heavy vehicle so quickly he was thrown forward in the turret. The huge 88mm shell intended for them whistled across their front. A second later they were hurtling back through the hedgerow. The Tiger fired again, and the shell was so close Grant felt the passage of air as it sped past them, to land in the field several hundred yards away. Then they were out of sight. Out of sight until the German heavy tank punched through the hedgerow to find them. He searched for a way out and saw the gap made by the now-destroyed STUG crew for their retreat.

"Angel, three o'clock, the gap next to the wrecked STUG. Take it!"

"I'm on it."

He gritted his teeth as they bumped over the muddy, rutted field. At any second, the Tiger would come through that hedgerow, and they'd be dead meat. Vernon was as ecstatic about being proved right, as he was terrified.

"I told you! A fucking Tiger, I knew it. A Tiger!"

"Shut up, Vern," they all chorused.

Their turret was pointed backward as they watched for

the enemy tank. Their 75mm gun presented little danger to the Germans, unless they got lucky. Minnie entered the field the other side.

"Jesus Christ," Solly exclaimed, "It's like a fucking car park."

"A tank park," Angel breathed.

"A German tank park," Vern corrected him, "Fuck me! Tigers!"

There were more than Tigers in the swathe of ground that stretched ahead of them, Panthers, Panzer IVs, and something else. The new, much vaunted Tiger IIs, a pair of them; sloped armor, huge, and menacing, their 88mm guns and massive armor able to dominate any armored confrontation. There had to be at least thirty tanks inside of a single square mile. He wanted to shout to Angel, 'Get us out of here.' Except behind them that Tiger was coming up fast.

The 745th Independent Tank Battalion resolved the dilemma for them. For once, Lindbergh came through.

"I'll be damned," he shouted to no one in particular. A company of Shermans broke through the hedgerow, and then another company, and another; until the entire Battalion was charging down the formidable German armored force. Lindbergh's M4 was in the lead, guidons streaming from the radio aerials. The turrets of the German armor begin rotating to face the enemy, and he held his breath, waiting for the inevitable slaughter of the 745th.

The next few minutes were a wild blur of movement, smoke and flame, and ear-shattering noise. The Panthers opened fire first. They were nearest to the 745th, and within seconds, three Shermans of Lindbergh's Battalion were destroyed. The American tanks returned fire, but there was no evidence to suggest they'd scored any substantial hits. Grant was mentally shouting at the Americans, "Pull back, pull back. Get out of there!"

Maybe Lindbergh was lucky, or maybe he'd arranged it in advance. It was probably the former. The fighters swooped, squadron after squadron of RAF Typhoons. One second, they'd faced devastating defeat, the next, it all changed. The German armor saw the threat and panicked. The menacing rows of heavy guns aimed at Lindbergh's Battalion swung away as the Panzers pedaled the gas. They didn't all make it.

"Angel, tuck her in close to the hedgerow. We'll stay here and watch in case they need us."

They hid in a patch of shade beneath the overhanging branches of a tree that grew right through the hedge. He opened the turret hatch and popped his head out. Solly emerged to join him. More rockets slammed into the retreating tanks, and the field was covered in roiling black smoke as they exploded, first a Panther, then two Panzer IVs. A Tiger vaporized as the gas tank exploded, and then more Typhoons attacked with cannons hammering to mop up the survivors.

"Most of 'em are getting away," Solly shouted, venting his anger that the hated Jew murderers may escape justice.

"Not all of them. The flyboys will be back with reinforcements. The heavy Panzers don't normally come out in the day, and when they do, they're juicy targets. Wait and watch."

They came over a minute later; first, eight Republic P-47 Thunderbolts, the big, heavy United States Army Air Force fighter bombers that had proved effective in a variety of roles. These P-47s were loaded with bombs, each aircraft capable of carrying more than a ton of ordnance. They rained on the Panzers, who by now were funneling through a gap in the hedgerow almost a mile away. The bocage, so impenetrable at ground level, was no obstacle in the air. The first bomb dropped, missed, and exploded close to a racing Panther. The pilot roared away to go around for a second attack, and the Thunderbolt behind him dropped another load. This time he scored a direct hit on the German, the gas tank exploded almost instantly, and searing flames swept through the vehicle.

"Fucking A," Solly cheered, "Another Kraut ain't gonna bother us, a Tiger, too. Vern will be happy about that one."

Grant didn't feel like exulting. He'd watched for the crew to bail out, but no one escaped the burning Tiger. He tried to envisage the unimaginable hell they must have gone through when the gas tank exploded.

If this is war, it's time mankind thought out a different way to resolve their differences.

The Thunderbolts were coming in one by one, dropping their bombs and zooming back up into the sky. The field was littered with burning armor, and then the bombers arrived to finish the job. Mitchells, B-25s, twin engine aircraft in RAF livery. More bombs dropped around the fleeing Germans, and five more smoking hulls blazed amongst the devastation.

Lindbergh's Company commanders recovered fast from the shock of the encounter. The Colonel was left floundering as they took the opportunity and charged in. The Shermans started to dish out some hurt to the retreating Germans. Solly chuckled in glee as a 75mm shell smashed into the rear of a Panther, and it came to a stop with smoke pouring from the engine compartment.

"Someone ought to tell those boys about turning and running from a Sherman. It's all we need to roast their asses."

"Yeah," Grant nodded, but something was nagging at his mind. It came to him in a flash. The Tiger, the reason they'd come through here in the first place. If he were running, they'd have a shot at his engine compartment.

"Driver, take us back through that gap in the hedge. Solly, get downstairs. We're about to see if we can put a shell up that Kraut's backside."

"You got it."

"Heads up, guys. We only get one chance at this, so make sure when we come up behind him, we hit him hard and fast before he gets in the first shot."

"Load AP," Solly intoned.

"AP loaded," Dale confirmed.

"A fucking Tiger! Damn, that's something to tell the grandkids," Vern shouted in glee.

"We haven't got him yet. Shut up and concentrate on fighting this tank."

Angel smashed through the thick bocage, but it was an anti-climax.

"Where is he?" Solly sounded puzzled, "Sarge, he must have hightailed it."

"Wouldn't you, with half the American and British Air Force dropping bombs and rocks on his head."

"I guess."

"Target, twelve o'clock." It was Angel who saw him first, "It's a Tiger. He's disappearing through the hedgerow."

At first he couldn't see him, but Grant took out his binoculars, and sure enough, he was there and running, with his ass toward them.

"Well spotted, Angel. Full speed, let's nail this bastard."

"He could put a shell into us before we get close. There could be a better way."

It was Dale who made the observation.

"I'm listening."

"We stalk him, and stay well back where he can't see us, until we can creep up on him. Then we let him have it. Injun style, that's what Dan Kuruk would have done."

He smiled. The implication Kuruk was an Indian bushwhacker didn't mean it wasn't a good plan.

"Angel, follow him, but stay well back. If he spots us, we're toast."

"Yeah, I kinda get that."

They plunged on across the field, slowing at the gap in the next hedgerow, and then stopping while Grant climbed down to check on the progress of their target. Each time they were a few hundred yards away. He remounted Minnie, and Angel eased through the gap and waited until the Tiger was again out of sight. A mile away, the battle still raged as Lindbergh's Shermans chased down the surviving heavy armor. He had a few misgivings about whether he was doing the right thing. The Colonel was clear after the arrest. Stick with the Battalion.

Except this is THE Tiger.

He knew it, was convinced of it. For him, the Battle for Normandy had condensed into this single tussle between two metal machines. It was as if the Gods of War had decreed the war would be decided between these two tanks.

A stupid thought, he chided himself. *Or is it? What soldier doesn't have some kind of weird superstition on the eve of battle?*

Men carry a rabbit's foot, St Christopher medallions, even a pair of the girlfriend's panties. I know of one guy who carried around a tame spider called Alex in a glass jar. He said it brought him luck.

"I lost him," Angel interrupted his thoughts. He slowed to a crawl.

Grant realized he'd been daydreaming about the Tiger, about the fate that had pulled them together from the first day they landed on Omaha. He jerked back to the present, to reality.

"What do you mean, you lost him?"

"I mean he's just not here. He's gone."

Grant surveyed the area around them with his binoculars. Angel was right. He'd gone. The entire region was a wilderness of high hedgerows, sunken roads, enough to lose a division of Panzers. No place to play touchy feely with a Tiger. Besides, he could hear the battle raging less than a mile away. Hammering machine guns, the crack of infantry rifles, and the bellow of tank guns and artillery. There'd be time to meet Mr. Tiger later.

"Swing her around. We'll rejoin the Battalion."

"You got it."

As they drove toward the crescendo of the battle that raged for Saint-Lo, he kept looking around.

He was HERE. I can feel him out there. Somewhere.

* * *

1 kilometer Southwest of Saint-Lo, 17.55, July 3, 1944

They sheltered in the sunken lane, and they'd been lucky to find it. He'd wanted to turn and finish the impudent Sherman that had bugged them for so long. Until Schelling, the driver, called him.

"I'm sorry, Obersturmfuhrer. It's the engine again."

"What now, Franz?"

"It's running too hot, Sir. If we keep going, it could seize the pistons. We have to stop and let her cool."

He felt his anger mount. They nearly had him, that damned grinning mouse painted on the side of the hull. He could even see it, blasted by an 88mm shell.

"For Christ's sake, when are you going to fix it?"

"We need a new engine, Sir. I keep telling you, this one is kaput."

"We don't have a new engine, Franz. You know why."

A silence. It was frustrating; while the Reich produced new, sophisticated weapons like the V1 and V2 rockets, they couldn't send replacement engines and other vital spares to their heavy Panzers in the field. He looked around, then looked down and spotted the sunken road. It was almost impossible to see unless you were virtually next to it, like now. He pointed it out to Franz.

"Very well, take us down there, and we'll let her cool for an hour. The rest of you stay sharp. If that Sherman finds, us, we'll need to open fire before he runs rings around us."

Franz eased the big tank into the narrow, sunken lane. It was only when they were out sight he realized the sides of the gully were so high they blocked the ability of the main gun to traverse.

If the American finds us now, God help us.

* * *

Gestapo Headquarters, Isigny, 18.35, July 3, 1944

Her body was a mass of pain. Every limb, every bone ached after the sadistic SS man Bachmann had finished beating her. He was an expert, and although she'd tried to endure the blows in silence, she soon reached a point where she had no alternative but to cry out. She screamed in agony. It was like a fire burning inside her. There was no respite; she was bound to a long, steel table, and he used a rubber truncheon mercilessly.

When she refused to cooperate, he injected something into her leg, and if she thought the pain had been bad, she knew it was nothing compared to what burned inside her.

"What information did you give to the enemy?" he intoned, for the tenth time. "Who are you reporting to? When will the Americans attack?"

"I don't know. I only cooked some food, no more."

"Where will the attack come? Do they have a date?"

"I don't know..."

Deep down, she suspected Bachmann was aware she had no information to give. But as long as she refused to answer his questions, it gave him the excuse, if one were needed, to torture her. She jerked as she felt his hand reaching inside her panties and groping her vagina.

"Leave her!" Father Bouchet shouted through his smashed teeth. They'd left him in chains, so he could watch. Every time they beat him, they also made certain her head was turned to watch his suffering.

Pervert!

She hadn't meant to say it aloud, but his free hand punched her hard in the kidneys, and she screamed again.

"You should be careful who you call a pervert, Caron.

You have little time left to you. I suggest you consider how you wish to spend your final hours. You can go to your death in peace free from pain, or in screaming, unbearable agony. It's up to you."

"I don't know anything."

In the end, he snapped an order to a guard waiting outside the cell, and he returned with another guard, dragging a heavy wooden bar between them. She wondered what fresh agonies she had to endure now, but the priest recognized it, and she saw his eyes close, as he understood what they meant to do to him. The bar had metal rings that suspended it from iron staples set high on the wall. They fetched a wooden stepladder, and then dragged the priest over to the beam. They carried him up, and one man held his hand while the other drove a nail through his hand into the beam.

Bouchet was whimpering in agony, and Margot wracked her brains for anything she could tell them that may ease his suffering. But she knew nothing. They left him hanging and screaming, and came back a few minutes later with another length of wood, which they propped against the wall below his dangling body. They then proceeded to nail his ankles to the vertical timber. He was quietly whimpering, and Margot suspected his mind had almost gone.

"What do you think of that?" Bachmann leered, "A priest suffering the same fate as the Jesus he worships. He should be honored, should he not?"

"You're sick!" she spat out, "You should be put down like an animal."

She thought he'd strike her again, and she'd gone beyond caring. Instead, he laughed.

"So now you know where you stand, Caron. You probably think I'm some kind of sadistic psychopath? Of course, you're probably right. The Third Reich has need of men such as me. Bold, brave men, men who are unafraid to get their hands dirty. The Fuhrer himself said that 'Everyone must know if he raises his hand against the State, then certain death is his lot.' I am merely an instrument of the Fuhrer's will, protecting Germany from enemies such as you and this priest."

By now, Bouchet had lapsed into unconsciousness.

"Why don't you kill us now?" she cried, "You must know I have no information to give you. If you're so bold and brave, finish this and go out and fight the real enemy, the Allies who are in process of liberating France."

He stared at her, wearing a puzzled expression. "But, my dear, do you wish to ruin my enjoyment? You're lucky. Your sentence has been delayed for now. You are to be taken to Saint-Lo presently for more intensive interrogation, so let's not waste your remaining time here."

He snapped out an order to the guard standing near the crucified priest. "Toss some water over him and bring him round. We'll start again."

CHAPTER NINE

Five kilometers outside Caen, 07.30, July 11, 1944

Captain Gunter Sturm had yet another bad night, tossing and turning in his bed at the Ardenne Abbey. It wasn't just the trucks racing in and out of Headquarters as they began to evacuate everything of strategic importance. Nor the smell of burning as frightened men began destroying the evidence of their crimes.

It was the idea that the side he fought on comprised of sadists, bullies, and murderers that gave him nightmares. He hadn't enjoyed a peaceful moment since he'd seen the Canadians shot down in front of his eyes by the SS. The knowledge that the French girl he'd saved, Margot Caron, was a captive of the Sicherheitsdienst weighed on his mind. When he learned she had a sentence of death over her head, he wanted to find Scharfuhrer Bachmann and shoot him down like a dog.

He felt so helpless, utterly helpless. If he could reach Saint-Lo where they now held her in the Gestapo prison, perhaps he could intervene and save her. But how could he abandon his post and travel across a battlefield without orders. They'd shoot him as a deserter. There had to be some other way.

He was finishing dressing when a knock sounded on the door.

"Hereinkommen."

A messenger entered, a private soldier, not SS. Sturm recognized him as one of the decoding teams who worked in the Army signals office. Like most of them, he was bedraggled, unshaven, and looked as if he hadn't slept for a long time.

"The Standartenfuhrer sends his greetings, Sir. You are to report to him immediately. He is in his office."

"Very well. Tell him I will be there in a few moments."

"Yes, Sir."

The man left, and he finished dressing. He briefly considered having a shave. After all, he was a member of the German Officer Corps. It wouldn't hurt to show an SS thug like Meyer how a soldier should present himself. In the end, he decided not to bother. It would give the impression he hadn't been busy like the rest of them, scurrying around, preparing to evacuate like frightened rabbits. So much for the much vaunted Waffen-SS, and their Fuhrer's promises of total victory.

As he walked down the staircase, he wondered if he'd done something wrong.

Am I in trouble for something I said?

The Gestapo and the SD were everywhere, rooting out so-called plots and insurrection. Most soldiers called it bullshit. They were trying to fight a war, not start a revolution. Meyer's door was open, and he went in.

"You wanted to speak to me, Sir.

"Yes, Captain Sturm. I want you to take a dispatch to Headquarters in Saint-Lo. The Allies are massing their armor and infantry around the town. Find out what resources they need to hold the town, but tell them we're stretched very thin. I must release some of my armored units to Caen. Otherwise we'll have nothing to hold them back, apart from a few lousy battalions of Ostvolk. Get over there right away."

"Yes, Sir, but, why not use the radio? Is there a problem?"

Meyer chuckled. "A problem? Every time I give an order over the radio for one of my companies to move to a new position, the British send in their aircraft to attack and destroy them as soon as they reach it, or even on the way. It's as if they can read our messages. I don't want to give away our order of battle, Sturm."

"No, Sir. But surely, the Enigma encryption system is unbreakable."

"The Enigma encryption system, yes. How do we know the Allies have not cracked our codes?"

"That's impossible! The Enigma uses millions, billions of alternative combinations. They cannot have cracked it."

"So how do you explain them knowing our plans, even before we do and put them into action? And only when we send the messages over the radio, using Enigma encryption."

The enormity of what Meyer was telling suddenly hit him. "Sir, if that's true, no matter where we go or what we do, they'll be waiting to destroy us."

"Exactly. That's what they're already doing."

"Standartenfuhrer, have you informed Headquarters of your suspicions?"

"They're not suspicions, Meyer, they're certainties. Yes, I have informed them. I have also informed Feldmarschal Rommel, Feldmarschal Rundstedt, even the Reichsfuhrer-SS, Heinrich Himmler. All to no avail, they said the same as you; it is impossible."

"And yet they are doing it."

"Of course. There is no other explanation."

He felt despondent. "This means we cannot even force a negotiated peace. There is no need for them to negotiate when they can forecast our every move."

Meyer grinned. "Now you know the truth, Sturm, you see we have lost the war, do you not?"

Sturm didn't answer. To say no to a question like that from an SS officer was tantamount to putting his pistol to his head. Meyer smiled at his silence.

"I understand why you will not answer, but of course you know we've lost. You think me cynical?"

"Of course not, Sir."

He bellowed a laugh. "I know I'm cynical, Sturm. I've had enough of trying to get our High Command to see sense. They're too busy squabbling for Adolf's favor to listen. As for our glorious Fuhrer, sometimes I wonder about his sanity."

Sturm walked over to the door and pushed it shut. Meyer chuckled.

"Good man. We don't want anyone hearing the truth, do we?"

"So why do we fight on, Sir?"

"Because we're soldiers, Sturm. This is what they pay us for, to fight and die for Fuhrer and Fatherland. It's glorious, isn't it? The Great Game."

Not glorious for those prisoners you ordered to be shot,

Standartenführer.

"If you say so, Sir."

"I do. Go to Saint-Lo, and find out what they need." He handed him a sealed envelope, "You may also deliver this to the Commanding Officer, SS Headquarters in Saint-Lo. Take a Kubelwagen, but watch out for enemy aircraft."

"Yes, Sir."

He walked out of Headquarters and found a Feldwebel in the transport section who reluctantly parted with one of the VW derived vehicles. As he drove away, he felt exultant. They'd sent him to the very place he wanted to go. All he needed now was to locate Margot Caron. He'd saved her once from American deserters. Now he needed to save her from his own people.

As he drove past flooded fields, burned out tanks and trucks with corpses lying alongside, unburied and unmourned, he wondered at himself. Why had this quest to save Margot Caron become such an obsession? He was a Wehrmacht officer, fighting a rearguard action against an overwhelming host of invading American, British, and Canadian troops. Some said there were also French troops pouring ashore. Yet he felt bound to concentrate his efforts on saving this one French girl.

The answer was simple. It wasn't just that she was pretty. No, it was more than that. When he'd saved her from the deserters, she became his responsibility. It was as if fate had placed him there at that particular time and place. As if his entire war had distilled into this single effort to salvage some common decency amidst the slaughter and outright murder.

Save Margot Caron, and he may save something of the soul of humanity with this single act. Saving Margot

Caron would go some way toward saving his own soul.

Is that a good enough reason to go to such lengths? I am prepared to give my life if necessary. Yes, it is enough.

Satisfied he'd put it straight in his mind, he drove on through the war-ravaged countryside toward Saint-Lo to free Margot Caron, or die in the attempt. An hour later, he swerved into a ruined barn as enemy armor appeared in the distance. They hadn't seen him, but they drove past his hiding place and stopped less than half a kilometer away. His route to Saint-Lo was now completely blocked. He camouflaged the Kubelwagen with bales of hay and broken pieces of farm machinery, and settled down to wait.

* * *

Five miles outside Saint-Lo, 07.30, July 11, 1944

On the way to Saint-Lo they'd passed a litter of destroyed armor. German armor, for the most part, and the majority had fallen victim to a succession of Allied air attacks. They were forced to stop at one time and take a break while an engineer unit bulldozed a couple of tangled wrecks aside to clear the road.

"Where the hell is their Air Force, the Luftwaffe?" Dale asked as they drove past the wrecked Panzers, "I mean, we were told they were this elite kickass outfit. So what are they up to, letting our bombers blast the crap out of their Panzers? Not that I'm complaining," he added hastily. "It's just strange. Like, do they know something we don't?"

"Like there're a few million Russians chasing their Nazi asses on the Eastern Front?" Solly grinned.

"Yeah, it could be that," he nodded his head, "If they're over there, they're not over here."

"Right."

"Fucking Tigers are over here," Dale asserted grimly, "You all laughed, but you saw that damn great tank. That wasn't any kind of a joke. Clever, too, the way he disappeared."

"Why would he do that?" Grant mused, more to himself. He'd been thinking about where the Tiger had disappeared to, what did they have to fear from a Sherman? He could have turned his turret through a hundred and eighty degrees and shot the shit out of them.

So why didn't he do it? Weird.

They stiffened as a jeep rolled up and halted next to them. A general was sitting inside, and he didn't look too happy.

"Sergeant, what're you men doing here? Are you part of the 745th?"

"Yes, Sir."

"Where've you been?"

Grant shrugged. "Here and there." He wanted to say, 'Fighting a war,' but he thought better of it.

"Why aren't you with your battalion? My men are getting shot to pieces while you sit here in the sun drinking coffee."

They hadn't seen any sun, not for several days, just a persistent, damp drizzle. And they weren't drinking coffee, although if that had any, they would have.

"We're waiting for the road to clear, General."

He pointed at the engineers toiling in the rain, their slickers gleaming as it fell on them in torrents. The General glared at the bulldozers, as if they were inventing an excuse. "As soon as it's clear, you join your unit. Have you seen any action yet?"

He thought about the brush with the heavy Panzers and their pursuit of the Tiger. They'd fought several actions since against entrenched Panzergrenadiers, including STUGs and anti-tank artillery, even a unit of Fallschirmjager who'd fought like demons.

"Some."

"Some." The General stared at him, "Define some, Sergeant." His voice sounded dangerous.

Grant gave him a rough estimate of the men and armor they'd destroyed, and the General managed to look impressed.

"You can back up those figures?"

"It's all in the log, Sir."

He licked his lips but eventually decided they were on the level. He even managed to smile.

"You've done well. Catch up with your Company. We're about to renew the attack on Saint-Lo. See if you can kill a few more of those Krauts."

"We will, Sir."

"That's the spirit. Carry on."

He leapt back into his jeep and drove away. Senior officers were more used to the bigger, more luxurious Dodge Command Cars, with comfortable seats and a quieter more powerful engine. Problem was, the Jerries knew that, too. They saw a Dodge Command Car, and they'd let all hell loose in an effort to kill it; after too many losses amongst senior officers, most decided to rough it in Willys jeeps.

"What was all that about?" Dale asked, watching the jeep disappear in the direction of Saint-Lo.

"I think that was the officer in command of VIII Corps, General Troy H Middleton," Grant told him.

"What did he want?"

"He wants Saint-Lo, I guess. That's where we're all headed."

The engineer shouted across to them and waved. The road was clear enough for a Sherman to drive through. They mounted up, and he gave the order for Angel to drive away toward Saint-Lo.

* * *

Three miles outside Saint-Lo, 09.30, July 11, 1944

There was no need for directions; flames lighted the countryside ahead of them as the battle for Saint-Lo got into gear. Angel headed for the columns of smoke that decorated the sky. As they drew nearer, they began to encounter the wrecks of American vehicles, and the reason for the destruction quickly became obvious. The first indication of trouble was the whistling noise in the air.

"Incoming!"

He ducked inside the turret and secured the hatch. Solly was already looking for a target, but when he found it, it was way out of range, a low hill commanding the approaches to the town. The shell exploded four hundred yards away, and Grant decided to take a look outside.

He threw open the hatch and looked in the direction of the hill.

The town will be a bastard to take, no question.

Protected by marshy ground and flooded fields, the

hillside sparkled with the flash of explosions as the German defenses threw out a curtain of heavy fire. He checked his map for the location of the biggest concentration of enemy guns. Hill 192.

Even as he looked at the surrounding countryside, he knew it'd be a hard job. The River Vire wound its way past the town, a natural line of defense. The Germans had flooded yet more fields, and the maze of bocage was a formidable defensive position. Of one thing he was sure, they were going to take a number of losses before they entered the town.

The rain still fell in constant miserable, cold sheets, destroying visibility and making the ground underfoot treacherous for the infantry who'd need to take the town. The hull of Minnie Mouse was slick and shiny, as if she'd been coated with gloss paint. In the sky the clouds were low, making air operations difficult, if not impossible. Any aircraft approaching would have to fly straight and low, right into the clusters of AA guns the enemy had sited around the town.

A bastard, no question!

He gave the order to advance, and they continued toward the devastation. An MP sergeant was directing traffic at an intersection, his face a mask of misery as he endured the pouring rain, with water streaming from his helmet and rubber poncho. They stopped to ask directions, and at first he glared at them.

"Are you the guys supposed to be taking that town?"

Grant nodded. "What of it?"

"Get a move on and get it done. I'm freezing my butt off out here while you boys travel in luxury inside those tin cans. Give that message to the guy in charge."

"Yeah, that should impress him. I'll be sure to mention it."

"You do that."

The MP pointed to a turning a couple of hundred yards further along the road.

"You turn in there, and you'll find them a few hundred yards along that lane. Can't miss 'em."

"Thanks."

"Don't mention it."

As they drove away, Grant looked back and saw him trying to light a cigarette. After a half dozen attempts, he cursed and threw it into the mud.

I pity the poor bloody infantry going up that hill.

Lindbergh was near the entrance to Battalion HQ, reaming out one of his company commanders, so he ignored them when they drove in. Probably he didn't realize they'd been missing again. They saw found Morgan's pitiful remnant of a company, two tanks, at the far corner. Dan Kuruk had managed to find yet another replacement Sherman; this one patched together after the crew perished when an AP shell exploded inside the hull. He came out to greet them, his dark, Indian face a picture of misery in the pouring rain.

"You made it back."

"Yeah, we had a disagreement with a Tiger."

"At least you're alive to tell the tale."

"Amen to that. They gave you another Sherman, I see."

He nodded. "The engineers patched her up, and it took us a couple of hours to wash away the blood from inside." He grimaced, "At least she'll keep us out of the rain."

He thought of that MP. "Right. Where's the Major?"

"He's with Lindbergh. Didn't you see him when you

came in? Our fearless leader is giving orders for the first attack. That'll be inside the next couple of hours. The 29th are going in, and we're their support."

"What're we up against?"

Dan shrugged. "The usual. Panzergrenadiers, our Intel suggests they have a couple of companies of heavy Panzers, and three or four rifle battalions. Enough to make it tough, you saw the approaches to the town on the way in?"

"I did. I only wish the rain would stop for the footsloggers."

"Don't we all. That muddy hill dominates the line of attack, and the infantry has to go that way. The moment they start, all hell's gonna break loose."

He stopped as Morgan walked toward them. He was smiling, although he looked tired.

"Where've you been this time? Chasing another Tiger?"

"Same one, Major."

"How can you tell?"

He shrugged. "I just know, Sir."

"Hmm. I've been having a row with Colonel Lindbergh. He's upset I keep losing tanks. He wanted to assign me to Headquarters Company, I guess so he could keep an eye on me. He didn't believe I had three Shermans left until I saw you roll in. You know we're about to move out?"

"I do, Sir. Dan told me."

He nodded, and they looked across to Kuruk's battered replacement. One of his crew was holding a poncho to ward off the rain while Dan painted the name on the turret.

"He's calling it Cochise again. I'm not sure it's lucky," Morgan muttered.

"They're alive, Sir. That's all the luck we need out here."

"I guess you're right. Grab some chow, and make sure you're ready to leave in," he looked at his watch, "an hour and forty minutes."

"Yes, Major."

They located a fuel bowser and filled Minnie with gas. To give Lindbergh his due, the Battalion had worked a miracle and brought up plenty of fuel and ammo to fill the empty tanks. Grant wondered if he'd missed his forte, a job in logistics. Behind the canvas-covered shelter, they could see many more drums of fuel, readied for the coming battle. There was another pile of stores further back, covered by a heavy tarpaulin. They were not drums of gas. These were coffins and bales of rubber body bags. As essential for the business of war as shells, bullets, and gas.

They heard the shouted orders, and the noise of engines starting up, plumes of smoke from the exhausts venting into the air, the stench of the fumes. Morgan's voice came over the Company net.

"A Company, prepare to move out."

"Three tanks, some fuckin' Company," Vern sneered from inside, "We..." His voice was drowned as Angel started up the big, 400 horsepower Continental air-cooled gas engine.

Grant watched the Major's Sherman move out and gave the order.

"Driver, move out."

They made it less than five hundred yards from the assembly point before the German artillery found them. A couple of shells smashed into the ground around them, and then the battle became a bloodfest. A German shell found a Sherman that became a smoking pyre. The infantry slogged through the mud, slipping and sliding on the treacherous hillside, keeping low to avoid the shrapnel. Grant began to wonder if this was the way to go about taking the town after whole platoons of infantry fell victim to the remorseless gunfire, and yet the Germans were too far out of range to hit back. The cloud base was still too low for effective air support, and at first it looked as if they'd beaten off the attack before they'd even got half way.

An enormous explosion sounded only yards away from inside an apple orchard they were driving past, and then another explosion, and another. He glanced through the trees and glimpsed the American artillery returning fire. A battery of 105 mm M2A1 howitzers had gone into action. Seconds later they were joined by two other batteries. The high explosive shells, each weighing thirty-five pounds, began to hammer at the enemy position up on the hill with a huge, rolling barrage. The noise was deafening. Each M2A1 was capable of a rate of fire of fifteen shells a minute, and the top of Hill 192 was wreathed in smoke and flames, almost like an erupting volcano.

From the infantry huddled in muddy ditches, he heard a mighty cheer. The men clambered out of their trenches and foxholes, even from behind stout trees where they'd been sheltering, and resumed their advance. Angel drove on, and behind them the howitzers continued to pound their targets.

Soon, they were leading a bunch of infantrymen, who used the bulk of Minnie for cover from the bullet and shrapnel filled slopes. Every hedgerow on the approaches had been turned into a strongpoint, and they had to be destroyed before they could advance further. Minnie led the way, and Angel smashed their Sherman through hedgerows twice the height of the tank, using the Culin device attached to the front.

They emerged into one muddy field, and an anti-tank rocked missed the hull by little more than a yard. The shooters were too slow to get out of sight, and Grant saw the movement three quarters of the way down the field as they disappeared into the hedge.

He grabbed the .50 caliber and fired a curtain of heavy slugs that sanitized the entire area. He'd no idea if he'd hit them or not, but no more rockets came from that direction. He thumbed the transmit button.

"Solly, keep her loaded with HE, and watch out for the heavy machine guns. They're here somewhere close by."

"You don't reckon they'll have a STUG stashed down the other end."

"I hope not. No, I don't think so. He'd have appeared by now."

The interior of Minnie reverberated as Vern opened up with the Browning. He'd seen a section of hedgerow drop away as if on a hinge, to reveal the deadly shape of a German machine gun. They got off a half dozen rounds that missed the crouching infantry before Vern's burst cut down the crew. The barrel of the MG42 pointed up in the sky as the burst sliced into the gunner, and he collapsed over the weapon. Angel hit the gas and pressed on across the field. Morgan was on the left flank and Kuruk on the right, the three Shermans on line abreast, able to bring all of their armament to bear. They were watchful for further German defenders, but they'd pulled back to the next field. Morgan called them on the net.

"Sergeant Grant, stay on point and push through the hedge. Let's look and see what they have the other side. Sergeant Kuruk, you and me will go in right behind him. Punch through hard and fast. With any luck, we'll hit them when they think they're lining up to engage a single Sherman. We'll give 'em a surprise and pound them into scrap before they realize it's a different game.

"Copy that, Sir."

They'll have the first few seconds to roast our ass before the other two tanks come through. This is going to be hairy.

Angel accelerated to deal the next hedgerow a mighty blow. The tough, wiry growth grabbed at Minnie's hull, and for a few seconds he thought they weren't going to make it through, but she eventually pushed into the next field with a mighty bellow of engine noise and exhaust smoke. It took them by surprise. The fleeing Germans from the first attack hadn't reached their friends at the other end of the field to warn them. Instead, they were in a straggling group, racing away from them, a half-dozen men in peculiar helmets and baggy smocks.

"Fallschirmjager," Solly exclaimed, "They're Hitler's elite troops. Damn, we need to waste these Nazi bastards."

Dale had already started shooting, and Grant grabbed for the .50 cal to join in the slaughter. He felt both sickened and exulted as they tore the paras to shreds, and their bodies littered the soaking field, the drizzle already washing their blood into the ground. This was close range killing, and as he knocked each man to the ground, he felt some more payback for David. Payback for Margot.

And yet these were men, and killing didn't come naturally to him. He was a lawyer, or had been once. Not a murderer. Shooting down running men didn't seem too many notches above murder. Even so, a kind of craziness took him over, took all of them over. It was an atavistic emotion; he was intelligent enough to realize that, a throwback to the human ancestors that once hunted wooly mammoths with wood and flint spears. Only they weren't mammoths; they were chasing Germans across the muddy field.

A bunch of field-gray soldiers appeared, struggling to push a PAK40 out into the open, but Solly was ready for them. Ready to take vengeance, ready with the HE shell Dale had loaded. The other Shermans had seen the danger, and two HE shells quickly destroyed the crew and the gun. The Germans pushed another anti-tank gun into the open from the other side of the field, and Solly was again ready.

"Target! Ten o'clock, anti-tank gun."

"Fire!"

The fumes filled the interior of the tank as the extractors struggled to clear them, but Dale already had another shell loaded, and Solly fired again. They smashed through yet another hedgerow into another field, and this time it came alive with enemy fire. They'd dug themselves slit trenches right across the field, which made it tough to hit them. The three Shermans blanketed the field with lead, and after they overran the first trench and buried the occupants in the dirt, the rest of the Fallschirmjager melted away.

They punched through more fields, and all the time the artillery duel continued. They finally reached the last of the bocage, and they were out in the open. The infantry came up behind them and assembled for the final push up the hill.

"They need heavy artillery," Solly commented as they

watched the preparations for the final assault.

"I think they got it," Grant replied.

A rumble announced the arrival of an American assault gun, a monstrous 155mm artillery piece mounted on a tracked Grant chassis. Named the M12 Gun Motor Carriage, it was capable of flinging a shell weighing a hundred pounds to a range of fifteen miles. A cargo carrier came up behind, loaded with replacement 155mm shells.

"Jeez, I wouldn't want to be on the receiving end of one of those," Solly murmured.

The crew of the M12 howitzer swung into action, readying the assault gun for the attack. Within minutes, the big gun started firing, and huge explosions marked where the shells tore into the enemy guns.

"Me neither," he murmured, watching the devastation.

He surveyed the track either side of where they waited. "What the fuck is that?"

A light vehicle had just emerged from a sunken lane some distance away, close to a small wood.

Strange.

* * *

One kilometer outside Saint-Lo, 09.40, July 11, 1944

Sturm was desperate. A battle was raging around the hill that commanded the approaches to Saint-Lo, and if he waited any longer, the Americans would arrive in even greater numbers, and he would never get through. He thought of Margot, cowering in a Gestapo basement, waiting for the knock on the door that would signal the arrival of her executioner. It was now or never. He left some of the branches on the hood of the vehicle and four hay bales in the rear, to change the distinctive silhouette of the Kubi. Then he started the engine and drove away.

There was a track to the east of his position. It looked like it may cut through a gap in the enemy lines and take him straight into the town. He floored the gas pedal, and the Kubi surged forward. He had to follow that route before the armor and infantry came up in greater force and made it impossible. He almost made it.

* * *

Three miles outside Saint-Lo, 09.55, July 11, 1944

"That's not one of ours!"

Even as Solly shouted, Grant could make out the field-gray camo paintwork and the sloped bonnet of the little German utility jeep. Some kind of VW variant, there was no mistake it was the enemy. Solly had already dived into the interior and was shouting for Dale to load HE.

"HE loaded."

"Target acquired."

"Hold it! Hold your fire."

Grant had grabbed for his binoculars and focused on the single occupant of the German jeep.

An officer, no question, and he's not pointing a gun at anyone. He could be an intelligence officer, worth his weight in gold for the information he has stored in his head. The guy could be carrying maps, orders, codebooks; you name it.

"I have to shoot. He's getting away."

"I said hold it."

Grant grabbed the .50 cal and let loose a stream of

bullets that chewed up the ground in front of the hood, forcing the Kraut to a halt. He applied the parking brake, raised his hands in surrender, and waited.

"Angel, take us over there. Vern, keep him covered. I'll talk to him."

He explained about the potential value an intelligence officer, but they grumbled nonetheless.

"Hell, Sarge, he's a Kraut. I've got him bang to rights. It's crazy to leave him alive."

"He's surrendered, Vern. You can see that. It'd be murder if you shot him now."

He heard the Southerner mutter something about, 'fucking lawyers,' but he decided to let it go. He also wanted to kill every Kraut he came across, but he knew it wouldn't bring back the people he'd lost. His brother David, and Margot, who he never even got a chance to know well. Although every Kraut they killed was another German who couldn't keep this fool war going when everyone could see they'd lost. He sighed, except this particular Kraut. He could be valuable. He climbed down from Minnie, drew his Colt .45, and walked up to the peculiar vehicle.

The man was a captain, sure enough. Wehrmacht, not SS. Grant took the Luger pistol from the holster on his belt and tucked it in the pocket of his jacket.

"Do you speak English?"

The man turned his head and nodded. "I do, yes. Captain Gunter Sturm, under the Geneva Convention, I..."

"Shut the fuck up, Sturm. I've got four crewmen on that Sherman who are all itching to put a bullet through you, so just answer my questions, and you may live long enough to get back to your shithouse of a Fatherland. Clear?"

He stared back. "Yes, I understand. Perfectly."

"Where were you headed, Saint-Lo?"

"Saint-Lo, yes."

"You're an intelligence officer?"

Sturm shook his head. "Not intelligence, no. I was a liaison officer for Feldmarschal Rommel's staff."

"Rommel, uh. I guess your troops are retreating to the town to prop up the defenses before we attack. It's okay, pal, it's no secret. So what are you, running away?"

They both ducked as a bunch of shells from Hill 192 landed nearby and threw mountains of earth and hedgerow into the air.

That's one way to do it. Let the Jerries clear the bocage for us.

When the smoke cleared, he saw the bodies strewn on the ground where the shells had hit. He felt like raising his Colt and shooting this man dead on the spot.

Fuckers.

"I was taking a message to the commander from the Ardenne Abbey."

"Ardenne Abbey?"

"Standartenfuhrer Meyer's headquarters."

"Standartenfuhrer? That's SS. You said you were Wehrmacht."

"So I am. As I said, I was a liaison officer."

Grant was suspicious. Solly Rothstein spoke some Yiddish, a bastardized form of German. He shouted for Solly to come down and held out his hand.

"Gimme the message."

The German hesitated, but after a few seconds handed it over. Solly snatched it away from him, with a scowl at the German. He left the man in no doubt what he'd like to do with him. He read the piece of paper and looked at Grant.

"This is crap, just a request for the local commander to arrange a guard and transport for the Divisional payroll and treasury. So this guy Meyer is sending the money back to Germany. Save it for a rainy day. I guess your man's a common thief."

Sturm looked puzzled, and he shook his head. "He is not my man. Meyer is SS. That message..."

"I'll bet he's planning to send back the loot they stole from French Jews before they murdered them," Solly snarled.

Grant watched Sturm for his reaction. There was just a resigned smile. He grabbed the lapels of his tunic. The guy was a Jerry, and he didn't trust him an inch.

"You knew about this?"

"No, I know nothing. Do I know about members of the SS and SD looting stolen artworks and valuables? Yes, I know, they make no secret of it. But I knew nothing of the contents of that message. My job was to assess the strength of our defenses, no more."

"How much have you sent back to the Reich to feather your little nest, Sturm? What do you have, a cozy little Hausfrau looking after it all for you?

He stared back with a firm gaze. "My wife is dead. One of your bomber raids destroyed our home." He closed his eyes; "Thank God she was asleep at the time. She wouldn't have known anything."

"A night raid? That's the Brits, pal, not us. USAAF bombs Germany in daylight. It's the Brits that go over during the night."

"Should that make a difference?" he replied, his lips twisted in irony, "She's dead. That is all."

Grant nodded in sympathy. "Yeah, that's a bad break. So you're just a messenger boy, is that right?"

"I told you, a liaison officer. That message, I was asked to deliver it while I was there."

"What else were you planning to get up to in Saint-Lo?"

"I, er, nothing."

Something in the man's reply didn't read right.

He sounds guilty. Why? He has to be hiding something.

Grant felt his anger intensify. He'd given this guy a break, and now he was lying to him. Maybe he should have let Solly again do his eye for an eye bit. He stared at the man, his eyes conveying a warning. He hoped this guy wasn't too stupid to understand he was in deep, deep shit.

I don't want to kill you, pal, but I'll give you to Solly if I have to.

"Tell me the rest of it. Why were you going to Saint-Lo? And don't give me that messenger crap, there's more to it, I know that. I'm not a fool. I've questioned plenty of guys in the past, enough to know you're lying."

"Those were my orders," Sturm almost shouted, "You can believe me or not. It makes no difference. If I'd known what was in them, I'd have tossed them into the River Vire before I passed on any dispatch that may help the SS loot the Divisional payroll."

"There's something else in Saint-Lo, isn't there? What is it, bank notes, jewelry? Tell me!"

The man shook his head. There was no fear in his eyes.

Does this guy want to die?

"A woman? A girl?"

He went rigid.

So that's it, Grant smiled to himself, *Some interrogation, all*

I've got out of him is the guy was going there to see his girl.

"She your girlfriend?"

"No!" he snapped.

"Sister?" Solly smiled, "What is she, on vacation in the Greater German Reich? Or maybe Hitler's girlfriend?"

"She is French."

"Name," he snapped out.

He felt himself going dizzy when the German said, "Margot Caron." At first, Grant refused to believe it, but how could this guy know of their connection? Sturm went on to explain how he'd rescued her from American deserters, only for her to be arrested by the SD. How she'd been transferred to a Gestapo cell in Saint-Lo and was under sentence of death.

With an effort, he brought his boiling emotions under control.

"Whereabouts in Saint-Lo are they holding her? Do you have the location?"

"Yes, I know the building."

"What is she to you, this Margot Caron?"

Sturm shook his head. "You would not understand. She is the end of war."

"End of war?"

"I've had enough of killing and brutalizing civilians. I'd already decided to surrender to the Allies. This war is nothing more than the mechanized slaughter of the innocents."

"You'd know about that, being a Nazi."

"I am no Nazi," he insisted, "But when I came across Margot Caron, I'd had enough. She is a symbol. That's what she means to me. If I can save her, perhaps my soul will not be totally forfeit."

"You're a Catholic, Sturm?"

"How did you know?"

"A lucky guess. So you planned to rescue her again, is that it? The shining white knight, you in love with her?"

"No."

"How did you intend getting her out, what's the plan?"

The German shrugged. "I have no plan. My intention was to get there first, and then make a plan."

"Now you do have a plan."

"Excuse me?"

"You have a plan. To be exact, you have a Sherman. Minnie Mouse is going in with you."

He shouted up to Dale, who was watching them from the turret.

"Come on down here. I want you to dump that piece of Kraut VW junk into the nearest ditch. Then I need a word with all of you."

The loader looked puzzled, but he climbed to the ground, started the Kubi, and drove it into a field. Halfway across there was a shellhole, and he put the wheels into it, so the hood was half buried in the mud. Then he ripped out as much of the wiring as he could, and for good measure put two shots through the gas tank. The Wehrmacht wouldn't be using that particular Kubelwagen in a hurry.

"The rest of you guys, come here," Grant shouted to them, "I want to talk to you."

They gathered around him, looking curiously at the German, and then back at their tank commander. He quickly explained the situation in Saint-Lo, that Margot Caron, the girl who'd cooked for them, was held awaiting execution.

"I'm going in to get her out, me and Minnie Mouse. This Kraut is coming to show the way. I'd appreciate some help, but if you don't like it, you can start walking back to Battalion."

His declaration was greeted by silence. Vern reacted first.

"Jesus, you only just met the girl, Sarge. I mean; we can't just go in there on a wing and a prayer. They'll murder us. They're fucking SS in that place."

He grinned. "They might. And then again, they might not. I'm planning to go in as soon as it gets dark, so they won't see us coming. We already captured a few SS, they're no big deal."

"They'll hear us coming," Angel said, his Hispanic faced stretched with concern, "You know the German Army has a headquarters in the town."

"Gestapo," Sturm said.

"Oh, great, that's just great." He shook his head, "It's crazy, just crazy."

"There're plenty of Krauts to kill," he said, "We could wind up with a medal if it comes off."

"Krauts to kill? Sounds good to me," Solly said.

"It could be a posthumous medal," Dale pointed out, with a slight smile.

"Maybe."

"I can get you in without being noticed," Sturm interrupted, "There is a way, a sunken lane with bocage on either side that will provide cover for most of the journey."

"Great," Dale stared at Grant, "So we get there alive, and then they kill us. It's not much of a plan."

"The entire town is in chaos," Sturm went on, "Every man has been called to the front, and the rear echelons are loading the trucks with equipment and heading west. They do not believe they can hold out for much longer."

"They think they've lost?"

He stared at Grant. "Yes, they think they've lost. Of course, the Fuhrer maintains we can still win the war, when he unleashes his secret weapons. But most do not believe it is more than a matter of time before Germany surrenders. The men in Saint-Lo are desperate. We can do this."

"Where is this French girl Margot being held?" Solly asked.

"Gestapo Headquarters."

He roared with laughter. "That's fucking rich. Gestapo Headquarters. What do we do, knock on the door and ask to be shown to Mam'selle Caron's suite?"

"Yes," Sturm said, "Something like that. There may be some shooting."

"You don't say."

They stared at the German. "Doesn't that bother you, a Kraut shooting other Krauts?" Solly grinned.

"They are Gestapo, so no, it does not bother me."

"In that case, I'm in. Just so there's no misunderstanding, I'm in this to kill Germans."

"Nazis," Grant corrected him, with a nod to Gunter, "I guess they're not all the same. Anyone else got anything to say?"

"I'm in."

"Me, too."

They were unanimous. "In that case, let's go to work. There are Krauts to kill, and the 29th Infantry needs our help." He looked at Sturm. "Climb on top of Minnie Mouse. You're coming with us."

CHAPTER TEN

Two miles outside Saint-Lo, 11.30, July 11, 1944

Commander of the 29th Infantry Division, Major-General Charles Hunter Gerhardt, thought back to his inspection in the early hours; row upon row of men, all of them waiting for the order to go, to attack into the maelstrom of German defenses that ringed Saint-Lo. He was aware of his reputation. The joke was he commanded three divisions in total. One was on the battlefield, another in the hospital, and the third in the cemetery. The last straw was when he set up a brothel for his men. The establishment was hurriedly closed on the orders of Eisenhower.

Rank upon rank of men stared back at him as he drove slowly past. Infantry, tank destroyers, M10s, some equipped with the latest 76mm gun that could penetrate heavy armor when loaded with high velocity armor piercing rounds. General Omar Bradley, Commander of the US First Army in Normandy, had called him shortly after midnight.

"Charles, we've had reports of enemy armor in the region of Saint-Lo. Intel figures it could be our old friends Panzer Lehr nosing around."

He shrugged. "As I remember, we kicked their asses last time they put in an appearance, General."

"True. Except this time we don't have the luxury of air cover. My weather guys tell me there's no sign of any let up in low cloud and rain."

Gerhardt glanced out the window of the farmhouse he was using as a temporary headquarters. The rain fell in sheets, and the clouds looked as if they were almost touching the hilltops.

"My tank destroyer battalions are equipped with M10s. I reckon they'll keep the Tigers and Panthers at bay."

"I sure hope so. You know how important this is to the Army?"

"I do, General."

Bradley had gone over it at least ten times in the past several days. Saint-Lo, the key to breaking out from Normandy, leaving the flooded fields and bocage behind, and starting the long push through the rest of France. Provided they took the town.

"Keep your eyes skinned for heavy armor. If we know how critical the town is, you can bet the Germans know, too. That means they'll throw everything into defending it, so it could be a hard slog. You're gonna take casualties, and they could be heavy."

"That'll give more ammunition to my critics," Gerhardt replied grimly. He'd known for some time his command of the 29th was on the line.

"Yeah. I'll cover your back, don't worry."

"Thank you, General."

"Provided you take the town. Otherwise, well..."

Otherwise I'll be looking at commanding a mobile kitchen.

"We'll take the town, Sir."

"When?"

Gerhardt thought hard. It was a tough target, no question. But he had a Division he was proud of, tough fighters, men who after only a few weeks were veterans of the bloody 'Battle of the Hedgerows.' Well supplied, well equipped, and well led. The Kraut strength was patchy at best, with a number of 'Ost' battalions, Russians and Ukrainians, who so far had indicated they'd surrender as fast as they could throw up their hands and shout, "Kamerad, Kamerad." Although they also had artillery, Fallschirmjager, Panzergrenadiers, and an unknown number of tanks, as well as the SS, there was always the SS.

"Tonight, Sir."

"Tonight? You're certain?"

"Nothing's certain in war, General. But if all goes to plan, we'll be inside the town by tonight."

"Then I wish you luck. One thing more, Charles, Intel has informed me there's a Gestapo Headquarters in the town. You know what to do."

"Gestapo? I'll make sure there isn't a brick left standing, Sir. My boys are not too happy with those SS and Gestapo bastards. Some of them are Jewish, and others have Jewish relatives. They can't wait to pay them back for what they've done."

"No war crimes, no shooting prisoners, Charles."

Gerhardt was offended. "No way, that's not my style. When we come up against SS and Gestapo, I have a way of dealing with them. Standoff and hammer the crap out of them with artillery." He chuckled, "We don't take too many prisoners that way. As soon as we get near, and I have the coordinates of their HQ, I'll pass them on to our artillery."

"That's the spirit, Charles. Save us all a deal of grief. Excellent. Call me when you're in the town, and I'll pass the news on to Ike. He's already planning the next stage of the offensive, something the Brits came up with. Cobra, I believe it's called."

"You'll be the first to hear, General."

* * *

Gestapo Headquarters, Saint-Lo, 12.30, July 11, 1944

Josh, where are you? I can't take much more of this. Every time I hear the sound of boots in the corridor outside my cell, I think they're coming to execute Father Bouchet and me. I can't help but worry the Germans may beat back the Allied offensive. Are you dead, Josh, lying in the burned out hull of a Sherman tank while the rest of the Americans are running back to the beaches, unable to defeat the might of the German Army?

She pictured the blackened bodies of the crew of Minnie Mouse, with a sneering SS tank commander laughing to his men as they drove past. She wanted to be dead, to end this terrible ordeal. She glanced across at Father Bouchet as he stirred, groaning in pain. They'd taken him down from the cross before they were transferred to Saint-Lo, and she'd assumed it was in preparation for the planned execution. He lay on the hard, concrete floor, moving in and out of consciousness. She crawled across to him.

"How do you feel, Father? Is there anything I can do?"
He smiled through lips that were cracked and bloody.

Inside his mouth, there was only his tongue. They'd smashed out his teeth during their frequent torture sessions.

"Perhaps a prayer would be the best option."

"I meant your wounds. You're still bleeding. I can see you're lying in a pool of blood."

He looked at his hands and then his ankles. "We have no bandages, and even if we did, they will come for us any day. No, prayer is our only comfort."

She ignored him, pulled off the tattered remains of her blouse, and began tearing it into strips. She gently wound a makeshift dressing around each of the four main wounds, one in each hand, and one in each ankle. Each time she touched the ruined flesh, he winced in agony.

"I'm sorry," she whispered, "but if I don't do this, you could die."

He chuckled, although it came out as a strangled noise from inside his throat. "I could die? I trust you're not serious."

"We're not dead yet, Father. The Americans could come at any moment and free us."

"Or the Gestapo may come and execute us."

"Let's hope it'll be the Americans. We should have faith in them. Their tanks will smash through the German lines and come to rescue us."

He didn't reply. As a member of the resistance, he had considerable knowledge of the capabilities of the German armor, and he knew the heavy Panzers would not be beaten easily. The Shermans, the bulk of the Allied armor, were lighter and less well armored. Their guns were of smaller caliber. Besides, their men lacked the experience of fighting on the Russian Front, which had forged the

Panzer crews into some of the best tankers in the world, those who had survived.

He was also aware of those that had not survived the vicious duels with the Soviet T34s, and as a result, large numbers of the Panzer crews in France were merely boys, drawn from the Hitler Jugend. Many SS troopers were unwilling low-grade 'volunteers' from the fighting in the East, and were likely to be less than committed to the Nazi cause. Then he considered the armor again and compared the relative size of the Tiger Is and the Panthers, the Tiger IIs, to the Shermans. It was no contest.

Even so, why bother to explain it to her. She'd told him over the past few days of her feelings for the American tanker, Sergeant Josh Grant. Love had struck her like a lightning strike, and doubtless the Sergeant felt the same way, yet how long could he survive against the might of the heavy Panzers? The odds were not good.

"Yes, they will penetrate through the German lines. Let us hope they are here in time to help us."

Before they take us out of here for that final, long walk, and then, oblivion.

* * *

One mile outside Saint-Lo, 17.30, July 11, 1944

They'd just driven down a slit trench that had sheltered an anti-tank crew. Two men with a panzerfaust, and Grant was ready for them. Angel went to full speed, bumping across the wet field, while Grant and Vern hosed them down with the machine guns. They were not men of the highest caliber, or maybe they'd just decided it wasn't worth fighting for a lost cause. They ditched the launcher, leapt out of the trench, and started to run. The machine guns cut them to pieces before they'd taken a dozen paces.

He heard the Company net come to life. "This is Morgan, who do I have left out there?"

He checked in, and Daniel followed suit. The Major sounded relieved

"Thank God for that. Form up on me. I'm in the field to the south of your position."

They acknowledged, and Angel plunged through the hedgerow to come up with Morgan's tank. Cochise made its appearance a few seconds later, and they formed a small arrowhead formation, ready for the next phase. Morgan had picked up a company of infantry, who were looking for the reassurance of heavy armor to hide behind, and a big gun to hit back with.

"Pull up alongside me," Morgan said, his voice grim and tired.

They halted either side of his tank and climbed down. Grant could see why the Major was upset. The field was strewn with bodies. American bodies.

They look so young, some of 'em are just teenagers.

"It was a hard fight." They looked up as an officer joined them. Like Morgan, he looked all in. The new arrival glanced at Gunter's German uniform but made no comment. It was that kind of a mixed up crazy war. The two officers moved away and chatted for a few moments, then returned. Morgan did the introductions. "This is Lieutenant Anderson, he's in command of Alpha Company."

A lieutenant, and he's a company commander. Jesus, it must have been bad.

"He's the most senior officer left standing," Morgan explained, "Probably the only officer. He's coming along with us so we can offer him close support, and his men will do their best to keep the Panzergrenadiers away from our Shermans."

"Makes sense," Grant nodded, "Sir, we're supposed to push on into Saint-Lo." He pointed toward the road lying a few hundred yards below their position, "That would seem like the quickest route to me."

He shook his head. "Not going to happen. Lieutenant, would you explain your orders to my Sergeant."

"Yes, Sir. The plan is to finish off the enemy here and dig in while the artillery pound the crap out of strategic targets inside and around the town; defensive strongpoints, artillery parks, assembly areas, and barracks. Oh, yeah, they've pinpointed a Gestapo facility in the town. Believe me, that's one target they're going to get a kick out of shelling. Those Nazi bastards are about to get a taste of hell."

Gunter gasped. "Sergeant, the Gestapo Headquarters, they cannot..."

He nodded and looked at Morgan. "Sir, there's a woman inside that prison, a hostage of the Nazis."

"A woman? What're you talking about?"

"The girl who cooked for us a few days back. We have to get her out."

Morgan's face showed understanding. "Yes, of course, I remember. That was swell cooking. I doubt my wife's chow will ever taste the same." He lost himself in his thoughts for a few seconds, but then his face darkened, "You were saying?" He looked even more tired, and something more, ill maybe. Grant noticed the deep lines etched into his face were even more prominent.

Either he's ill or he's going through a divorce.

"The girl who cooked for us." He grinned, trying to lighten the moment; "I guess your wife ain't no great shakes in the kitchen."

He scowled. "No, Sergeant, she is not."

"She could always take some lessons," Solly tried to cheer him up. He considered himself something of an authority on food and occasionally harbored plans to open a kosher restaurant.

Morgan shook his head. "Too late for that, I'm afraid."

Solly's enthusiasm bubbled over, "It's never too late. She can't be much more than thirty years old, Sir. She could..."

The officer's eyes were red, and tears began to form in the corners. "She's dying, Corporal Rothstein. On this occasion, I assure you it is too late."

Grant put a hand on his shoulder, a gesture of reassurance. "Cancer?" His uncle had died prematurely of that dreaded disease.

"Cancer, yeah. She was getting treatment, but I got a letter from her to tell me we've reached the limit on our insurance. She'd need, well, a lot of money to give her a better than even chance. Telephone numbers, they said, it could run to a hundred thousand dollars over the next three years. Without it, well, you know."

"It's a lot of cash. Can't you, you know, can't you raise it? I mean, I don't mean to pry..."

"If we sold everything, the house, cashed in our investments, borrowed every penny, we could maybe raise a quarter of it."

He cut off the discussion to stride away and stand

on his own for several minutes while he wiped his eyes. When he walked back, his eyes were even redder, but he'd recovered his equilibrium. He forced a grin.

"Just some grit in the eyes. Forget my problems. Let's go kill some Krauts. Where were we, this girl in Saint-Lo, was it?"

"Yes, Sir. We need to get her out before the attack starts."

He looked puzzled. "Sergeant, they're about to shell the place in, when is it?"

He looked at the Lieutenant.

"Four hours, Major, the artillery barrage starts just before dark."

"There you are, four hours. It can't be done, Grant, I'm sorry. She'll have to take her chances."

"I'll go in on my own," he snapped, "I'm not leaving her to be pounded to gristle by our own artillery."

"Sergeant, that'll do!" Morgan murmured, "You obey orders, otherwise you know what'll happen. You're already in the shit as it is. You do this and Lindbergh would have you shot at dawn."

Grant felt a dark mist closing around him.

We have to go in and get her, goddamnit. We have Gunter Sturm, and he knows a way in. We could snatch her from the prison, kill a few Krauts, and get out while the going's good. There has to be a way to persuade him, something anything, but what? Shit! There is something.

"If you won't do it for Margot, Major, do it for your wife."

Morgan stared at him. "You'd better explain yourself. You're one step away from a court martial, Sergeant. And that's after I break your nose."

He explained at some length. They clustered around while he told them about the SS Divisional payroll, as well as the treasury, and how the SS planned to grab it for themselves. Gunter filled in the gaps, with the exact location and the estimated amount.

"It's the payroll for the past five months. It was delayed while they were in Russia, and somehow it's only just arrived in France. Then there are the allowances for expenses, together with the Divisional treasury."

"How many million?" Solly stared.

"Forget it," Morgan snapped, "It's not our money. It belongs to the soldiers who earned it."

"You mean it belongs to the SS," Gunter reminded him, "You would pay them to continue killing American soldiers?"

"I, er..."

"If we take that money," Grant said quietly, "It's possible some of them may desert. It could save lives. Many lives."

"Forget it," Morgan said again.

"Major, we could help," Lieutenant Anderson offered. He looked around at his depleted force, a miniscule total of thirty-four men left standing, "Hell, chances are we'll all be dead the way things are going. We may as well die fighting for something worthwhile."

"Lieutenant, if..."

"I could put my kids through school," his Company Sergeant, Wade Jenkins, interrupted, "It'd be a dream come true. Worth fighting this war for."

"Worth dying for?"

Jenkins shrugged. "I'm taking that risk every hour of every day, and there ain't any kind of a reward."

Morgan shook his head in disbelief, but then he looked

down sharply at his hand. He suddenly realized he was holding the letter from his wife. He thought for long moments. Finally, he looked up.

"It'll save lives, you say?"

"No question," Anderson jumped in.

"Hundreds of lives," Solly added, "They'll desert in droves if they can't pay them."

Grant could see in his eyes his dreams of relocating his family on a farm in Palestine. Angel visualized his dream of his own pizza bar, and his face twisted in a smile. For once, Vern was silent. He stood next to Dale, and they chatted like old friends, about alligator farms, probably, and college tuition. They all needed just the one thing to make their dreams come true. And it lay less than two miles away.

Morgan stared at Gunter. "You can get us into the town, no tricks?"

"Yes. I can give you no guarantees about what happens after. But it should work. Then again, this is war, Herr Major."

"Yeah."

An hour later, the attack started forward. Morgan had made it clear there was no way they'd abandon the 29th to go off on a freelance operation. They'd only break away when they'd cut their way through the defenses in their sector. The first problem was the Fallschirmjager, Panzergrenadiers, and infantry tucked deep into more slit trenches that crisscrossed what seemed like every field.

They fought like demons, the three Shermans and Anderson's infantry. Inside of the first hour, they were well ahead of the Allied line, pushing out a salient in the enemy lines.

"Anti-tank gun, twelve o'clock. Bastard just popped up. He's..."

Solly had already fired. There was no waiting for orders. The German soldiers disappeared in chaos of smoke and flame, leaving the gun bent and twisted, and Minnie rolled on. Grant heard him shout, "No hard feelings, this is business, pal."

Gunter Sturm held a steel stanchion behind the turret, clinging on for dear life as the Sherman bucked and lurched over the fields. There simply wasn't room to fight the tank and accommodate another man inside the cramped interior. Not without risking everything. A pile of cash was worth fighting for, but who could spend it if they were dead.

A machine gun slashed across the field they were crossing, but their infantry was advancing behind the tanks, so they were effectively safe from the gunfire. Bullets pinged against the steel hull, and both Grant and Vern sprayed down the enemy with machine gunfire. They were on the left of the trio of tanks, with Morgan in the center and Cochise on his right. The drivers kept their speed low to allow the soldiers to keep up. When they smashed through the next hedgerow, they went through in a solid bunch, tanks and foot soldiers together.

Solly was about to open fire on an armored vehicle waiting the other side of the hedge. At the last moment he saw it was an American that had somehow got ahead of the rest of the Division. An open turret M10 tank destroyer, what the Brits called a Wolverine. Built on the hull of a Sherman M4, they'd only enjoyed limited success, until the army fitted a few M10s with the 76mm M1 main gun. The effect was immediate, an increase in kills as the more powerful artillery penetrated thicker armor. German armor. Tiger armor.

The Sergeant in command of the gun crew stared at them in consternation for a moment, then relaxed and jumped down. They'd come out in a shallow bowl in the ground that was enough to hide them from enemy gunfire. Morgan, Kuruk, and Grant joined him, and they shook hands.

"I'm Greg Allendale," he introduced himself, "This ugly monster is mine. It looks like we've jumped ahead of the rest of the Division, so me and the boys decided to wait for them to catch up."

Morgan nodded. "Very wise. Have you seen anything ahead we need to worry about, any heavy armor in the vicinity?"

"Damn right we have, Major. A couple of Panthers moving up to the town, together with three Panzer IVs and a Tiger."

"You think they're at Saint-Lo now?"

"Yep, no question. They'll have hunkered down somewhere they can wait for our boys to approach, and then, 'wham.' They'll let fly with those 88s and 76mms, and all hell will break loose. That's why we're here. Ain't nobody getting inside Saint-Lo unless we take out those Jerry tanks. Otherwise they'll tear the Shermans apart like they're made of paper."

They looked at each other. Morgan indicated they needed to have a quiet word, so they moved a few yards away.

"What do you think?" Morgan asked them.

"Another five men ain't going to make much difference," Dan Kuruk replied, "There're already plenty of us. I make it about forty-five. If the crew of that M10 wants to join us, it'll make it a round fifty. That sounds like a good number to me."

Morgan looked at Grant. "What about it?"

"I agree. We need them. We should talk to them."

Allendale was curious when they returned, and he called his crew to join them for a chat. It took all of four minutes.

"I'm in."

"Fuck, yes."

The Sergeant nodded at them. "We're with you. Equal shares?"

"That's right. Equal shares."

"What're we waiting for?"

They surveyed the advance of the 29th Division. The battle had flared and raged, and without any doubt, the defenses were collapsing. The time to enter Saint-Lo was now. The first task was to bring Gunter down from Minnie's hull. They asked him which road they needed to enter the town unseen. He glanced around for a few moments looking puzzled, and then his expression cleared.

"For a moment I thought was lost. It's okay. We're too far north. The track I'm looking for is further to the south. We need to cross the next two fields, and we should be able to cut the road and head east into Saint-Lo."

"We'll take the lead," Grant suggested to Morgan. He nodded his agreement.

"I don't like someone else leading the unit into battle, but I guess you and Gunter have got some kind of an understanding, so we need to listen to what he has to say. I'll position the M10 right behind you, and I'll follow with Kuruk in the rear." He looked around for Lieutenant

Anderson, "Distribute your men amongst the vehicles. You can ride on the hulls. Watch for snipers, and if we see any armor, we'll take care of it. Oh, yeah, look out for Panzergrenadiers."

"Understood, Major. We've done this before."

"Good. Let's do it."

Half a dozen infantrymen swarmed up on the hull of Minnie Mouse. They gave Gunter hard stares, but when Grant explained he was the key to getting rich, they had a change of heart and slapped him on the back. The rest of Anderson's men boarded the other vehicles. He took a last look around and waved for them to go forward. Allendale was out of radio contact, which forced them to use hand signals.

"Driver, advance."

They rumbled forward at a faster pace than before, with the infantry riding on the tanks. They were forced to dismount when the armor punched through the hedgerows, and they waited while the Shermans checked out the adjacent fields for signs of the enemy. There were none. They'd entered a poorly defended region, and within minutes they reached the track. There was still no sign of the enemy.

"If we follow this lane," Gunter explained, "it will take us into the south of the town, and with any luck, they won't see us. At least, until we get nearer."

Grant surveyed the outskirts of the town less than a mile in front of them, the town where Margot was held in a Nazi prison under sentence of death, either from the Gestapo, or from the Americans when they started the shelling.

"I can't see any sign of defenses, why is that?"

"They expected an attack to come from the north, not from this direction."

"Except not all of our troops have come in from the north."

The German shrugged. "They'll be panicking by now. All they can think about is getting out rather than how to defend a position that's indefensible."

Grant nodded. "Okay, we'll go in."

"Any problems?" Morgan radioed.

"We're good, Major."

He held up his arm, feeling like a nineteenth century cavalry commander leading a procession of mounted troops. Then he smiled to himself. That's exactly what he was doing. He held up his hand.

"Advance!"

They rumbled forward, threading their way through the narrow lane, wedged between high hedgerows on either side. After the first two hundred yards, the bocage suddenly ended, and in front of him he could see a collection of farm buildings that straddled the road. A few hundred yards further, the first of the houses of Saint-Lo came into view. There was no sign of the enemy. It worried him.

If I was a German commander, that's where I'd put my tank, inside one of those buildings. I could be staring into the muzzle of an 88 and not know it.

There was only one way to handle it. He used the Company net to call up Morgan and Kuruk to tell them of his suspicions.

"I want both of you back up a hundred yards, then punch through the bocage on the other side and come around the rear of that farm. If there is a Kraut tank in there, I want you ready to bust his ass with a couple of AP

319

shells. Sir," he added for Morgan's benefit.

"That's okay, Sergeant Grant. You're doing fine. Let's go, Sergeant Kuruk."

He waited for the two Shermans to maneuver out of sight, and then used hand signals to warn Allendale in the M10 what he planned. The other man waved an acknowledgement, and Grant gave the order.

"Driver, advance."

It came when they were only one hundred and fifty yards away from the big stone barn. At first it was a slight movement in the stonework, like it rippled. He was already grabbing for the transmit button when the long barrel pushed out of the building, sending more blocks of stone tumbling to the ground.

"Enemy armor!" Angel shouted, starting to swerve away.

"Tiger!" Vern shouted, "Oh my Lord, we're gonna die."

For once, he was right. The subject of his nightmares appeared in front of him. Huge and menacing, with the massive, long barrel of its 88mm main gun overhanging the hull like some monstrous appendage. They were so close Grant could see the strange anti-magnetic Zimmerit coating, with its peculiar rippled effect. The hull was painted in a gloomy dark green and gray, and it seemed almost as big as a house. In fact it was almost as big as a house.

"AP loaded!"

"Fire!"

The shell hit the mantlet of the big tank while it was emerging from the wreckage of the building. They missed. The Tiger fired, and the massive shell whistled overhead, missing them by what seemed like inches. The next one wouldn't miss. Already, the infantry had leapt off the hull and were diving for cover, and then the M10 fired. The shell smashed into the frontal armor of the Tiger and did little or no damage. Then Solly was ready.

"Fire."

The crash echoed through the hull as the shell spat out at the enemy, and the extractors sucked out the stinging fumes of the propellant. This time it was a hit on the turret armor, but the shell failed to do any obvious damage. He was about to order a change of direction when the Sherman jerked to a stop, as if they'd hit a solid wall. The next shell from the Tiger flashed past the front of Minnie, a near miss. It wouldn't work again. Next time they'd be ready for them. But what would work?

The M10 fired again, and their 76mm shell did some real damage. It impacted on the hull just below the turret where the charge exploded, although it had failed to penetrate the thick armor. Whatever it struck, the turret seemed to jam. Angel veered away to the west and the M10 to the east, to offer a harder target. Yet the big gun stayed still, unable to fully rotate the turret to bear. The German commander was no fool, and Grant heard the Tiger tracks squeal as the huge tank started to slew around, turning the entire hull to aim the 88, like a massive assault gun.

It was an act of desperation, but if they succeeded, they still had those big AP shells that could turn a Sherman into a flaming coffin. For half a minute they played a game of hide and seek, reversing and driving forward, while the German maneuvered for a shot.

It worked for a time, until the M10 stalled when the driver failed to see a stone wall with a pond in front of it. The vehicle plunged downward, and the tracks slid into the muddy bottom, the bulk of the vehicle settling against the wall. The driver hit the gas to try and get them out, and the tracks spun, but the angle was too much. Nothing short of a tow would pull them out. The Tiger scented prey like the carnivore after which it was named, and the monster tank began turning to line up on the helpless target.

"Angel," Grant shouted, "Head for the Tiger. Solly, keep firing. Distract the bastard, or Allendale and his men are toast."

The hatch of the M10 had opened and the crew was jumping to safety, but they were almost out of time. The Sherman had little protection against a Tiger, but the M10 had even less, with frontal armor an inch thinner than the M4. The German gunner opened up with the MG34, and heavy rounds chewed up the farmyard as the Americans dived behind the temporary safety of the stone wall.

They drew near, and Solly poured shot after shot at the German, but they were shooting at the front, and the heavy armor held off their AP shells.

"We need to get behind him," Grant shouted, "Angel, Solly needs a rear or side-on shot. Do what you can."

"Every time I move, he moves. I'm doing my best here."

"I know. But we have to nail this bastard before he gets in a good shot."

"Too right we need to nail him."

He grinned, that was Vern, probably pissing his pants. But they were no nearer to killing the Tiger, and the game had become a deadly dance. The German could absorb incredible punishment while it waited for a single mistake, a mistake that would enable them to fire a shell to destroy their enemy. And then Angel made that mistake. It may have been fear, or just the effect of the adrenaline slopping around his system, but instead of stopping the left track to slew left, he stopped the right track. They went right, under the direct line of sight of the huge barrel. Minnie and her crew were less than a second away from death.

There was no time to consider what might have been. One second they were ahead in the game, the next, they were about to die. The German stopped dead, about to take the shot, and Grant waited, his heart icy. His mind was numb to anything other than that huge, yawning black hole in front of them, and the monstrous shell that was about to turn a sophisticated piece of American engineering into so much scrap. The shot crashed out, a huge explosion, but oddly it wasn't as loud as the previous 88mm shell. They heard another explosion as the German fired again.

He opened his eyes and found they were alive. Minnie Mouse was still intact. Not so the Tiger, which had become a sea of flames as the gas tanks caught fire. Morgan had come up with Kuruk in the nick of time, and both Shermans slew the beast with shells into the vulnerable engine compartment. He saw the hatch open, and a black clad tanker attempted to escape.

The furious flames were too much, and the German's body slumped over the turret, the black uniform billowing smoke and flames. Then the ammunition cooked off, and a rumbling explosion inside the burning Tiger almost blew the turret off its mountings. When the noise died away, the big gun sagged down, pointed at the ground.

"Thank the Good Lord, I never want to see one of those again."

Vern had left his co-driver's position and emerged into the turret. Without asking, he threw open the hatch, put his head out, and retched over the side. He puked for a long time, and when he was finished, he climbed down to the ground and walked over to the pond where the M10 lay, with the nose under the water. He dunked his head in the pond and kept dunking for a long time.

Morgan and Kuruk stopped next to the stone wall, opened the hatches, and stared down at the crew of the tank destroyer.

"You guys look like you could do with a tow."

Allendale and his crew came out from behind the wall. The Sergeant gave them an embarrassed smile.

"That mud at the bottom of the pond, it's like glue. We could do with AAA."

"Better hurry it up, Sergeant, they're getting closer."

He meant their side. The artillery had emplaced only a half-mile away, and it didn't take a genius to know they were close to beginning the final assault on the town with a preliminary artillery barrage. Gestapo Headquarters would be one of the first targets. Allendale's crew dragged out the heavy chains and fastened them to Morgan's Sherman. His driver back away and slowly the M10 eased out of the mud. They unhitched and climbed aboard. There was a bad moment when the engine refused to fire, but after several attempts, it roared into life, spewing mud and pond water into the air from the blocked exhausts.

When they were ready to go, Morgan called them over for a brief chat.

"If we don't make it into the town inside the next hour, the artillery will likely flatten that Gestapo building. I'm afraid your girlfriend won't stand a chance."

Grant nodded. They were so near, yet so far.

"Major, if it's okay with you, I'd like to stay on point,

and Gunter can guide us in. He's done all right so far."

"You go ahead, same as before, the M10 right behind to deal with the heavy armor. Always assuming their driver can stay out of the ponds. Move out."

Grant vaulted onto the hull and climbed down inside the turret. Gunter climbed back on the hull and sat next to the rear of the turret. He took a last look round to make sure the engine of the M10 was still running, and then gave the order. Angel set the tracks moving on the last stage of their journey.

As they neared the town, he was surprised not to see German strongpoints. It looked as if they might make it, as far as the Krauts were concerned; as for their own artillery, that was something different.

"You must take that street there," Gunter shouted over the noise of tracks and the roaring of the engine, "It will take us to the Headquarters, what used to be the Town Council building. There is a wide paved area in front where our troops parked their vehicles. Be careful when you take the corner, in case they have armor drawn up for the defense."

He passed the warning on to Angel, and they rumbled through the streets of Saint-Lo. He was aware they were the first Americans into the town, and he wondered what Major-General Charles Hunter Gerhardt would think about that. Maybe they should have warned him. After all, Morgan was on the Battalion net and could have got a message through.

Then again, what could he say? "Sorry, General, but we disobeyed orders and charged into the town ahead of our main force. We had to rescue a French girl held captive in a Gestapo prison. As well as the SS payroll."

Maybe not, the only way was get in and out before anyone knew they'd been there. In the smoke and chaos of the attack, no one would ever know who'd done what. Especially after an artillery barrage leveled the Headquarters building, together with most of the town. Provided they got out in one piece, the only losers would be the Gestapo and the SS.

Isn't that what we're in this war for, anyway?

Angel jerked to a halt just before the intersection. Grant climbed out of the turret and walked forward. The soldiers riding the hull wanted to climb down, but he told them to hold tight. The last thing he wanted was a squad of American troops alarming the locals. He peered around the corner and ahead of him was the target. Two huge oak and iron doors guarded the Gestapo building. A guard stood in front, complete with helmet and MP38 machine pistol. As if to dispel any doubt about the occupants, the Nazi Swastika flag flew from a flagpole. The paved area in front was a vehicle park, with a half-dozen trucks drawn up near the doors. A sound made him look to see Solly come up to join him.

"The Nazi fuckers are preparing to leave, and those trucks will be to carry away our money."

He chuckled. "We haven't got our hands on it yet, but it looks that way."

"We don't have much time."

"No. We'll shoot up the vehicles and personnel with machine gunfire as soon as we round the corner. That'll stop 'em getting away."

"They'll lock and bolt those doors as soon as they hear us start shooting."

"That's why you have a main gun."

Solly smiled. "And there's me thinking it's just for killing Germans. Now I know it's for relieving them of their dough as well."

"Right. I'll talk to the others. We need to coordinate the attack."

Allendale, Morgan, and Kuruk had stopped their vehicles and climbed down for a look-see. Grant stopped them before they gave the game away and explained the layout just around the corner.

"Remember, we're stuck for time. The Krauts are trying to hightail it, and they're loading their valuables on the trucks right now. Our own army is about to level the place with high explosive. Between the two of them, we have to drive in fast, shoot up the trucks and personnel, and put a shell through the main doors. Don't shoot at anything else. There are prisoners inside."

"Don't forget the money," Allendale reminded him with a glare, as if they were about to leave without it.

"And the money, yeah. As soon as the door blows, and when we know the troops in the square are all dead, Lieutenant Anderson's infantry will go in and secure the building. The armor stays outside, in case they get a chance to call for reinforcements."

"What about you?" Morgan asked, knowing what he had at stake.

"I'll go in with the infantry. Solly, you'll have command of Minnie Mouse. Look after her for me."

He chuckled. "It's a deal. Just look after my share of the dough, Sarge." He looked around and grinned, "This is going to be a piece of cake. Take the loot, kill a few Krauts, and off to Palestine to settle on a nice little kibbutz. What could go wrong?"

Before anyone could reply, the first Panzer nosed around the corner.

CHAPTER ELEVEN

Two kilometers outside Saint-Lo, 20.30, July 11, 1944

"We had a call from Standartenfuhrer Meyer's headquarters, Sir. They've sighted American armor inside Saint-Lo. We're ordered to go there immediately and destroy them."

"American armor inside Saint-Lo? How the hell did they get there? They told us the American attack had stalled?"

"Perhaps their information was incorrect, Obersturmfuhrer," his radio operator said tactfully.

"You mean they lied, Wilhelm?"

Schneider didn't reply. They were all too aware of Lenz, only a couple of meters away. He would be listening intently, desperate to pass on any defeatist or treacherous talk to his relative, Standartenfuhrer Schulz. Rolf surveyed the ground on the approaches to the town where a furious exchange of fire had taken place earlier. A few stray shells still arced overhead, but in the darkness it was impossible to make out who was shooting at whom. He sighed; there probably weren't American tanks inside the town. They were just panicking. But he had his orders, and there was only one way to find out.

"Franz, drive into Saint-Lo. We'll take a look and see if this report is true. Heinrich, load AP, in case we're facing enemy armor. All of you stay alert. We don't want any nasty surprises."

"Jawohl, Obersturmfuhrer."

He kept his head outside the turret, enjoying the cool night air, despite the cold drizzle. With any luck, the report would be a false alarm, and they could rejoin their unit. They were sorely needed. The 12th SS Hitler Jugend had linked up with Panzer Lehr to make an armored force that should have been formidable. Until the bombs and shells had ripped the guts out of their armored divisions.

Their mission was to keep the enemy out of the town, presenting them with an overwhelming armored force. No man was in any doubt the American assault on Saint-Lo would be decisive. If the town fell, the arteries that led east would be wide open. The future of France was at stake. And if the Russians and the Allies kept squeezing, well, their next step would be the Reich itself.

He felt his anger rise, thinking of the number of times he'd heard the military experts, the Generals, even the Fuhrer in the early days, warn of the perils of a two front war. Yet after the sacrifice of the lives of millions of German soldiers, and with the Reich itself laid waste by the enemy bombers, they'd fallen neatly into that trap.

He saw a flash as a shell fired. It came from inside the town, so perhaps they were right. Another shell exploded, a medium.

Shermans, probably.

As they drew nearer the town, he felt something strange.

That feeling again, clammy, ice-cold, it gripped his body to warn him he was going to meet his fate.

Will I die in that crappy little town? Will it all end in a blinding flash when an AP shell penetrates the hull of my Tiger? Is that Sherman waiting for me, the one I first saw on the beach? Yet how is it possible the American tank is inside the town, the one they painted the name Minnie Mouse on the hull? Out of all the thousands of American tanks they landed on the beaches, it hardly seems possible it could be THAT tank.

And yet, he couldn't shake off the feeling. Somehow, he knew. They were here. He looked at each hand, one by one. They were both shaking.

What would it mean if they met inside the town? A Sherman would need to get very close to destroy them, probably a hit from the rear. So why was he so worried? If his crew were doing their job, they'd be fine. Besides, no one but a fool would allow enemy armor to get that close. Yet inside the narrow streets of a French town, they would be close. Close quarters fighting. There was a risk.

He contemplated buttoning up inside the turret, but then he laughed at his fears. He was in command of the mightiest tank on the battlefield, and here he was behaving like a frightened kid. An American tank opposed him that had the absurd name of Minnie Mouse painted on the hull. He reminded himself, tigers ate mice.

That's the way it would be, in the event they tangled with the inferior American machine. It didn't help a lot. He couldn't help feeling uneasy. He kept his head out of the hatch, ignoring the chill rain that soaked him to the skin. If this was to be the end, who cared about a little rain? He chuckled to himself, what was he thinking.

We'll find that Minnie Mouse, gobble her up, and spit out the bones. Hals und Beinbruch!

* * *

Town of Saint-Lo, 20.55, July 11, 1944

"Shoot the fucker!"

"There's another one right behind him."

"Jesus, another. That makes three."

"AP loaded."

"Fire!"

They'd been lucky. For some reason, the Panzers hadn't been aware the American tanks were so close. Solly's first shell scored a lucky hit on the base of the turret, an inch below the mantlet, and the first Panzer IV came to a stop with smoke pouring out of the hull. The second and third tanks put on speed, and the turrets began to turn. Allendale's M10 fired, and the longer, heavier 76mm shell turned another Panzer IV into a smoking, flaming ruin. The third vehicle halted abruptly, allowing Morgan's shell to whistle past and bury itself in a nearby building. The German driver slammed his vehicle into reverse, and a couple of seconds later he was out of sight.

Morgan charged across the open ground, pursuing the fleeing German, and Kuruk went with him. Anderson's infantry had dismounted and were milling around, uncertain about what to do. It was still an enemy held town, and at any second they were liable to run into more German armor.

The M10 came alongside Minnie, and Allendale climbed on top of the turret to shout across.

"What's the deal, Josh? Do we leave 'em to chase down

that Panzer while we carry on to the target?"

"That's what we're here for," Lieutenant Anderson called up to them, "You need to give the order."

His men were grouped around him, waiting on his reply. Waiting to go in and grab the dough. Grant realized he was the de facto commander. They looked to his commands to keep them alive, and to make them rich. But they were right. Two Shermans could deal with a single Panzer IV, and right now they had the advantage of surprise, which they were about to lose if they didn't move fast.

He looked across at the stone edifice opposite. The sentries were gone, and the massive doors firmly shut. It had to be now or never. If he left it too late, they could meet German reinforcements, or the American barrage would start.

"We go in. Stand by, wait for us to blast the main doors."

The soldiers looked content with the plan. They wanted to make sure of their money.

"Solly, load HE. As soon as we've fired, I'll go with the infantry to find Margot. Look after Minnie. She's all we've got to get us home. Gunter, I want you with me."

"Of course," the German replied calmly.

He looked at the infantry. "Are you ready?"

"I know my job, Sergeant," Anderson snapped.

He nodded. "Stand by."

A second before Solly fired, a German machine gun crew doubled around the corner and set up an MG42 directly in front of the doors.

"Fire."

When the smoke cleared, the doors had disappeared, along with the machine gun and its crew. There were just scraps of wood, steel, and flesh painted with blood.

Anderson raced forward, leading his men, and as soon as they were inside, the shooting started. Grant shouted," She's all yours, Solly," as he grabbed his M2 carbine, vaulted to the ground, and ran.

Dale had taken over the gun, and Vern would load. It would never have worked before. Vern would have made it impossible, loading for a black gunner. On the other hand, money changed everything. Even prejudice.

He dodged across the square with Gunter at his heels, but there was no attempt by the enemy to stop them. They were either dead, or they'd run. He almost tripped over a German helmet in the doorway, recovered, and sped through the front into the building. Bodies were strewn in the hall, some killed in the blast, others gunned down by Anderson's men.

"The basement," Gunter shouted over the racket, the sound of automatic fire, rifle bullets, and the crash of tank shells.

It seemed unlikely the Germans had brought up more armor. With any luck, Morgan was disposing of the last Panzer IV. The cell had to be in the basement, of course. It was always in the basement where evil men carried out their dark deeds. Hidden from the harsh, bright glare of public scrutiny. Half of Anderson's squad was racing up the wide staircase, while the rest of them busted into the Gestapo Commandant's office on the first floor. Gunter had told them the treasury was in a storeroom inside.

Good luck to them, to all of them. I don't want the money. I want the girl. Margot.

They reached the foot of the staircase, and a hail of bullets chipped stone from the wall behind them, forcing them back. Someone down there had a machine pistol, and they weren't about to surrender.

"Give me your pistol," Gunter pleaded, "I will distract him while you take the shot."

He was wary about giving a weapon to an enemy, but he decided it was worth the risk. The guy hadn't brought them this far just to sell them out. He handed over the Colt.

"What're you planning to do?"

"Kill him," the German answered. His voice was casual.

"It may not work out the way you're planning, buddy. He could kill you, unless you're careful."

"Another death?" Gunter smiled, "Why would one more concern you, Sergeant, when there have been so many? What is important is that we free this girl before they kill her."

"Sure, but you don't want to die in the attempt."

"Do I not?"

He hesitated only a second, then he was gone, sprinting around the corner, and another fusillade of shots exploded from whoever was back there. Grant followed, and as he left the safety of the stairwell, he was forced to duck low as bullets chipped stone next to his head. The unknown shooter had been waiting for them, and Gunter was stretched out on the floor, blood oozing from his body. He looked dead, but then his head moved a fraction. More gunshots cracks out, and in the flashes he could see the German sheltering in a recess, or maybe it was a doorway. Whatever, it was impossible to get in a clear shot.

Gunter's sacrifice was all for nothing.

It was an impasse. The German broke the silence first.

"Drop the weapon, American. Unless you want to die like your treacherous friend."

He spoke English with a harsh, guttural accent. He studied the other man. His face was almost a caricature of sneering brutality. If anyone wanted to look the evils of the Nazi regime in the face, this was it. The man held an MP38, and Grant wondered how many shots it had fired. Not enough to be empty, almost certainly. Which meant there'd be enough left in the clip to finish him off. Besides, the guy had the drop on him.

Maybe he could bring up his M2 up and pull the trigger before the other man reacted, but he doubted it. This was a Jerry who lived for the kill, and he'd be praying that Grant made the move. He looked down as Gunter's lips moved, framing a word, two words.

Just two words, but he couldn't make them out. A trickle of blood seeped out of his mouth, and he saw the man's head move slightly. A nod, and then it came to him.

Do it, that's what he said. Does he have some kind of a plan? But he's dying, his blood leaking out to the cold, dusty floor.

"I said drop the weapon, American."

He glanced at the man, and then at Gunter again. His right hand was held in an awkward position beneath his body.

Does he have a gun in that hand? He has to. Otherwise, we'll both die.

"Okay, pal, take it easy. I'm putting the gun down."

He carefully placed the M2 on the stone floor and stood up to face the German.

"I didn't come to kill you, pal. I just want the girl."

He knew there was no way the sadist would give him anything, but he needed to give Gunter time to make his move. He edged forward, moving his arms to attract the attention of the Nazi, keeping it friendly. Hoping it would take his attention from the bleeding soldier on the floor. Assuming he was right, and Gunter did have a gun in his right hand.

The Nazi's sneer widened. "You're so stupid, you Americans. Do you honestly believe you can defeat Germany with such a feeble, weak attitude to war?"

He pronounced Germany, 'Chairmany.' Grant suppressed a smile. It wasn't even remotely funny.

"We're not doing so badly, last time I checked."

The sneer disappeared and his expression darkened. "You've achieved nothing! We have secret weapons which the Fuhrer will unleash on your puny armies and send them home in coffins."

Grant nodded. "Uh huh. He's leaving it a bit late, isn't he, your Fuhrer? A lot of your soldiers have died here in France, Africa, Italy, and in Russia. When do these things appear, these secret weapons, this year, next year, or the year after, maybe? If I was Adolf, I wouldn't leave it too late."

He was taunting him deliberately and knew he was taking a chance. The SS man raised his weapon, and Grant stared into the small, dark hole at the wrong end of an MP38.

"The Fuhrer will show them to the world when he is ready. And you, American, will not live to see it. You have come here to die."

Grant tensed, about to lunge for the M2. He knew he'd miscalculated. Gunter wasn't going to make a move. He only had that one tiny chance to grab for the gun. He started to move, and the German's eyes widened as his finger tightened on the trigger. It was the last move he made. With a supreme effort, Gunter twisted his body over to free the Colt .45 automatic, and he fired a single shot. It struck the Nazi in the throat, and he staggered backward, clutching at the wound. Blood was pouring down his uniform even as he tried to bring the MP38 back to the aiming position. It was too much for his waning strength, and he dropped the weapon as he fell to the floor. Blood oozed onto the stone in a gathering pool.

Grant snatched up the M2 to cover him, but he was a gonna. He turned to Gunter.

"That was some shooting. How bad is it?"

"I'll live, for now," he replied, "Let's go find the girl."

He helped the German to his feet and gestured at the Nazi who was gasping for breath through his ruined throat.

"What about him? We should put him out of his misery. It'll only take a single bullet."

"No! He deserves a slow death, and that will be more mercy than he showed to his victims."

Grant shrugged, and they walked past the shuddering body. At the end of the corridor the cell door was closed but unlocked, and they pushed their way in. Margot was inside, her face covered in cuts and bruises, and her eyes screwed up in pain. Father Bouchet lay nearby, his hands and ankles covered in dried blood. There was a third man in the cell. An SS officer, Grant corrected himself; the cuff titles were different. The initials SD were embroidered in silver on a black patch.

So this was a member of the infamous Sicherheitsdienst, the Nazi SS intelligence service, a Standartenfuhrer, from his rank badges. The rank of colonel, he recalled from his briefings. They said that any prisoner of his rank should be taken to Headquarters for interrogation. Yet this man wasn't going anywhere. He had his arm locked around Margot's throat. His other hand held a Luger 9 mm Parabellum pistol, pointed at her head. His expression was calm, and he studied them for a moment before he spoke.

"If you want her to die, carry on and arrest me. Otherwise, get out."

"No!"

It was Gunter who shouted, and the SD officer shot a glance at him. "No? You want me to kill her?"

"Let her go. If you want a hostage, you can have me."

The man smiled. "I think not. I hardly think a captured German has the same value as an attractive French girl. Get out of here, and perhaps I will let her live."

Grant considered taking the shot, but it was risky, too risky. He stared at the Nazi.

"Listen, pal, let her go. We'll take the priest as well, and we'll leave you here unharmed. Otherwise, we'll have to kill you. If you shoot the girl, well, that's up to you, but you die. However this goes down, I promise you we're not leaving her here with you. Your only chance to live is to let her go."

He thought for a few moments and then nodded. "I have your promise, your word of honor?"

"I'm no fucking Nazi. Yeah, you got it."

"And you?"

He looked at Gunter, who inclined his head. "As an officer of the Wehrmacht, you have my word I will not attack you, provided you let the prisoners go."

The Standartenfuhrer smiled and nodded. "Very well, take her."

He lowered his pistol, and Grant rushed forward to grab Margot before she collapsed. Gunter staggered over to the priest and inspected his wounds.

"This man needs a hospital and quickly. What did they do to him?"

"They crucified him," Margot said, "They tried to get me to give them information."

"What information? All you did was cook some food."

"I'm sure they did it for their enjoyment. They must have known after the first torture sessions I had nothing to give them."

He looked at the SD officer, who shrugged. "It's war, mein Herr. Nothing more."

"Yeah." He looked at Margot, "Can you walk? I need to help Gunter with the priest. He's been shot and won't manage on his own."

"I can manage, but I hate to leave this monster alive."

"I gave him my word. Let's not give him the satisfaction of knowing we're no better than him."

She glared at the SD man for a few moments, and then spat in his face. "Next time I see you, I'll kill you. When you leave here, you'd better get back to Germany, because nowhere in France will ever be safe for you."

Her voice was eerie, cold and calm, and not a man in that room doubted she meant it. He inclined his head but kept silent. Grant went to help Gunter with the priest, and between them they carried him outside the cell. Margot followed, and they dragged the semi-comatose man to the top of the stairs and out to the lobby. Anderson stood there supervising his men as they carried sealed wooden boxes out to the waiting M10. His face wore a beaming smile.

"It's all here, just like you said. Jesus Christ, we're rich." His face fell as he looked at the priest, "What happened to him?"

"The same as Jesus Christ, but he'll make it if we get him to a medic. How did we make out with the money?"

"Pretty good. It's all Swiss francs. Apparently, the SS were worried the war may go against them and German currency could collapse. They swapped their money for Swiss currency."

"How much do we each wind up with?"

"About fifty thousand dollars, that's a rough estimate. Maybe a little more."

"Fifty thousand dollars?"

"Yep. Not bad for a few hours of work."

"Right. We'll help these people outside and make preparations to leave."

"To leave? Our army is on the way into town."

"That's right. After they've flattened it with artillery."

The Lieutenant was silent for a few seconds and then nodded. "Maybe we'd better get out of Dodge."

"Good plan. We need transport for the civilians. There's no way they can manage on the hull of a tank. The German is in a bad way, too. Too much jolting and he'll bleed out."

"I'll send a couple of my men to look around. There has to be a car somewhere around here. Jefferson, Engstrom, on the double. I need you to..."

The crash of a shell landing somewhere in the town cut him off.

"Forget the car," Grant said quickly, "If we don't get out now, we're dead. Margot, let me help you onto the hull of Minnie. Someone give these two guys a hand. We're leaving."

Another shell landed, this time closer and in the next

street, and they manhandled Gunter and Father Bouchet onto the hull of Minnie Mouse. Margot cradled the priest in her arms as the infantrymen climbed aboard. At that moment, Morgan and Kuruk appeared, taking the corner at high speed and halting in a shower of ripped up cobblestones. Anderson's soldiers swarmed up onto the hulls as the Major leaned down, his expression grim.

"Grant, we need to leave."

"You don't say. Did you get that other Panzer?"

"He won't be returning to the Fatherland, that I promise. Now let's get out of here." He paused and looked uncomfortable, "Uh, did we get the, er..."

"The money. Yeah, Swiss francs, no sweat."

"How much?"

"Enough to pay for your wife's treatment, Sir. Now let's get moving."

Solly looked at him curiously. "I thought it was..."

"Shut up, Solly. Angel, get us out of here. Major, if you don't mind, I'll take the lead, with the M10 behind, then you and Dan. It seemed to work before."

"Sure."

Morgan understood. Grant wanted to get Margot away first, and if there was any trouble from the German garrison, the armor at the back would form a barrier to protect her. That was Josh Grant's theory, anyway.

Explosions like the Fourth of July; flames, flares, a myriad of colors, and plenty of whizz-bangs lighted the town, but this was no celebration, unless it was a celebration of death. As they exited the town, buildings behind them crumpled from shells landing, and then a direct hit on an ammunition dump caused an explosion that rocked the vehicles on their springs. Behind them, more buildings toppled, razed by the destructive force of hundred of shells.

They made it to the outskirts of the town without any sign of the enemy. He breathed a sigh of relief, what had seemed like an impossible dream had come true. He'd freed her and dealt a solid blow to the Nazis. Solly popped up beside him and stuck his head out of the turret to suck in the fresh air. He caught Grant's eye.

"A hundred thousand dollars each, Sarge? No way."

No one could hear them over the roar of the engine, the grinding of the tracks, and the explosions from the artillery barrage. They could have sung a Wagnerian opera and no one would have heard.

"So?"

"I heard it was more like fifty."

"Yeah, I heard the same."

"Morgan's going to be disappointed when he finds out the real figure."

"He won't. Find out, I mean. He'll have my share."

Solly's eyes widened. "Your share? You're kidding me. All this, and you come away with nothing?"

"I got what I wanted." He glanced at Margot, who was trying to make the priest more comfortable. Father Bouchet seemed to have come round, and she was whispering to him as she worked.

"Worth fifty thousand dollars?"

He looked at her for long moments and felt the powerful emotion of tenderness at the sight of her beauty.

"Every penny."

She glanced around, saw him staring at her, and smiled back at him.

Oh yeah, she's worth it. That's one girl in a million, almost worth fighting a war for.

They rumbled out of town, heading in the same direction as they came in. As the last house slipped behind them and the sunken lane came into sight, every man breathed a sigh of relief. No matter what happened now, they'd done it. Pulled off the impossible, at last something worth fighting for. They were almost home free. It was a miracle. Some of them pulled out concealed bottles of booze, brandy they'd 'liberated' on the way across Normandy, and took a few swigs. Some high-fived each other, and on the hull of each tank, men chatted about their plans for the future. Josh allowed himself to relax.

We made it.

* * *

Outside Saint-Lo, 21.20, July 11, 1944

"Obersturmfuhrer, are you sure this is the way?"

"Dammit, Heinrich, I don't know. I can see the town right ahead of us. If it hadn't been for that damn hedgerow, we'd have been there by now. These Frenchmen need to put up some road signs for their country."

"The Fuhrer says it's our country," Lenz reminded him.

"Well the fucking Fuhrer isn't here, is he?" Manhausen snarled, "He's hiding in some fucking bunker in Berlin or wherever he goes these days."

He immediately wished he could take it back. There was a silence, as they digested what he'd said. It was treason, no question.

"I didn't mean it like that, not the way it came out," he said quickly.

344

He knew it was too late. Lenz would gleefully recount his remark to that SD relative of his.

Fuck him!

"Sir, there's movement up ahead," Franz shouted a warning, "Armor, coming up fast."

The driver's night vision was legendary. Rolf could see the shadows up ahead in the sunken lane, but that's all they were, shadows.

"Relax, Saint-Lo is in our hands. They'll be our own Panzers, probably coming out to reinforce the defenses.

"They don't look like our Panzers, Obersturmfuhrer."

"They must be ours. Panthers, perhaps."

A shaft of moonlight suddenly lit up the dark, moving shapes ahead of them.

He screamed a warning. "Shermans, dead ahead! Gunner, load AP, driver, get off the track."

He slid down into the turret and slammed the hatch closed. His heart was thudding from the adrenaline pouring through his system, and he squinted through the vision port at the oncoming armor. Another shaft of moonlight lit up the turret of the lead tank, and he felt his guts turn to ice as he recognized the cartoon character painted on the side. Minnie Mouse.

"Gunner, have you got a shot?"

"Almost, Sir. They keep dropping out of sight in this damned sunken lane."

"As soon as you see them, kill them. The lead tank, hit it," he screamed, "Keep hitting it until it's no more than scrap."

"Sir?"

He knew he'd let it get to him, the superstition that had followed him all these past weeks.

Why am I worried? It's only a Sherman.

"Destroy him, Boll. Kill him!"

He wiped the sweat from his forehead. Strange, the night was cold.

* * *

Town of Saint-Lo, 22.00, July 11, 1944

"Tiger!"

Vern's shout interrupted his reverie, and he looked around. He saw nothing.

"Shut up, Vern. There ain't' no..."

"Over there, he just left the track, and he's driving into the field. I tell you it's a fucking Tiger."

As his eyes pierced the gloom, he made out a shape, dark, huge and menacing, moving through the field, and just visible through gaps in the hedgerow. The hull was massive, with a flat section at the front of the vehicle, just below the Henschel turret. The gun was enormous, obscene in its outsized length. It looked almost as if the mechanized monster would tip over from the weight of the barrel.

It was like something from a nightmare. It was death, and he couldn't help the shout.

"Tiger!"

CHAPTER TWELVE

Half a mile outside Saint-Lo, 01.30, July 12, 1944

Major-General Charles Hunter Gerhardt stood beneath a canvas shelter hastily erected between two vehicles, one a Willys jeep and the other a 'deuce and a half' truck. He was listening to the reports from his men.

"We're inside the town, Sir. Some of the lead elements of the 29th are fighting their way through the defenders, and we had a report of American armor attacking Krauts hard inside the town itself."

Gerhardt winced, as he did every time someone used the pejorative term, 'Kraut.' With a name like Gerhardt, it wasn't too hard to work out he had more than a few ancestors who were Krauts. He sighed; he'd forced himself to ignore it ever since Hitler came to power and began this insane war. The report about their armor inside the town didn't ring true, and he questioned the officer, a very young, newly promoted Captain. They'd lost more than a few officers since they landed at Omaha, and promotion was quick.

"Which armor, Captain? Who sent them forward? Where's Colonel Lindbergh?"

"Here, Sir."

The elegant, patrician senior officer stepped forward. He looked like he'd just attended a dinner party.

"Lindbergh, what's this about your armor inside the town? Could it be true?"

"Er, well, Sir, I'm not sure. Maybe it's another unit."

"Sure. Like the 12th SS Panzer Hitler Jugend that's been bugging us all this time."

"I meant a company from another battalion, General."

"Which battalion? Unless they've put bigger engines in those Shermans to drive faster, who else could it be?"

"Er, no one, Sir."

"You're damn right, no one. If there're American tanks in there, they have to be the 745th. Find out who they are, and tell me how come they made it in while the rest of your outfit is sitting on their butts out here getting wet."

"Yes, Sir, right away."

He went off to find someone he could dispatch to check it out. Gerhardt watched him go.

"Useless tailor's dummy," he muttered under his breath.

"Sir?"

Shit, I didn't mean for anyone to hear that.

"Nothing. You can halt the artillery barrage in one hour. We don't want to kill our own soldiers. Get the men moving. It looks like Saint-Lo is ours. All we need do is walk in and hang our shingle on the door."

* * *

Town of Saint-Lo, 04.30, July 12, 1944

"All of you, off the hull and board the other tanks."

"Off the hull?"

"Now!"

He watched as infantrymen helped Margot and Father Bouchet down to the ground and across to the other two Shermans. Margot looked up at him, shoving away a soldier who was trying to hurry her along.

"Josh..."

"It's okay, Margot. We'll be fine."

"You cannot do this. Not on your own."

"I don't have a choice."

"That's crazy! Why don't you have a choice?"

A good question, how can I explain to her that premonition I had when we came ashore? How do I tell her I knew it would end like this, just Minnie and the Tiger; it has to be.

"This won't take long."

She gave him a sorrowful look. "Josh..."

Already they were bundling her on top of Kuruk's Cochise, and he turned away. It was time to call Morgan.

"Major, I'm going after the enemy armor. Take care of these people."

"What kind of enemy armor, Grant? Why are you sending those people across to me and Dan?"

"Just get those people to safety, Sir."

A pause. "Why do this on your own? What's so important?"

There it is again. The one question I can't answer.

"It's something I have to do, Sir. Give my regards to your wife."

"My wife? Of course, but..."

"Good luck, Sir. Take care of them."

Especially one of them.

He shouldn't have made that comment about Morgan's wife. It was a death thought, and the last thing on his mind was dying. Not when they'd just located and rescued Margot after he'd thought her dead. However, it was too late to change anything; it was something he had to do. Alone. It had been bugging him ever since they came in on the LST and saw that big mother up on the cliff top.

Why am I so certain it's the same one? Why do I think it has to come down to this, a one-on-one duel with the biggest, meanest Nazi bully on the block? I just know.

"Driver, advance. Gunner, load AP."

"AP loaded."

"Stay sharp, this is a Tiger."

"They're big, bad fuckers," he heard Vern say. No one contradicted him.

We all know that, Vern.

"Driver, make a one hundred and eighty degree turn. We're heading back into town."

"Into town? You sure, Sarge?"

He smiled at Angel's astonishment. "I'm sure. This is a Tiger, and out in the open we're dead meat. The only chance we have is inside the town where he can't maneuver."

"They're shelling the town," Solly reminded him, "We might take a hit from our own side."

"So could the Tiger. Do it, Angel."

The tracks squealed as he spun Minnie around, knocked over a stone wall and plunged back toward Saint-Lo. A stray shell burst close by, and Grant ducked inside the turret as steel fragments sliced through the air. He popped his head back out in time to see the enemy tank fire. The boom of the big 88mm main gun, and a second later, the whistle of the shell sped past them, a miss, but not by much. The gunner had offset the shell to allow for their forward speed and miscalculated. The projectile struck a rusting tractor a hundred yards away and blew it to small fragments.

That could have been us. Dear God, I've led them into this.

Seconds later, they were inside the town. As they passed a narrow intersection, he glimpsed the Tiger moving toward them, only fifty or sixty yards away. The German commander glanced his way for a split second, and then they were once again out of sight. In that split second, he'd seen the man's face.

He knows, the same as I do. Good.

A shell smashed into a spot on the tarmac a split second after they'd rolled past. They avoided three more shells that demolished a house in the next street, and debris bounced off the rear of the hull. They were lucky; inside the town it was impossible for the German to get a clear shot. Out in open country, it would be a different story. They'd be dead.

He briefly considered closing the hatch, but in the close, dark confines of the built up area he needed his vision to be one hundred percent. They passed Gestapo Headquarters as the familiar building loomed out of the night. It had already been partly destroyed by artillery shells. Getting them out had been a close thing.

The Tiger could well know the reason they'd come into town ahead of the main force. After all, they were SS, and everyone knew they were linked to the Gestapo. If the tank commander worked it out, he could be waiting for them in ambush, expecting them to appear in a predetermined place. In which case, he needed to do the unexpected.

"Driver, take the next three left turns. Get us moving in the opposite direction."

"Out of town? You sure?"

"I'm sure."

"You got it."

The Sherman lurched when Angel swung through the first ninety-degree turn, just as a huge shell smashed into the house ahead of them. He looked in the direction it had come from.

The Tiger commander's clever, very clever. He stopped short of Gestapo Headquarters, waiting for us to present him with a clear shot. If I hadn't given the order to turn, it would have been 'farewell Minnie Mouse.'

They squeezed through the narrow streets, and he had another thought.

If the German can predict our movement, he'll expect Minnie to go around the block and come up behind him. It wasn't my intention, but the three turns will do exactly that.

"Driver, skip the next turn, keep heading south along this street. When you see a junction, take a right."

A pause. "You got it."

He smiled; he could almost hear Angel muttering, "Why don't you make up your damn mind?"

He could sense their anxiety, their terror; it was like a dark fog that clouded the interior of the hull. Yet they trusted him to make the right call. He needed that trust, needed them to jump when he told them to jump, because a split second's delay could kill them all.

They turned south, and now they were heading out of town. He tried to work out where the Tiger could be waiting.

Where will he set an ambush for us to fall into their trap? The Gestapo Headquarters, it commands the center of town. Is he waiting behind a wall of the ruined building, with the long barrel poking through a hole in the masonry?

More shells were smashing into the town, churning the rubble over and over. There were plenty of walls to shelter behind, enough concealment for a company of Tigers.

He had to take a risk, a hell of a risk. Then again, in war everything was a risk. He had to assume the Tiger was waiting for him in the center of town, and that meant the Gestapo building, which offered the most concealment. As soon as Minnie approached, he'd have time to line up a clear shot. At short range, the 88mm would penetrate their frontal armor like paper.

Dammit, it'd penetrate their frontal armor at most any range.

More shells were falling around them, and he forced himself to ignore them. He had to outthink that Tiger.

"Driver, new direction, head toward the east side of town. Skirt around the outskirts to the north, and then come back in to the center. We're heading for the rear of the Gestapo building.

A pause, this time longer, a lot longer. Followed by a sigh.

"The outside? You sure this time?"

"I'm sure. Real sure."

"You know there's a Tiger out there hunting our ass?"

"I know."

Another sigh, "You got it."

Grant turned it over and over in his mind.

Do I have it right, or has that Nazi SS bastard outthought me again?

He was so preoccupied he almost missed the enemy troops who suddenly appeared fifty yards in front of them, two soldiers, one supporting an MG42 on his shoulder, and the other behind the butt, about to hose them down with a stream of 7.92mm Mauser bullets. It wasn't these two men who would kill them. It was the missile team who followed.

Two Panzergrenadiers, one with an anti-tank launcher on his shoulder and the other carried spare missiles. He ducked down into the turret and slammed the hatch closed. The first salvo from the machine gun smacked into the hull. Some of the bullets ricocheted off the hatch before he got it closed.

A close one!

"Vern, anti-tank crew missile ahead! Nail them. Solly, shoot those bastards!"

As he spoke, he grabbed for the machine gun. Before he could cut loose, Vern fired, loosing off a stream of lead at the enemy. A half second later, Solly fired his first round. There hadn't been time to switch to HE. The shell was AP, ready for the Tiger, but the projectile exploded next to the soldiers, adding to the carnage created by Vern's machine gun.

"Good shooting, men. Angel, don't slow, roll over 'em."

"You got it."

They barely noticed the slight jar as the tracks churned over the bloody remains of the four Germans. Then they were past. He opened the hatch and looked back. A mess of blood and tissue lay on the narrow street, mixed with fragments of metal flattened by Minnie's tracks. He didn't feel any emotion at the ghastly sight. It was just part of fighting a war. Even the urge for the revenge he'd sought when he came over from England had evaporated, and he'd begun to see his brother's death in some kind of box. A box called war, and in war, people died. He hadn't forgotten, would never forget, but the time to mourn would come later.

He needed to concentrate on the now. This was unfinished business. Ever since that dark, dismal morning on Omaha Beach, he'd been heading inexorably for this day. The day when accounts would be settled, the day that would decide who would live. And who would die.

"We're coming up on that Gestapo building," Angel sung out, "What do you want me to do?"

"Hold it! Halt right here until we can take a slow look around."

"You got it."

They were behind the big building, and it was unrecognizable, a heap of broken masonry. As they looked, another shell smashed into the ruins. Without doubt, they could drive straight into the rear, and with any luck they'd come up behind the Tiger, who he assumed would be waiting for them to approach from the front.

We'll only get one chance, he cautioned himself. *If the German gets wind of us, he'll bring that big gun to bear, and it'll be the end.*

He felt uneasy. He'd worked out how to outwit the German, and he was convinced he'd done the right thing. Except they still hadn't located the hiding place of the Tiger, and there were several places big enough to hide an armored vehicle inside the ruins. If they chose the wrong one, he'd be waiting for them. The seconds ticked by. They watched and waited with the engine ticking over.

Which way?

"Angel, you see anything in there?"

"Nothing."

"Solly?"

"Nope."

He briefly considered climbing out to take a look around, but these Germans weren't fools. They'd likely have someone watching, and the town was still full of Germans like the four soldiers they'd killed only moments before.

There's bound to be snipers around somewhere.

He had to choose. Any longer and the enemy would spot them. He wracked his brains as he studied the wreckage of the building, working out angles, lines of fire, trying to decide the best place for a heavy tank to wait in ambush. And then it hit him. He never knew why it came to him so suddenly, only that they were seconds from disaster.

"Driver, back up, back up! Fast! Gunner, load AP. Stand by to engage! Target is behind us!"

Minnie's tracks squealed as Angel hit the gas and shot back. The part of the building where they'd been waiting disappeared in a massive explosion.

The bastard!

He'd anticipated their every move, and instead of waiting to ambush them inside the building, he'd hidden in another building across the street, knowing they'd try to get up behind him.

Angel drove recklessly in reverse, hardly aware of where he was going, just getting them out of trouble. Solly rotated the main gun to target the enemy, but he didn't fire. There was still nothing in sight. Grant studied the big building across the street. It looked like it had been some kind of auto repair shop, big, timber double doors, peeling paintwork.

There! The end of a 88mm barrel is poking out through the gap between the doors, unseen in the darkness. Nice try, Kraut. You almost had us.

Then he lost sight of it as Angel retreated further along the street, out of sight of the German. He stopped at an intersection.

"What do you want me to do now, Sarge?"

He quickly explained where the German had to be hiding.

"Angel, we'll use the same plan. Try and get behind him. Quick, you need to..."

"Sarge."

"Not now, Solly, we're..."

"Sarge, we're fucked. Finished."

"What?"

"He's coming out. Take a look."

He swiveled his head to look around. The huge, menacing shape of the German tank had pushed out from cover and waited less than one hundred yards away. They'd outthought him every time.

The gun looked huge. It was huge. A massive cannon, and inside the breech there'd be an AP shell that was about to blast Minnie into oblivion. He didn't move. Nothing moved. Everything had come to a standstill like a frozen tableau.

"You want me to put a shell into him?" Solly asked quietly.

"Negative. Before you can rotate the turret to bring the gun to bear, we'll be dead. He's got us cold, Solly. I'm sorry, guys."

"There must be something."

"No."

We could bale out. We might make it."

"No, we won't."

He didn't know why he denied them the chance of making a run for it. Only that he was certain it was the wrong move. He didn't know why.

"Sarge, we could..."

"Wait."

* * *

Town of Saint-Lo, 05.42, July 12, 1944

"What are you waiting for, Obersturmfuhrer? Give the order. Shoot the Ami! If you refuse to fire, you would be a traitor to the Reich."

They were staring at him, but Lenz had gone too far.

"How dare you, Sturmann Lenz! I make the decisions about when to shoot, not you. In future, keep your mouth shut."

It wasn't to be. The fourteen-year-old loader was bolstered by his hatred of the enemy, by adulation of his Fuhrer, and the knowledge he'd always have the support of his uncle, the SD Standartenfuhrer.

"I will not be silent," he snarled, "Not this time. There's an enemy out there, and you hesitate to shoot. This is treason, Obersturmfuhrer, no question. Either you kill that tank, or I will report your actions to Standartenfuhrer Schulz. You know the penalty. They'll shoot you as a traitor."

He smiled. The fanatical little shit had made up his mind, and he knew nothing would change it.

Fuck him, and fuck his SD uncle!

"Leave it, Siegfried," Unterscharfuhrer Boll advised the young loader, "If you rat on Obersturmfuhrer Manhausen, you're on your own. You'd be making a big mistake."

"I don't give a damn what you think." His voice had risen to a shrill scream, almost as if his voice hadn't broken, "This is treason against the Fuhrer. Perhaps you're all in it together. I'll give him your names, and we'll see what the Gestapo makes of your excuses. Don't ask me to change my mind. It's made up. You're a bunch of traitors, all of you."

No one spoke. It was a pivotal moment; his outburst meant they faced an inevitable future, arrest, and incarceration in a Gestapo dungeon, torture, and death. It had gone too far now, much too far. No matter what happened, they would have the threat hanging over their heads.

"Why won't you shoot?" Boll asked quietly, so Lenz couldn't hear.

"I don't know, Heinrich. It's just, well, a feeling."

"If you're not going to shoot, perhaps we should get out of here. I don't understand your reasons, but if we don't kill that Sherman, he'll come at us."

Rolf suddenly glimpsed troops racing past an intersection less than four hundred meters away.

Americans. Enemy troops. They're here.

"Yes. Tell Lenz to load HE."

"HE, Sir? That's enemy armor we're facing."

"There are American soldiers up ahead. They'll be here shortly."

"Yes, Sir. But the Sherman..."

"Do it, Boll."

Why can't I give the order to destroy that tank? What is the thread that connects us, and has connected us for the past month? Why do we keep meeting? I only wish I knew the reason. And what do I do about Lenz? The entire crew is in mortal danger. He'll carry through with his threat, no question. The Gestapo is far more dangerous than the Americans.

"The breech is jammed."

He looked down to where Lenz was struggling to unlock the breech mechanism and switch shells.

"What do you mean, jammed?"

"It's the powder charge. Somehow it's jammed inside the loading mechanism. It must have been faulty. I can't extract it, and the gun won't fire, not without blowing us sky high."

"Boll, check it out."

"I'm looking now, Sir.

Rolf waited; all the while he was watching the Sherman.

Why don't they do something? They think the Tiger has them beat, of course, so what would be the point? Or is it something else? Does my opposite number in the tank named Minnie Mouse feel some strange connection, like I do? Maybe.

"It's fucked."

He looked down at Boll, who had his arms covered in thick grease.

"What do you mean?"

"Somehow a double charge got loaded in the breech by mistake, and the second charge displaced the first, so it jammed it at an angle inside the barrel. If we'd fired just now, the gun would have exploded. Lenz, the little fucker, he screwed up. Nearly got us all killed."

"I, I...it wasn't my fault. Standartenfuhrer Schulz will tell you I am a dedicated..."

The report was loud in the confined space. A single

shot fired from a 9mm pistol. Boll stared at his victim, at the body of Lenz as it slumped to the steel floor of the tank. They were silent for several seconds, and then he handed the gun to Manhausen.

"I'm sorry, Sir. Arrest me if you wish. He nearly got us all killed. He'd become a dangerous liability."

"You mean when he messed up loading the gun, or with his SD relative?"

"Does it matter? Either way, I confess to my crime."

Rolf sighed, as if he didn't have enough trouble. "A pistol misfired, went off by mistake, Heinrich, that's all. There was no crime. I suggest we concern ourselves with what we do about that Sherman."

He handed the gun back to Boll.

"If we'd tried to kill it, we'd all be dead," Boll pointed out.

"I realize that."

"Do you think it is fate, Obersturmfuhrer? You know the Reichsfuhrer SS believes in fate, and in the stars. So does the Fuhrer, I believe. They say it enables them to foretell the future."

"They didn't foresee the crappy mess we're in, Heinrich."

No one said a word. Not until Franz finally asked if he should drive them away.

"The moment we move, he'll start shooting," Rolf said.

"So what do we do?"

"I don't know."

* * *

Town of Saint-Lo, 05.55, July 12, 1944

"What do we do?" Dale asked, "Do I load AP or HE? I mean; they could be about to bail out. Maybe there's something wrong."

"Just hold it. Wait."

"Wait for what?" Solly snarled, "They're fucking SS Nazis. We're here to kill them, not have a pow-wow with them."

"I said wait."

They heard the tone in his voice. It was something he'd learned in the courtroom when questioning a witness, what he called his, 'don't fuck with me' voice. People just listened. They waited, and someone murmured, "Jesus!"

The hatch of the Tiger opened. A man appeared and climbed down to the street, followed by the three further members of the crew, three of them. He'd always heard it was a crew of five in a Tiger. He cautioned himself to remain alert in case they pulled something.

Is this a trap? What's the fifth guy up to inside that steel hull? But why would they need to do that? They have a Tiger.

"It looks like they're going to surrender," Angel said, "Jesus, they'll never believe this back at Battalion. We've beaten a Tiger."

Did we? Or was it something else? Like fate.

"They're just kids," Solly exclaimed, his voice shocked. He was staring at them through his periscope.

"I'm getting out to take a look at them."

"I'll come with you," the Jewish gunner added, "Be careful, they're still Nazis, even if they are kids."

But his voice had lost some of the hard bitterness. Killing children was not the reason any of them had joined

362

up. Even Solly. The two Americans climbed out of the hatch and down to the street. They approached the black-clad tankers, and as Solly had said, they were kids. Children. Except for one of them, obviously the commander. An officer, a hard-bitten veteran, his eyes were watchful, and his face bore the scars of many conflicts. Grant decided it was for him to kick off. They were the victors.

"The name's Sergeant Josh Grant. What do you want?" He didn't offer to shake the hand offered by the German officer.

The man's lips twisted into a cynical smile as he withdrew his hand. "I am Obersturmfuhrer Rolf Manhausen. What do I want?" He sighed, "I want the war to end, and I want these children of mine to live long enough so they can go home to their families."

"Is that all?"

The scarred officer nodded. He looked haunted. Beaten. "That is all."

"You know you've lost. I mean; Germany has lost. You're finished, pal."

He nodded. "I think we all know that, although some will not admit it. They'll keep fighting until the very end, until the Allies batter down the gates of Berlin and destroy what is left inside the rubble left by your bombers."

"Why didn't you shoot? A Sherman is no match for a Tiger. We all know that. You could have killed us."

"I don't know. It was something. I had some kind of a feeling. I saw you come ashore on June 6th."

"That was you? Up on the cliff top?"

"I was there, yes. Perhaps you felt something?"

"Maybe."

"What will you do with us?" the German asked him.

He studied the man for several seconds, undecided about how to play this. Then he looked at the kids who comprised the crew of the Tiger.

What kind of men send their children to do the fighting for them? They belong in a school, not in a heavy Panzer.

He made up his mind.

"Get out of here."

The German looked puzzled. "I'm sorry?"

"Leave, vamoose, go away. Go home."

"You're serious?"

"Yeah."

"And my tank?"

"I assume you can't fight with it. Otherwise you would have fired on us. Something's wrong?"

"The main gun, yes. It is jammed." He grimaced, "In truth, all we have had is trouble these past few weeks. It was not well made."

Thank the good Lord for that.

"Take it and ride all the way back home to the Reich. Those kids should be in school."

"I agree. And thank you, Sergeant."

"Yeah. Maybe you should thank fate."

"I do. By the way, we have a body inside the hull, one of our crewmembers. I would like to remove it. Perhaps we can..."

"Absolutely not. You'll take him home. Treat him with respect. His ma and pa will want to bury him properly."

They stared at each other for several seconds. Manhausen drew himself to attention, clicked his heels, and was about to throw up his arm in the Nazi salute when he thought better of it. Instead, he brought up his arm in a traditional army salute. Grant responded American style, flipping him a cross between a salute and a wave.

"Thank you, Sergeant."

"Yeah."

The SS officer turned to his men and shouted an order. They stared at him and then at the Americans in disbelief. One man asked a question, but Manhausen snapped a few words at him, and they scrambled back into the Tiger. The engine misfired a few times and then started. The once feared monster rolled away, the start of a long journey home. He grinned at Solly.

"I guess that's it. Time to get out of here. We're done. For now."

"Yep. What's next, Sarge?"

"Next? There's a war on. There's still plenty to do, Germans to kill."

The gunner gave him a rueful glance. "It seems a crying shame, now we're rich."

"It'll make it more worthwhile to survive."

"Damn right. There's no way the Krauts are going to get us now. Not after this. I still can't believe it. We beat a Tiger."

"A messed up Tiger. Besides, we let them go, so no one will ever know."

"So? We did it.

* * *

Town of Saint-Lo, 06.38, July 12, 1944

"Obersturmfuhrer, can he do that?"

"Do what, Heinrich?"

"Send us back to the Reich?"

"No, he cannot. He had an alternative, he could have destroyed us."

"Yes, I understand, but he did not. We still have a working Tiger. We could fix the..."

"We nearly died, but we did not. Be thankful that American tanker gave you your life, my young friend."

Boll didn't reply. He didn't get it, didn't get it at all.

Neither will the Reichsfuhrer-SS, and that will be the trickiest part, Rolf chuckled to himself.

Himmler wouldn't be impressed. He resolved to deal with that when he got to it. It wasn't the only problem he had to face. There was the business of Lenz; they'd have to concoct a story to explain the death of the nephew of a senior officer of the Sicherheitsdienst.

There was also the question of Standartenfuhrer Schulz proceeding with the arrest warrant. He was sure to face an SS honor court, and the outcome wouldn't be good, especially now Lenz was dead. His probable fate would be a punishment battalion and an early death. He had to do his best to protect the teenagers of his crew in the meantime. As soon as they were clear of the bombardment of Saint-Lo, he'd find a way to surrender to the Americans. At least they'd survive, albeit in a prisoner of war cage. It was better than lying forgotten in a muddy grave in an anonymous French field. And afterward, he could keep his promise and get them back to Germany, and into the schoolroom where they belonged. He had a suspicion the end was not too far away.

"Sir, there's something strange up ahead."

"What is it?"

"Christ, it's Standartenfuhrer Schulz. He looks, well, odd."

Rolf opened the hatch and looked out. He did indeed look odd. The normally immaculate intelligence officer was covered in mud, and even his face was smeared. He'd lost his cap, and his hair hung in tangled knots, flattened by the rain. He looked around in terror as they approached, and then saw it was a German tank. He waved, and Franz slowed to a stop. Manhausen looked down at him.

"Standartenfuhrer Schulz."

His eyes widened. "You!"

"Yes. Do you have a problem, Sir?"

"I'm trying to get away. The battle is lost. The town is lost, and the Americans are coming."

"It looks that way, Sir. But why are you leaving, surely you should be defending the town to the last man?"

"Waste of time, Manhausen. We must retreat. I require you to carry me to rejoin our lines."

It suddenly came to Rolf that the body of Lenz was still inside the hull. He deserved to know his nephew was dead, so he spelled it out as gently as he could. The reaction was not what he expected.

"Dead? What do you mean dead?"

"We had no choice, Sir. He was going berserk. He'd lost his nerve. He became a risk to all of us, so I had no choice."

"You shot him?"

A pause. "Yes, I shot him."

A cunning look came over the SD officer's face. "You are already under open arrest, is that not so, Manhausen?"

"It was you who gave the order, Sir."

"Yes, I did. And with good reason, fleeing the battle when the Fuhrer ordered every man to stand fast. Who is your second-in-command?"

"Unterscharfuhrer Heinrich Boll."

"Very well, call him up here."

He leaned down and called for the gunner to appear. Boll looked sheepish as he stared down at the SD officer, the uncle of the crewman he'd so recently shot dead.

"You wanted me, Sir?"

"Yes. Unterscharfuhrer Boll, by the authority vested in me by the Fuhrer, I place you in command of this tank. Obersturmfuhrer Manhausen is under close arrest. You will relieve him of his sidearm, and he can assume the duties of the man he killed. My nephew was your loader, is that correct?"

"Yes, Standartenfuhrer."

"Very well, Manhausen will serve in that capacity. I will accompany you until we reach our lines, and then I will arrange a firing squad for Manhausen."

"A firing squad?"

"Of course. He shot my nephew, killed him in cold blood. I will insure he receives the maximum punishment. Death. Take his weapon. That's an order. Pass it to me."

Boll gave Manhausen an apologetic glance and put out his hand. Rolf unholstered his Luger and gave it to him.

"Hurry, man, give it to me. Unless you want to stand in front of a firing squad with him."

"No one will face a firing squad, Standartenfuhrer."

Boll's voice was calm.

"Eh? What are you talking about?"

"This."

Boll worked the action to chamber a round, pointed the pistol at the SD officer, and fired. And fired again, and again. Until the fourth bullet spat out the barrel, and without a glance at the body of his victim, he handed the gun back to Rolf.

"This is yours, Obersturmfuhrer."

He took it. "But, why?"

"You know why. I killed Lenz, not you. The treacherous little bastard deserved to die." He pointed at the body that lay in the mud, "Besides, that cowardly shit was running away from the fighting. You heard him; the Fuhrer decreed a single punishment for cowardice. Death. I just carried out his orders."

He smiled and ducked back inside the hull.

Rolf shook his head. It was over. With the death of Schulz, there'd be no need to concern himself with the open arrest.

Thank God! Now, how do we find the nearest American unit to whom we can surrender?

"Which direction, Obersturmfuhrer," Franz called from the driver's position.

He only needed to think for a couple of seconds. "Northwest, Franz."

"Northwest? But that is..."

"I know what it is, my friend. I promised to get you all back to school, and I believe that's the quickest route to get you there. It will take time, a long time, and we'll spend time in a POW camp. It could be a year, maybe more. But I will do everything I can to keep the promise I made to that American Sergeant."

The driver sounded uncertain. Eventually, he said, "Yes, Sir."

The Tiger swung around until the nose was pointing northwest, toward the American lines.

They drove across the Normandy countryside for many nights while he tried to find a safe approach to the

American forces. During the day, they sheltered wherever they could find somewhere out of sight of the marauding bombers and fighters, ruined buildings, sunken roads, and thick woods. On one occasion they camped in the lee of a platoon of Panzers, wrecked during an Allied bombing raid. Rolf insisted they bury the bodies of the dead crews before they could rest.

They were tired and hungry, and Rolf decided to risk driving in the daytime to find an American unit so they could surrender. Dawn began illuminating the Normandy countryside, and he anxiously searched the skies for marauding aircraft. Abruptly, Franz shouted, "Sir, over there. It's an American unit. Do you want me to take avoiding action?"

He looked toward them and saw a mixture of infantry and armor. One Sherman in particular looked familiar, and he smiled.

"No, drive toward them, Franz, but make it slow. Very, very slow."

He began to fasten a white piece of cloth to the radio aerial. He hoped it would be enough.

* * *

Town of Saint-Lo, 18.40, July 23, 1944

"Tell me where the fuck you've been, Sergeant Grant? I ordered you to stay close to Battalion."

He was standing rigidly to attention, looking at the smooth, unlined face of Colonel Martin Lindbergh III. He couldn't help compare his ragged and stained uniform to Lindbergh's immaculate outfit.

"That's correct, Sir. However, we ran into enemy armor, so I had no choice but to engage."

"No choice! What the fuck do you think you're here for, Sergeant?"

"To help defeat the Germans?"

Lindbergh scowled. "Don't fuck with me, soldier. You're here to obey my orders, nothing more, nothing less." He glanced aside with irritation when Major Morgan tried to intercede, "Major, whatever you have to say, I'm not interested. Put this soldier under close arrest. Dereliction of duty, disobeying orders, you name it. You're finished, Sergeant, finished. And you can forget your rank. I'm dropping you back to private soldier. Good God, I'm trying to fight a war here."

"How?"

He jerked around at the interruption and found himself staring at Major-General Charles Hunter Gerhardt.

"Sir, I didn't realize you were there. I'm sorry."

"Yeah. I asked you a question, Colonel. How?"

"How what?"

"Exactly how are you fighting a war? By arresting your most successful tank commanders? You think that's a recipe for success?"

"N-no, Sir, of course not. But we need concerted action, leadership from the top, and men need to know where they stand. They have to obey orders."

"This NCO destroyed more enemy armor than any other commander in your unit. Sergeant Grant also survived and brought his crew back in one piece. Isn't that what fighting a war is all about? Kill the enemy and bring your men back alive?"

"We have to obey orders, General. It's fundamental to

the way the Army functions."

"So is killing Germans, Colonel. And knocking out a Tiger is quite something, you have to admit."

"We only have his word for it," Lindbergh smirked, "He could be lying. He's already under open arrest as it is. He's probably trying to avoid a court martial."

"A court martial for what, Colonel?"

"For murder. He shot and killed an SS Noncom, a soldier who had just transferred to active service from guarding a camp."

"A camp? You mean a concentration camp?"

"Yeah, I believe it was. Some place in Poland."

"Poland."

"Right, nothing to do with us. Besides, I don't believe this claim of his about a Tiger." He snorted, "If it's true, where is this fictitious Tiger?"

General Gerhardt was staring over Lindbergh's shoulder. He smiled. "I do believe it could be that one, Colonel, the Tiger that's coming in under a flag of surrender. It looks real enough to me."

The Colonel swung around, and his mouth opened and closed like a goldfish. Gerhard turned to Grant.

"Is that the one you defeated?"

"It looks like the same number and markings. Yeah, that's the one, General."

He nodded. "Very well. Here's how this is going to go down. Major Morgan, your company is a credit to the Battalion. You've fought the enemy, given them a bloody nose, and lived to tell the tale. I guess you're due for a battalion. The 745th is yours. Just try not to lose any more tanks. I have a bad enough reputation as it is."

"Yes, Sir."

While Morgan smiled, Lindbergh scowled. "You can't do that, General. The Battalion is mine."

Gerhardt's expression was cold. "The Battalion is mine, Colonel. I decide who stays and who goes. Do you keep up with the news?"

"The news, Sir?"

"Yeah, the news, current events. Like what's happening on the Eastern Front, where the Russians are hitting the Krauts damn hard."

He looked puzzled. "I try to keep up with current events, of course. As a senior officer, it's important to know what's going on."

"So you heard yesterday about the discovery of a concentration camp at Majdanek? It was the big news on the radio. The entire Army is buzzing with it. Probably the whole world."

"I, er, did hear something about that."

"Right. So you know the Krauts built this concentration camp to be a kind of murder factory. When the Russians went in there, they found thousands of people starving. They were more like skeletons than human beings. They also found bodies piled everywhere. It was like a scene from hell. The Russians located a few of the German guards hiding nearby, and they shot them dead on the spot. I have to tell you I'd have done the same. They weren't men. They were beasts. Now you're telling me you want to punish Sergeant Grant for doing what every soldier in this army would have gladly done?"

"Well, er, I'm not, er..."

"Colonel, you're not really a people person, are you?" He smiled, and Lindbergh shuddered, "There's an opening in my logistics department. I reckon they need someone with your grasp of, uh, whatever it is you have a grasp of. You're dismissed, Colonel."

He stalked off, muttering threats and curses that everyone around him was careful not to overhear.

"Sergeant Grant, this arrest thing is bullshit. It's finished, as from this moment."

"Yes, General. Thank you, Sir."

"No problem. In recognition of what you've achieved, I'm issuing a field promotion, as of now. Congratulations, Second Lieutenant Grant."

"Sir?"

He held out his hand and they shook. "You're an officer. It's no more than you deserve. What are you planning to do next?"

His mind was whirling.

The court martial, it's all over. Lindbergh gone. And a lieutenant, well, I can live with that as long as I can fight. Margot!

He saw her face peering through the back of the press of soldiers around the General.

"Sir, I need to make arrangements to reinstate the Battalion cook."

"Cook?"

"You won't believe how good she is, Sir. If you'll stay here for lunch, you'll eat better than you have since you left the States."

"Is that right? I'll take you up on that. And afterward?"

"Saint-Lo, Sir. There're plenty of Krauts still in the area, so we need to finish the job and clear up the last pockets of resistance."

"Good man. You'd better see to that Kraut tank first. Those Germans need to go in the pen. I'll see you at lunch, Lieutenant. Dismissed."

They exchanged salutes, and he shook off the congratulations to go find her. She was waiting for him.

"Did I hear right? Lieutenant Grant?"

"Second Lieutenant. I can't believe it."

"You deserve it, my love."

Vern interrupted them. "Hey, Sarge, Lt, whatever it is. I hate to barge in, but did you hide our stash okay? I mean, it is safe?"

He thought of the deep well they'd uncovered outside Saint-Lo. After him and Solly dropped it to the bottom, they'd thrown a couple of tons of rocks on top.

"Safe as Fort Knox, no sweat!"

"It better be," he mumbled as he walked away.

He looked back at Margot. "What about Father Bouchet, did he get back okay?"

"He did. They put him in the field hospital, and they say he'll recover. He says he can't wait to get out of there and start killing the Nazis."

"I don't blame him after what they put him through. And you, any problems?"

Her face still betrayed the scars of her incarceration. Cuts and bruises, and her eyes had lost a little of their fierce shine, but only a little.

"No problems, not anymore." She put her arms around him, and the kiss almost sucked the breath out of him. When they separated, her face had creased into a broad smile.

"You made some crazy boast about my cooking to the General, is that right?"

"I'm sorry."

"No, it's fine. If I'm cooking for you soldiers, it means we can be close together. Show me to the field kitchen. I have an idea for a meal which should please the General, and a very special second course for you."

He hadn't been aware of telling her about his preferences for meals. "What's that?"

"As an officer, you will have your own tent, is that correct?"

"I guess so. As soon as I can get the stores to issue me one."

"You'd better hurry. I cannot unveil my second course until we're safely inside."

For a second, he didn't get it. Then realization dawned. He gave her a quick kiss and darted away.

"I'll be back real soon. This won't take long. Don't go away."

"Never."

CPSIA information can be obtained at www.ICGtesting.com
Printed in the USA
BVOW03s1353270215

389261BV00002BA/78/P